ROTH FAMILY FOUNDATION

Music in America Imprint

Michael P. Roth

and Sukey Garcetti

have endowed this

imprint to honor the

memory of their parents,

Julia and Harry Roth,

whose deep love of music

they wish to share

with others.

The publisher gratefully acknowledges the generous support of the Music in America Endowment Fund of the University of California Press Foundation, which was established by a major gift from Sukey and Gil Garcetti, Michael P. Roth, and the Roth Family Foundation.

In addition, the publisher gratefully acknowledges the generous contribution to this book provided by the Research Opportunity Grant from the School of Arts and Sciences at the University of Pennsylvania.

And the publisher gratefully acknowledges the generous contribution to this book provided by the Gustave Reese Endowment of the American Musicological Society.

The Amazing Bud Powell

Powell

Black Genius, Jazz History,
and the Challenge of Bebop

Guthrie P. Ramsey, Jr.

UNIVERSITY OF CALIFORNIA PRESS
Berkeley · Los Angeles · London

CENTER FOR BLACK MUSIC RESEARCH
Columbia College Chicago

University of California Press, one of the most
distinguished university presses in the United States,
enriches lives around the world by advancing scholarship
in the humanities, social sciences, and natural sciences.
Its activities are supported by the UC Press Foundation
and by philanthropic contributions from individuals and
institutions. For more information, visit www.ucpress.edu.

University of California Press
Berkeley and Los Angeles, California

University of California Press, Ltd.
London, England

Center for Black Music Research
Columbia College Chicago

For illustration credits, please see page 229

Library of Congress Cataloging-in-Publication Data
Ramsey, Guthrie P.
  The amazing Bud Powell : Black genius, jazz history,
and the challenge of bebop / Guthrie P. Ramsey, Jr.
      p.   cm. — (Music of the African diaspora ; 17)
  Includes bibliographical references and index.
  ISBN 978-0-520-24391-0 (cloth : alk. paper)
  1. Powell, Bud—Criticism and interpretation.
2. Jazz—History and criticism. I. Title.
  ML417.P73R36   2013
  786.2'165092—dc23   2012039182

Manufactured in the United States of America

22 21 20 19 18 17 16 15 14 13
10 9 8 7 6 5 4 3 2 1

In keeping with a commitment to support
environmentally responsible and sustainable printing
practices, UC Press has printed this book on Rolland
Enviro100, a 100% post-consumer fiber paper that is
FSC certified, deinked, processed chlorine-free, and
manufactured with renewable biogas energy. It is acid-
free and EcoLogo certified.

For Kellie Jones, the first I ever met

Contents

Acknowledgments

Although I completed a dissertation on Bud Powell what seems like ages ago, I cannot claim that he's always been "on top of my desk" in the ensuing years. There were many other projects to complete, including my book *Race Music: Black Cultures from Bebop to Hip-Hop*; writing, recording, and performing my own music; curating the exhibition *Ain't Nothing Like the Real Thing: How the Apollo Theater Shaped American Entertainment* for the National Museum of African American History and Culture; many smaller writing assignments; wonderful collaborations with other artists and scholars; and much more. Mr. Powell patiently waited his turn.

When I started to think about him seriously again, and with more maturity, the lessons of his musical life and the issues surrounding them became clearer and more salient. Powell became a wonder. I first and foremost thank him for sharing his beautiful gift with the world, and I hope, with this book, that others will find a greater appreciation for the profundity, sublimity, and courage that I've found in his work.

The many roads traveled from graduate school to an endowed professorship have been filled with people and institutions that have supported my work in numerous ways. At the University of Michigan, a scholarly and musical community sparked my excitement for intellectual pursuits and showed me how they might intersect with my ongoing interest in performance. The Thurgood Marshall Dissertation Fellowship at Dartmouth College allowed me time and resources to complete my dissertation on Powell. Tufts University's collegial faculty and inspiring students provided great opportunities to understand how teaching could impact one's intellectual life.

I can never thank my colleagues at the University of Pennsylvania enough for their very special brand of support, liveliness, fierceness, and thoughtfulness. The energies of the departments of music and Africana studies have guided and encouraged all the quirky turns in my career path and all the extra-musicological projects I've taken on. I couldn't ask for a better collection of people to work among. My friend and colleague Tim Rommen has always been valuable as a sparring partner and arbiter in all things musical and intellectual through the years. Penn undergraduates never disappoint in helping to create an atmosphere in which ideas take form and then move out into the world. Graduate students in my various seminars through the years have read and responded to drafts of this book in its various stages, and it is better because of their keen eyes and sharp intellectual insights. In this regard, I must thank in particular Garry Bertholf and John Meyers for their readings of an entire draft. To the former students on whose dissertations I had the honor of serving as advisor, your insights and energy remain with me always. The office staff in both the music and Africana studies departments continue to amaze with the level of support they provide in all things great and small. Thank you. I also thank the faculty and students at Princeton and Harvard Universities for opportunities to teach and to engage your intellectual communities. I also wish to acknowledge Tony Peebles and Fredara Hadley for technical support and Chuck Stewart and Michael Cuscuna for the photographs in this book.

The Jazz Studies Group at Columbia University, founded by the eminent scholar Bob O'Meally, created a space for the most advanced and motivating interdisciplinary thinking about this art form. The conversations, presentations, and debates among regular attendees and guests always provoked new ways to think about—and in certain cases introduced me to—some of the ideas in this book. The staff and resources of the Center for Black Music Research, Columbia College Chicago, for many years have been a source of information and direction. I also thank the McColl Center for Visual Art in Charlotte, North Carolina, for the wonderful artist-in-residency that allowed me the time, space, and place to put the finishing touches on this book.

I cannot list all of the friends and family who have made my life richer and, in turn, my work more enjoyable. My parents, Guthrie Ramsey, Sr., and Celia Ramsey Wynn, together with my wonderful siblings and beautiful children, have shared with me many experiences and memories to cherish outside my professional life, all of which have made the writing easier. The young ones coming along particularly inspire me: E.J., Zoe, Lyberty, London, Jada, Myles, and Levi. They touch my life in amazing ways. My in-laws, an extraordinary group of writers and thinkers, have kept me on my toes, always pushing me toward new ideas and ways of doing. I particularly thank Hettie Jones for reading a draft or two and for readily offering me her ideas about craft and clarity. And to Amiri Baraka, I extend thanks for clearing the philosophical and political space many years ago for the kind of work this book represents.

Although I've had many mentors along the way, I must make special note here of Samuel A. Floyd, Jr., and Richard Crawford, two gentlemen who have had and will always have the greatest influence on my work as a scholar. Their standards of generosity and rigor have made me the scholar I am today. I don't have the words to fully express the depth of my gratitude to them. I owe thanks as well to the trailblazers of the particular brand of jazz studies to which I aspire, one that seeks to understand how the details of sound organization signify in the social world. For providing excellent examples before me, I acknowledge Mark Tucker, Robin D. G. Kelley, Ingrid Monson, Scott DeVeaux, Farah Griffin, Jeffery Magee, David Brackett, George Lewis, David Ake, Eric Porter, Tammy Kernodle, Robert Walser, Ronald Radano, and many more too numerous to name here. My editor, Mary Francis at the University of California Press, is the best in the business and continues to be an ideal partner in this process because of her intellectual gifts, experience, drive, and "cool breeze" manner. I'm looking forward to working on more projects together.

Musician, engineer, and producer J. Anthony Thompson has helped me to stay in the groove for the past few years, collaborating on various musical projects and providing a great example of how to push things to the finish line. My big "Cuzzo," Ernest Perry Lyles, never leaves my side in whatever endeavor I take on. He's always there, providing whatever is required, be it motivation or productive distraction. My friend and brother Tukufu Zuberi, a scholar of many talents, has been a constant source of inspiration and support through the years.

This book is dedicated with humble appreciation to the "eye-minded" one, Kellie Jones, an astonishing partner, friend, and scholar who continually brings much knowledge, light, sweetness, and power to the world, and to whom I extend gratitude for sending some my way every day.

Charlotte, North Carolina

Introduction

In August 1966, William Powell, Sr., found himself speaking to the press about times past as he prepared to bury his son, the gifted jazz pianist, Bud Powell. He reminisced about giving a four-year-old Bud his first piano lesson after being cajoled by his wife, Pearl, to provide some instruction to keep the child from banging on the piano, something Bud enjoyed doing. "That started it," he told the *New York Amsterdam News*. As he recounted memories for the reporter, William expressed pride in his son's accomplishments, no doubt to fend off his sense of loss and regret. He ticked off a list of his son's accomplishments, from his diligent study of classical piano as a child to his years as a teenage titan in jazz. Powell, Sr., wanted the world to see Bud as he himself recalled his son in early life: "We used to call him 'happy' because he was always laughing and was a healthy youngster."[1]

At press time, his son's remains had been held in New York's Kings County Morgue for more than forty-eight hours since his passing on July 31. Awaiting legal permission from his next of kin to carry out an autopsy, hospital authorities tried to reach out to his estranged wife, Audrey Hill, then living in California, but their efforts apparently failed, since Bud's father had to send the morgue a telegram that would allow his body to be released shortly thereafter.

By the time of his death, Powell's health struggles were well known throughout the international jazz world. Before he had come back to New York in August 1964 (he had lived in Paris since 1959), the press had hailed his impending homecoming with enthusiasm, despite reports of his life-threatening illnesses and hospitalizations in Europe. Powell recuperated and aspired to make a comeback in the United States. When he arrived in New York, "cured of TB and fat as a *Bürgermeister*," he was immediately booked at Birdland for an extended engagement, for which he received favorable reviews.[2] Powell's former manager, Oscar Goodstein, no doubt planned the appearance with high hopes that the pianist could return to one of his old gigs in grand form. Could he recapture some of the magic of years past now that he was well and had the added mystique of a Parisian pedigree?

How the engagement went depended on whom you asked and which night they saw him. Greeted by a seventeen-minute standing ovation when he first took the stage, the night of August 25 was filled with promise. But when he didn't show up for the gig one night in October and went missing for two days, it became clear that returning to New York was perhaps not the best idea for his health. Powell was fired from the gig, and things would get worse. His devoted friend and caretaker Francis Paudras—the man credited with saving Powell's life, who had accompanied him to New York—returned to Paris without him. Powell would now have to work out his life and career issues without the benefit of his trusted "supervisor." When he had first landed in New York, Powell declared that he was looking forward to managing his own finances. That time had come.

Money turned out to be just one of his many challenges. If Powell planned to get solvent by jumpstarting a recording career, his discography tells of the bleak results. He recorded only sparingly between September 1964 and January 1966. Beyond the first album, titled *The Return of Bud Powell*, on the Roulette label, the rest were recordings that lacked the necessary quality to be released to the public. The recordings have, however, inspired lots of debate, detective work, and speculation among Powell discographers as they've tried to figure out the who, what, when, and where of these scant, intriguing unissued records. Everyone agrees on one thing: Powell only hinted at the virtuoso prowess he had once flaunted with ease.

These final contributions to his body of work were a far cry from the high hopes he and Paudras had held as they planned their stateside trip: "Bud was going to be back on top, buoyed by the certainty that he has recovered all of his powers, ready to plunge into a new life, freed from the spectres of the past."[3] But as Paudras's copious, personal, and poetic account of Powell's last days in his book *The Dance of the Infidels* details, the misfortunes of the pianist's past were always close at hand, ready to swallow him whole. Indeed, as Paudras points out, more often than not Powell's psychological issues positioned him on the weaker side of interactions with the businessmen, police, psychiatrists, attorneys, and even journalists with whom he had to contend throughout his entire adult life. When all was said and done, and as Powell and Paudras would soon learn, the mid-1960s New York jazz scene could not offer him the new life of prosperity, calm, and artistic acclaim he so desired.

Reality hit as soon as he stepped off Air France flight 025. With all of the excitement generated in the press and by Birdland's publicity machine, Powell's upcoming residency was eagerly anticipated. However, as Paudras would learn, the American way of jazz business was stark, unglamorous, and undignified. Goodstein had booked them into a rundown, roach-infested single hotel room with a kitchenette for the entire stay. The advance consisted of the following, according to Paudras's dramatic account: two one-way plane tickets, thirty dollars between them for immediate expenses, nine hundred dollars for back dues he owed the musicians' union, room and board deducted from Powell's future earnings, and seven hundred dollars for an attorney to clear up various legal actions before he had expatriated himself. And then there were the narcotics testing, fingerprinting, and police notification that would all verify that he had been cleared to receive a cabaret card, which would in turn allow him to perform in a New York nightclub. That engagement, of course, was the reason for the business trip.[4] It *had* to work.

There was much to cheer them on. *Time, Newsweek, Down Beat*, and the *New Yorker* covered Powell's return to the American stage and praised him with solid, enthusiastic reviews. Musician friends offered a steady stream of admiration and love—Max Roach, Thelonious Monk, Barry Harris, Babs Gonzales, Elmo Hope, Mary Lou Williams, the Baroness Nica de Koenigswarter, and others celebrated his return. Each had supportive contact with Powell between the time he arrived and the time he passed away. But during those two years, his life unraveled—gradually and in dramatic fits and starts—in a manner that was all too reminiscent of his old struggles. His body, now ravaged from the effects of tuberculosis, could not heal. He chain-smoked and craved alcohol. One drink would immediately debilitate his performances and severely rattle his emotional balance. Drugs abounded in this atmosphere. And to make matters worse, sometimes Powell would suddenly disappear, sending everyone into a panicked search around the city.

By this time, Powell appeared to be closer to his French guardian than to his own family. His mother had died and his father, by Paudras's account, had no room for Powell in his home or psyche. When Bud showed up one night at his father's Harlem apartment, unannounced and drunk, the elder Powell called Paudras to come and take him back to the hotel and warned Bud to not come back; his presence was too much to handle. Bud's then teenaged daughter, Celia, and her mother, Frances Barnes, had moved to North Carolina. At Paudras's invitation, they made the trip to Birdland, reuniting father and daughter for the first time since she was a little girl. They moved back to Brooklyn, and Powell soon began living with them. He began to drink heavily, too, growing weaker and weaker physically.

His last public performances of note took place at Carnegie Hall at a Charlie Parker memorial concert in March 1965 and at Town Hall on May 1 of the same year. Reports from observers of those concerts toggle among shock at his deteriorating physical appearance, memories of his once stunning musicianship, and disappointment in his failure to live up to them. Some called the Town Hall date (which was arranged by Bernard Strollman, Powell's attorney since his return to the United States) simply disastrous. But all around him remained hopeful that they could get a glimpse of the musician who had rocked the jazz world to its core and helped to shift its aesthetic center.

He was hospitalized on June 28, 1965, and given a moderate chance of survival because of his serious pulmonary complications and other issues, including jaundice and abdominal dropsy. He remained at Cumberland Hospital for five weeks, some of that time spent in critical condition. Powell was not a forgotten man, as evidenced by the many visitors, cards, and letters that came to the hospital. Mary Lou Williams and Max Roach, old friends from the glory days, both visited before he was discharged in August.

Amsterdam News reporter George Todd visited Powell as he convalesced in Brooklyn. Described as "the home of friends," the apartment in which Powell stayed was on the second floor, and the climb, Todd noted, exhausted Powell to the point of breathlessness. Powell could not, or at least would not, respond to questions. Celia Powell and Frances Barnes cared for Powell in his last days. Even with this support system, however, his physical and mental health continued to spiral downward. His drinking also increased, which meant, of course, that his music languished. Insisting on drawing Powell out and apparently keeping the best face on for the press, Frances told George Todd that she'd been in love with the pianist since she was fifteen and that Powell had planned to spend his time composing new music.[5]

Concerned friends reported by letter any information that they learned about Powell to his friend Francis in Paris. The news was mostly bad. Making matters worse for Paudras, he was in a battle with Strollman over some recordings of Thelonious Monk's composi-tions that Powell had made when he lived in Paris. A letter from Alan Bates announced that Powell once again had been institutionalized by November 1965, this time in Kings County Hospital, where he was making progress and losing some excess weight, although his teeth were rotting from neglect. He was allowed to play in "a half-assed band" in the hospital twice a week.[6]

By April 1966, he was living in Brooklyn with Frances Barnes and her and Bud's teenaged daughter, Celia, and he was struggling physi-cally but mentally stabilized. A circle of Paudras's friends plotted in vain to take Powell back to France, where they believed he would thrive once in his friend's constant care again. Their hopes were dashed by news reports that he had fallen seriously ill in early July. After another stint in Cumberland, Powell was transferred to the psychiatric hospi-tal in Kings County, where doctors, against his wishes, were planning shock treatments to his brain. Frances intervened, but he couldn't hang on. Earl "Bud" Powell was given the last rites of the Catholic Church and passed away on the night of July 31, 1966, at the age of forty-one.[7]

The jazz community, together with Powell's family, associates, and fans, honored his memory in grand style and with reverence. His body lay in state for three days at Unity Funeral Chapel in Brooklyn, surrounded by impressive floral displays, provided by his family, Duke Ellington, Max Roach, Mary Lou Williams, and Alfred Lion, among others. Close to five hundred visitors—an interracial crowd of young and old—paid their last respects at the police-managed event. Following this, a New Orleans–style funeral was held in Harlem. The procession, which was led by the Harlem Cultural Council Jazzmobile and an honor guard, slowly filed up Seventh Avenue toward St. Charles Catholic Church on 141st Street, which he had attended as a child. It was truly a jazz community affair: pianist Barry Harris was among the musicians performing; Nellie Monk, Thelonious Monk's wife, was on the committee planning the funeral; and Max Roach and Local 802, American Federation of Musicians, were among those recognized for their role in the financial arrangements. Powell was laid to rest in a family plot in Willow Grove, Pennsylvania, the town outside of Philadelphia where his mother had lived.

BUD POWELL: THE EXCEPTIONAL ARCHETYPE

The extent to which the public and the jazz community celebrated Powell's life is a testament to his contributions to American music. This book discusses some of the reasons that he continues to be one of the most intriguing musicians of his time. *The Amazing Bud Powell* is not an exhaustive biography. Rather, it puts what we know about Powell's life and music in dialogue with ideas that made possible, among other things, his reputation as a musical "genius" and bebop's social identity as a singular art form. Jazz letters have circulated these notions about Powell's impressive artistic stature, and these sentiments are directly aligned with the music's ever-evolving social pedigree.

Throughout this book—which is the first extended scholarly study of its kind on Powell—I explore questions concerning the relationships among Powell as a figure in American music, bebop as a sonic discourse, and the writing of jazz history as a political activity that engages many issues beyond musical aesthetics. Within these connections, Powell emerges as a complicated subject, both typical and exceptional among his peers in modern jazz. Powell was an archetypal bebop musician, and his accomplishments, much like those of Charlie Parker, Dizzy Gillespie, Kenny Clarke, Max Roach, and Thelonious Monk, inspired the expansion of artistic horizons for black artists across varied media at midcentury and beyond.

And yet within this paradigm of African American experimentation, narratives of Powell's exceptionalism abound, and this book treats, but does not attempt to resolve, these tensions. Like the dissonant intervals that define the art of bebop itself, they are allowed to languish here, resisting my desire to manage—to make stable, consonant, and neat— what is truly a robust, multidimensional, and unruly historical subject. With that in mind, then, Powell's life, music, and the analyses of them reveal a complex and dynamic picture of one of the twentieth century's most beautiful and fiercely adventurous musical minds. His artistic commitment not only codified bebop piano, but also beat a path for the language of musical abstraction that would stun the jazz world during his final years.

This book is about more than one musician's inspiring accomplishments. It is also about the various meanings that can be derived from the bebop movement, in which Powell was an innovator. Powell's amazing muse—his expansive musicianship, riveting improvisations, and inventive compositions—can be best understood within the broad social, musical, historical, and especially marketing frameworks in which listeners experienced and understood him. Thus, this book considers the relationship between the sonic details of bebop—particularly Powell's engagement with them—and the "performance rituals, visual appearance, the types of social and ideological connotations associated with them [the musical details], and their relationship to the material conditions of production."[8] This book, then, is also about how bebop and the social networks in which meanings about it were made, and how all of these things suggest that jazz had experienced a generic shift. Jazz, according to many, had become a new "genre," and it did so partly because of Powell's important contributions.[9]

The idea of genre in this study involves many factors, including the pressing business of labeling in popular culture; the tidal wave of "Negro" artistic experimentation and the surging black political efficacy that characterized the 1940s; modern jazz's evolving critical discourse; the gendered musical language of bebop genius; and the potent atmosphere in which new identities and identifications were being made at this historical moment. During these years and set against these influences, Powell began his rise as a bona fide giant of modern jazz piano—just as black popular music and the social sphere it inhabited were experiencing the tumultuous changes mentioned above. His work is, therefore, ideally suited to an exploration of shifting notions of genre in jazz. Why? Because he was one of the key musicians who supported jazz's perceived move outside the tight constellation of "vernacular" styles such as blues, gospel, jump and urban blues, rhythm and blues, and, later, rock 'n' roll. And he is an exceptional example of this shift because even while he helped to codify bebop's language, he developed an idiosyncratic, forward-looking voice within it.

THE SOCIAL CONTRACT IN BEBOP'S CHALLENGE

Jazz is singular in that its social mobility—its ability to move among "folk," mass culture, and "high" art discourses—has been the subject of meticulous scrutiny. Through the years, divergent theories about it have surfaced as observers debated whether jazz was the music of an ethnic, subcultural folk, a popular music intended for mass audiences, or a cultural expression of the highest order, one requiring an elitist, specialized training to adequately comprehend its value. As such, we hear in its history the audible traces of this struggle for a cultural and social identity, the commercial interests of the music industry, and the "changing orientations and perspectives among working-class and middle-class African-Americans, especially black youth and young adults."[10] To this latter point, I note that at the time that Powell was building his early reputation, jazz occupied a similar cultural-social position to the one that hip-hop has held for the last thirty or so years.

When bebop drummer Kenny Clarke said he resented the label "bebop," he joined a chorus of critics who understood the power as well as the limiting effect of musical labels. Yet labeling has been a major preoccupation in the world of arts and letters, particularly in the specific case of music, where the act of categorizing performs many functions. Stylistic distinctions, for example, tell us much more than which musical qualities constitute a piece of music. They shed light on what listeners value in sound organization. Categorizing also inherently comments on the nature of power relationships in society at large—it tells us who's in charge and running the show. As bebop musicians were keenly aware, if you named it, you could claim it. In the "on the ground" listening experience, labeling establishes the rules of the game, allowing listeners to perceive the relationship between the idiosyncrasies of a single piece of music and the larger category of sound organization to which it belongs. Thus, a good deal of cultural work is achieved by the act of stylistic labeling: it provides a social contract between music and audiences, one that conditions the listeners' expectations on many levels, particularly in the area of meaning. When one considers, for example, the range of musical tributaries flowing through Powell's aesthetic sensibilities—as this study does—it becomes obvious how labels can constrain or discipline interpretations of a musician's work.

African American music in general is a particularly rich site for exploring issues of stylistic labeling. Critics, scholars, and listeners have recognized that the singular historical experience of African Americans is perhaps the most compelling reason that the conventions of black music have inspired such powerful reactions. The ideology of race has, of course, contributed to the dynamic reception of the history of music labeled "African American." And beyond this aspect of their shared social histories, the genres jazz, gospel, rhythm and blues, soul, blues, and hip-hop contain strong familial relationships based on common characteristics that many, despite contestation, continue to trace to an African cultural legacy, as well as other sonic tributaries originating in Europe and elsewhere. Despite their commonalities, however, these genres have distinguished themselves and are marked with social, historical, geographical, and commercial particularity.

Generic labels such as "jazz" guide listeners toward the "proper" responses as dictated by a social contract established by the label itself. They establish a framework for the communication of meaning, provide a context for interpretation, and serve as a starting point from which to discern changes or innovations. To be sure, positioning a musical practice in this or that category carries important consequences: it connects the music and musicians to commercial institutions, genre-specific interpretations, and traditional audience bases. Thus, when sound organization is assigned a genre designation, the name speaks to both purely musical issues and to larger social orders. Musicians are keenly aware of this fact.

I should back up a bit here and make clear how I'm using the terms *genre* and *style*. Important and helpful accounts tracing the etymology of these terms already exist, so I will not recount them here.[11] I use *genre* to refer to the broadest categories of musical and social practices. The term *style,* for me, designates subsets of such practices. These groupings are always flexible and situational. For example, we use the term *black music* to indicate a large range of styles closely associated with the social and historical experiences of African Americans. Samuel A. Floyd, Jr., among many other writers, links these various styles by identifying a common set of conceptual approaches. When we turn to jazz specifically, the labels Dixieland, swing, bebop, modal, free, fusion, and acid represent substyles that have been subsumed under the "jazz" genre.[12]

Because musical practices tend to be dynamic, categorical designations are always moving. Consider the relationship of blues and gospel. On the purely stylistic level, they shared many common qualities in the 1920s. But as we see in the music of Thomas A. Dorsey, the "father" of gospel music, for example, socially grounded beliefs about each category of music (blues and gospel) began to codify. Thus, although they continued to share formal conventions, they became separate genres of music, a move that the commercial market perpetuated and helped to solidify. Categories or distinctions such as these performed a good deal of cultural work. They carried the baggage of social hierarchies: some genres fit into the "art" category of culture, while others were viewed as mass or folk culture. To further clarify this point, bebop permanently changed how jazz was viewed in the value system of American musical culture and represented an important rupture that was felt beyond the music world. This book seeks to index some of those changes by considering Powell's career and music. Indeed, the specifics of his art and the identity he fashioned with it bring into sharp relief some of these shifting perceptions.

THE BEBOP FIGURE IN JAZZ HISTORY

One way to interpret these changes in the music's social pedigree is by considering jazz historiography, or the history of writings on this topic. As such, my work engages a wide range of literature with the deliberate intention to contextualize Powell's work. I should mention at the outset that I situate my own work within two broad historiographical streams. During the 1960s, the final years of Powell's life, two vibrant studies appeared or were underway, and each of their premises is central to this book's methodological approach. They are Gunther Schuller's *Early Jazz: Its Roots and Musical Development* (1968) and LeRoi Jones's (Amiri Baraka) *Blues People: Negro Music in White America* (1963).

When it was published, Schuller's work promised to be a model for future jazz studies: a book-length treatise on jazz that explored its sonic qualities with rigor. In his opening paragraph on its origins, Schuller gives what one has come to expect from his writings: an emphasis on the notion of development: "Jazz . . . was not the product of a handful of stylistic innovators, but a relatively unsophisticated quasi-folk music—more sociological manifestation than music."[13] Schuller moves on to give the most thorough technical discussion in any jazz narrative to that date of the transformation of African and European musical practices into an uniquely African American one. Schuller considers form, timbre, melody, harmony, rhythm, and improvisation with the tools of western music analysis. The remainder of the book maintains this standard, with formalist, technical explanations of a large body of jazz recordings.

Some saw this approach as purging the sonic of its social (or even cultural) meaning. In his essay "Jazz and the White Critic" (1963), Amiri Baraka argues that "Negro music is essentially the expression of an attitude, or a collection of attitudes, about the world, and only secondarily an attitude about the way music is made." Furthermore,

Baraka believes that white critics' approach to jazz criticism stripped "the music too ingenuously of its social and cultural intent. It seeks to define jazz as an art (or folk art) that has come out of no intelligent body of socio-cultural philosophy." Baraka draws a hard line with what he sees as the search for organic unity and structural coherence: "In jazz criticism no reliance on European tradition or theory will help at all."[14] At the same time, however, Baraka insists on the uniqueness of the *American* experience and argues for "standards of judgment and aesthetic excellence that depend on our native knowledge and understanding of the underlying philosophies and local cultural references that produced blues and jazz in order to produce valid critical writing or commentary about it."[15]

With *Blues People,* Jones attempts to develop what he sees as a more appropriate theory for black music. Its reach has been broad: one writer hails it as "the founding document of contemporary cultural studies in America" because of the way Baraka combines aesthetic judgments with poignant cultural and political critique.[16] Not everyone agreed with this "social" interpretation of black music. In his famous review of *Blues People,* the African American novelist Ralph Ellison draws a line between art interpretation and sociology, arguing that "the blues are not primarily concerned with civil rights or obvious political protest; they are an art form and thus a transcendence of those conditions created within the Negro community by the denial of social justice."[17]

My work here flatly rejects the notion that music itself can transcend, in the sense suggested here by Ellison, the conditions of its historical and social milieu. Yet historical actors have certainly used music to assert their own senses of beauty as well as to make sense of, confront, negotiate, and/or change their social, political, and economic conditions. Music's ability to do this kind of cultural work is, in fact, one of the reasons we find it such a powerful medium. *The Amazing Bud Powell* attempts to uncover the cultural work of Powell's music partly by dealing with issues, methods, and questions appearing in *Early Jazz* and *Blues People.* How, I ask, do we make sense of Bud Powell's music as that of someone whose talents could never lift him above the challenges he faced as a uniquely gifted but disabled black American man at a time of tumultuous transitions in the material conditions of African Americans across the board? What were his musical contributions, the structure of his sound language, the broader stylistic worlds he engaged, the conditions of the music's reception, and the critical discourses that surrounded and tried to make sense of it? In what social orders did bebop emerge, and how did musicians such as Powell navigate them?

. . .

My first chapter discusses the idea of bebop's pedigree as a serious art: how that concept emerged and which musical, social, literary, and pedagogical discourses support the claim. From today's vantage point, the "art of bebop" notion condenses a collection of disparate yet interdependent factors: formal musical analyses, commercial interests, subcultural visual styles, western ideas about musical "complexity," aesthetic multiplicity and sonic assemblage, traditions of avant-garde black youth culture, violent state-sponsored suppression, the cultural politics of geography, a jousting written criticism, a discerning and thoughtful audience base, and a politically focused body of interdisciplinary scholarship. Powell's points of intersection with these variables form an important thread in this book.

In chapter 2, Powell's artistic agency, together with his life's challenges, is situated in the context of modern jazz's growth in the music industry and in the broader world of black artistic experimentation in the 1940s and 1950s. At the same time that Powell was building a name in the jazz world, poets such as Langston Hughes and Gwendolyn Brooks were refining, and indeed remaking, the black artistic landscape through their bold experiments with the written word. Painters such as Norman Lewis were also troubling artistic waters with the visual language of abstraction as practiced by the always politicized creative imagination of the black man. The chapter places Powell's life as a musician squarely within the context of the various identifications he made during bebop's early development. By *identifications,* I mean the specifically musical and social associations he made among the choices that were available to him. In my view, it is impossible to fully appreciate Powell without considering, in some relevant way, the work and lives of his contemporaries. He and the other modern jazz musicians all "made" bebop within the music industry's business practices and venues. As we learn, Powell's genius was geographically, historically, and culturally specific. It did not, and in fact could not, transcend its milieu—indeed, his genius was a product of its time, place, and artistic position with other musicians in bebop's orbit.

Chapter 3 focuses on three broad social orders: art discourse, the idea of "blackness" in historical jazz criticism, and American psychiatric practice. I treat each of these as important structural factors with undeniably direct and indirect bearing on our contemporary under-standing of Powell and his accomplishments. The role of race "thought and practice" in jazz's literary aesthetic discussions and in the pianist's experiences with psychiatric institutions throughout his adult life ani-mates and connects these seemingly incongruent discursive spheres of influence. As we shall see, the compelling literature that established an art discourse in jazz aesthetics was shaped by ideas about race and blackness within energetic discussions about the "Africa" in the music. Taken together, these factors—the industries of music criticism and psychiatry and each of their roles in creating a jazz-art idea—pro-vide compelling contexts for understanding some of the very powerful social ideas associated with Powell's exploits as well as his reputation in American music history. The chapter helps to move my discussion beyond sound organization in order to explain the ways in which vari-ous social orders have inspired meaning in Powell's music.

Much has been written recently about the "masculinist" discourses that have informed jazz's public persona since its early years. Bebop, with its storied history of gladiator-style jam sessions/cutting contests patterned on athletic conquest, is legendary in this regard. Moving beyond this proving ground for musical "manhood" through spontane-ous technical display, chapter 4 considers other factors. This key sym-bol of modern jazz masculinity can also be understood by engaging the histories of attitudes about a range of topics, including gendered ideas about musical instruments and commercialism, rhythmic coherence and the body, racial social orders, artistic heroic individualism, and the creative hierarchies assigned to both composition and improvisa-tion. All of this is meant to deconstruct what constitutes jazz manhood or, in Powell's specific case, to declare how the notion of his genius is a very gendered proposition from top to bottom. When situated within historical patterns of the larger American musical landscape, the jazz manhood complex takes on a more comprehensive import.

Chapter 5 provides a technical working through of the particulari-ties of Powell's contributions within the developing language of mod-ern jazz. The presentation of this part of my discussion may challenge some readers not familiar with music theory. I have nonetheless tried to make the main ideas accessible to nonspecialists. Throughout the book, I show that modern jazz's quite fascinating historiography has forwarded theories of its sound organization and cultural politics from the very beginning. Together with the details of Powell's musi-cal rhetoric, we witness a new style crystallizing through the recordings of a gifted yet challenged musician. As I stated above and reiterate throughout this book, with bebop, jazz expanded its social pedigree and became "art"; and it also morphed jazz itself into a genre distinct from other contemporary vernacular forms. This trajectory is easily traced from Powell's earliest recordings to his later work.

In many ways, this book, one that centralizes the contributions of Bud Powell, details the collision of two vibrant political economies: the discourses of art and the practice of blackness. The "race" discourses that have formed a persistent source of controversy in jazz history are important (and certainly fascinating) enough to scrutinize here. As we will learn, the story of bebop is about the discourses of art and blackness meeting head-on and tussling it out in both musical and critical terms. Modern jazz occupies a singular position in American musical thought and scholarship. The so-called bebop revolution has been generally perceived as a radical break with "tradition," particularly because of the perceived absence of social dancing in its aesthetic. This turn has signaled to some the music's break with black vernacular expression and even the harsh realities of race in twentieth-century America. I argue, however, that the social energies resulting from this fissure spiral out into broader questions of artistic production in American society. As such, chapter 6 concludes with Powell's move to Europe in an attempt to escape the complexities of race and art in America.

1

"Cullud Boys with Beards"

Serious Black Music and the Art of Bebop

Little cullud boys with beards
re-bop be-bop mop and stop.

Little cullud boys with fears,
frantic, kick their draftee years
into flatted fifths and flatter beers
that at a sudden change become
sparkling Oriental wines rich and strange . . .
Langston Hughes, "Flatted Fifths"

In her treasury of private memories, Bud Powell's daughter, Celia, recalls her father as an uncomplicated man, "content with the simple things in life, not wanting much more than a meal and to play."[1] But in the public world where he established his fame, Powell cut a more challenging figure. His work represents, for many, a pinnacle of artistic achievement among the pantheon of brilliant jazz pianists. His relentless flow of musical ideas—their unsettling rhythmic disjunction; those explosive launches into beautifully crafted passages of push, pull, run, and riff, punctuated by the perfect landing at ferocious speeds—remains an inspiring, though intimidating, factor for pianists who come behind him. Indeed, his brilliance in the bebop idiom pushed jazz musicians of all stripes to high standards of performance that have rarely been matched. His contributions have been as germane to the modern jazz pianist's training as Czerny five-finger exercises and Bach Inventions are to that of classically trained pianists. Despite his importance to jazz, he remains one of the music's lesser-known figures. Yet he was a towering pianist who inspires awe and respect among those in the know.

As one of the select group of gifted mid-twentieth-century "cullud boys," Powell can teach us much about what made his chosen idiom such a dramatic and poignant musical statement. Here and in following chapters, I discuss some of the themes and issues—musical and otherwise—that show how Powell's bebop worked as a commercialized, racialized, gendered, and age-specific enterprise. Throughout his lifetime, jazz developed from a cultish, ethnic-infused vogue to the sound of American pop to a demanding avant-garde. Within this dynamic continuum of pedigree shifts, Powell's work can also be seen as entangled in the aesthetic legacies of musicians such as Duke Ellington, Art Tatum, and Teddy Wilson, among others whose artistic lives helped to create a cultural space for the learning, practice, and dissemination of the art of jazz. At the same time, there are those who believe that we should retain the political edge that bebop once possessed as a stand-alone tradition. Eric Lott, for example, has lamented what he sees as the casual commercialization of a style that at one time represented the political and aesthetic avant-garde: "We need to restore the political edge to a music that has been so absorbed into the contemporary jazz language that it seems as safe as much of the current scene—the spate of jazz reissues, the deluge of 'standard' records, Bud Powell on CD—certainly an unfortunate historical irony."[2] Bebop is, indeed, an abundant site of expressive force.

Despite Powell's brilliance as a pianist, composer, and innovator, his work remains a curious and understudied force in jazz history. Indeed, looking for Bud Powell involves a search through "cullud boys' beards and fears": it's an investigation of the meanings embedded in all manner of styles, musical and otherwise, and how all of them signified in the world. Black male musicians of the 1940s streamed self-conscious ideas about who they were in the world through their art. In the flatted fifths, rhythmic disjunction, and sheer velocity of bebop convention, we can find Bud and his peers. But we also find him (and others like him) in other forms of representation, such as photography, and even in the other kinds of art that shaped his social world, such as poetry and the visual arts. In other words, we must examine the world into which Powell walked, a world in which life and musicianship challenged the post–World War II world on many levels. When we look for Bud, we sift through many riches.

THE MUSIC, THE WRITING, AND THE ART IDEA

Powell's accomplishments invoke a generation of musicians whose innovations during the 1940s and 1950s are some of jazz's greatest artistic triumphs. Through them, jazz became a bona fide "Art," an expression that is considered by many to be an elitist music deserving formally trained devotees, a vigorous criticism, and a rigorous scholarship. With bebop, the accepted wisdom goes, jazz shed its populist impulses and moved up the cultural ladder. This book meditates on, among other things, this dramatic transition through the example of Powell's musical contributions.

But "Great Art-Jazz" did not just happen; it had to pay its dues. In the scholarly world, for example, jazz would need to be analyzed with tools from beyond its immediate cultural borders. Jazz needed to be imbedded into the nineteenth-century Eurocentric notion of Great Art's transcendence of the social and political "everyday," and this move was a major hurdle for this body of music. And naturalizing the shift has been achieved primarily, though not exclusively, by the acts of formal musical analysis and written criticism. Let's begin with "analysis," by which I mean the study of musical structures as applied to specific works and performances.

One of the goals of formal analysis—to expose organic unity—is a musical value in which few major jazz musicians have expressed much interest. Enter Joseph Kerman, one of musicology's progressive voices during the 1980s. This was a time when analysis of this kind came under increasing scrutiny as well as the time when the first dissertations on jazz began to appear in the field. Kerman argues that musical analysis is not a politically benign act, but "an essential adjunct to a fully articulated aesthetic value system": western art music of the common practice period. Musical analysts extended their techniques to all of the music that they valued, and eventually to jazz, as part of this book exemplifies.[3]

At the same time, it should be understood that this brand of formal analysis, embedded as it is in nineteenth-century western European music history, has done little to raise the music's prestige among the average jazz fan. Many Powell enthusiasts, for example, have never required musical scores or scholarly treatises to validate or affirm their devotion. His recordings, together with the lore, myth, and gossip that circulated around him, have sustained his reputation as one of jazz's greatest, and indeed most mysterious, stars. Even casual knowledge of Powell and his exploits seems to anoint the jazz fan with insider, aficionado status. His work has remained important because of the extent to which jazz pianists have imitated his innovations, the scholarly analysis that it (and the work of his colleagues) has stimulated, and the devotion and awe that exists among his fans.

FROM THE JOOK TO THE CLASSROOM:
BEBOP'S PEDIGREE OF BLACK MULTIPLICITY

Powell's and his colleagues' version of serious black music has often inspired the notion that theirs was an aesthetic in opposition to crass commercialism and, I would argue, to certain aspects of art discourses as well. A recurring theme in bebop literature (one that still shapes its reception), for example, presumes that modern jazz intentionally tried to sever itself from the entertainment business, from the "jooks" and nightclubs of its origins, and from its social legacy in the black "vernacular." It is quite remarkable that such a diverse range of writers—music scholars, journalists, cultural critics—frame bebop's profile in the same way: as a challenge to a diverse set of orthodoxies.

Musicologist Frank Tirro writes, for example, that bebop musicians attempted "to create a new elite." The cultural critic Cornel West believes that "bebop musicians shunned publicity and eschewed visibility." Likewise, journalist Nelson George argues: "The bebop attitude overrode any lingering connection to the black show-business tradition that turned any cultural expression into a potentially lucrative career (though eventually that would happen to the beboppers as well). Its adherents found it a higher calling than mere entertainment." Music historian William Austin maintains that Charlie Parker's "music required for discriminating appreciation as thorough a specialized preparation as any 'classical style.' . . . He stood for jazz as a fine art, knowing that this meant exclusiveness. . . . Thus with 'bop,' jazz met the difficulties that had bewildered critics of new serious music ever since 1910. The best work was so complex in harmony and rhythm that it sounded at first incoherent, not only to laymen but to professionals very close to it. Good work could no longer be discriminated with any speed or certainty from incompetent work." English music critic Wilfred Mellers writes that although Parker's roots in the black music tradition are evident, the "expressivity" of his rapidly paced music shares "affinities with the development in European art-music that was (contemporaneously) associated with Boulez, Stockhausen and Nono."[4]

Writers who valued beboppers' achievements borrowed critical rhetoric from the most prestigious and status-building model available to them—the modernist strain of western art music. But where did this leave Powell and his associates? Did the rhetoric of elite modernism serve well their aspirations?

One important writer believed it did not. Martin Williams, the influential jazz critic and compiler of the landmark anthology *The Smithsonian Collection of Classic Jazz,* writes that Charlie Parker helped renew jazz "simply by following his own artistic impulses."[5] Williams argues that bebop musicians made a self-conscious effort to change the social function of jazz. But he characterizes the result of this effort as a kind of "dream deferred," questioning its success because although social dancing is, for the most part, not done to modern jazz, "for a large segment of its audience it is not quite an art music or a concert music. It remains by and large still something of a barroom atmosphere music. And perhaps a failure to establish a new function and milieu for jazz was, more than anything else, the personal tragedy of the members of the bebop generation."[6]

Williams writes in the same essay that although Parker and others "repudiated what they thought of as the grinning and eye-rolling of earlier generations of jazzmen. . . . [they] courted a public success and a wide following that were defined in much the same terms as the popular success of some of their predecessors."[7] Naturally, the process of elevating bebop to this lofty new pedigree meant critically endowing the musicians themselves with artistic autonomy. But at the same time, Williams seems to recognize that jazz was not completely free from its social roots, that it seemed stuck between aesthetic discourses. So what is the truth about modern jazz's pedigree?

Bebop musicians such as Powell did represent an elite group, and my discussion of his music will show that he merits this claim. But his elite status, like the pedigree of bebop itself, is quite a complex matter. At one time the word *elite* described "someone elected or formally chosen"; by the end of the nineteenth century, however, the term "became virtually equivalent with [the] 'best.'"[8] Writers have framed beboppers' achievements in this latter sense, and more specifically, as an elitism within the framework of western art music. Yet I believe it is important to show that bebop retained powerful connections to black communal values and to the commercial, popular music industry. Ultimately, I wish to show through Powell's music that any argument about bebop as fine art should take into account its dynamic relationship to art discourses, black culture, and commerce.

In order to parse this relationship, one has to move beyond the sonic. Bebop was, of course, sound, but it also embodied a look composed of the berets, goatees, and thick horn-rimmed glasses that were popular among the postwar "Museum of Modern Art set."[9] The clothing worn by the beboppers represented an "intellectualized" adaptation of the zoot suit, the dress code for World War II–era hipsters.[10] Photographs of bebop musicians show that many chose to chemically straighten their hair in the "conk" style popular among many urban black males in the 1940s. Along with the look came an insider language. Trumpeter Miles Davis is only one of many who recalls that early beboppers cultivated a colorful vocabulary that grew out of black slang or jive talk, a popular dialect in the jazz world during the late 1930s and early 1940s.[11]

The bebop look and language gave the popular press an image to promote (or denounce) and lent more than a dash of human interest to the scene. Both *Life* and *Ebony* magazines featured articles in the late 1940s that focused primarily on these features. These seemingly peripheral aspects of bebop culture reveal much about the music's political import. Robin D. G. Kelley argues that clothing such as the zoot suit (and variations thereof) does not carry a direct political statement in itself, but its cultural context renders it into a statement. Bebop musicians belonged to a larger underground culture of black working-class youth, in which the "zoot suit, the conk, the lindy hop, and the language of the 'hep cat' [were] signifiers of a culture of opposition among black, mostly male, youth."[12] Such acts have traditionally allowed the construction of a collective identity that challenges dominant stereotypes and forms insularity.

Consider, for example, Miles Davis's account of Dexter Gordon coaching him in the art of "bebop hipness" in 1948. Gordon urged Davis to buy new clothes and to try to grow a moustache or a beard to affirm his affiliation with the bebop subculture—onstage and off. Davis recalls that after he had saved enough money, he purchased a big-shouldered suit that felt much too large for him. Gordon's response upon seeing Davis in the suit resembles an initiation rite: "Now you looking like something, now you hip. . . . You can hang with us."[13] Bebop dress negotiated a musician's identification as an insider of bebop subculture.

Kelley connects bebop's sonic language to the hipster vocabulary that Miles Davis refers to above. Young black males, he writes, "created a fast-paced, improvisational language that sharply contrasted with the passive stereotype of the stuttering, tongue-tied sambo."[14] Dizzy Gillespie also recognized the relationship between the spoken words of the hipster and the musical rhetoric of bebop: "As we played with musical notes, bending them into new and different meanings that constantly changed, we played with words."[15] Gillespie's "play" represents some important cultural work, firmly situating bebop within the priorities of black vernacular culture.

Moving back to the musical, how do we interpret bebop's artistic pedigree through the lens of its sonic complexity? Did its intricate approach to harmony and rhythm and its virtuosic solos situate it outside the realm of black popular culture? Certainly this notion of complexity is crucial among those who believe that western art music is superior to other musical forms. Ethnomusicologist Judith Becker has argued that many believe "that Western art music is structurally more complex that other music; its architectural hierarchies, involved tonal relationships, and elaborated harmonic syntax not only defy complete analysis but have no parallel in the world."[16] And many jazz writers believe this sentiment to be true because a good deal of jazz literature assigns jazz prestige by arguing that it is just as complicated (and that it is complicated in the same way) as western art music. As I will show later, Powell's music certainly embodies a good deal of melodic, harmonic, and rhythmic complexity—so much so that it would seem to support a perception of bebop as art music. Yet we will also see how Powell's early career in swing grounds the music in the repertory, not to mention the social histories, of other 1940s black popular music. (This is not a new point by any means; it is simply amplified in the specific case of Powell.)

Susan McClary has made clear how "within the context of industrial capitalism, two mutually exclusive economies of music developed: that which is measured by popular or commercial success and that which aims for the prestige conferred by official arbiters of taste."[17] The bebop-as-fine-art notion seems to have moved jazz from McClary's first musical economy to the latter. The much-promoted idea that jazz is "America's classical music" seems to suggest that philosophy. But successful music making in the United States has always depended on attracting and satisfying the needs of paying customers, and bebop was no exception.[18] Beboppers worked under these assumptions, as Gillespie himself has pointed out: "We all wanted to make money, preferably by playing modern jazz."[19]

The bebop movement as a whole conveyed a string of tensions: popular versus elite, commercial versus esoteric, vernacular versus cultivated. Bebop's ability to communicate this aesthetic of multiplicity says much about the source of the music's appeal in its own time, and even more about the nature of American music making. Some writers have tried to capture bebop's essence in ways that indicate this multiplicity. Albert Murray links bebop, for example, to the Kansas City jam sessions of Charlie Parker's youth: "Whatever they play becomes

good-time music because they always maintain the velocity of celebration. . . . What you hear when you listen to Charlie Parker . . . is not a
theorist dead set on turning dance music into concert music. What you
hear is a brilliant protégé of Buster Smith and admirer of Lester Young
adding a new dimension of elegance to the Kansas City drive, which
is to say the velocity of celebration."[20] This kind of "driving celebration" is front and center in Powell's music, as we shall see in much of
the commentary about his music.

Music scholar Samuel A. Floyd, Jr., has said that "works of music are
not just objects, but cultural transactions between human beings and
organized sound—transactions that take place in specific idiomatic
cultural contexts that are fraught with the values of the original contexts from which they spring, that require some translation by auditors
in pursuit of the understanding and aesthetic substance they offer."[21]
This book is ultimately about what transactions might have taken place
during a Powell performance. How was the sound organized? In which
specific contexts did Powell create his music, and in which contexts did
it circulate? What aesthetic substance did he offer?

Powell's contributions are, of course, best interrogated by exploring
some of the ideas, activities, and discourses that have shaped our modern-day understanding of bebop. It should come as no surprise that old
and new ideas about race percolate through many of these issues. Jazz
is a powerful example of the many cross-pollinations occurring among
the various cultural tributaries flowing into African American culture.
As such, explanations of jazz that consider it essentially and solely
"African" do not take into account history, human agency, or the fact
that jazz shares a legacy with the European aesthetic value system. In
other words, to analyze jazz, one must take seriously the breadth and
diversity of African American culture, understand the qualities that
make black music distinctive, take artistic human agency into account,
consider jazz historiography, and, finally, consider the historical speci-
ficity of the work or artist in question. Numerous contested histories
are dialogically and vibrantly present in both the art and the letters of
modern jazz.

NOTES FROM A BLACK YOUTH UNDERGROUND—AND ITS CRITICS

The bebop movement began as the avant-garde music of 1940s black
youth culture, much as Louis Armstrong's music did in the 1920s and

as hip-hop did in the late 1970s and early 1980s. As bebop drummer and pioneer Max Roach implores:

> I often have to remind my cohorts, musicians of my generation, that rappers come from the same environment as Louis Armstrong—they came from the Harlems and the Bed-Stuys, the West Side of Chicagos. The rappers didn't . . . [go] to the great conservatories or universities so they could deal with literature and "learn how to write poetry." And Louis Armstrong didn't go to the conservatory where he could learn to write music. And if he had, we wouldn't have this great music that the world is listening to now. So thinking about that, I have to remind them that these guys are making history, like [John] Coltrane and Pops [Armstrong].[22]

Roach's words not only grapple with the issue of youth culture, but also call up a fundamental tension involving "high" and "low" culture in the United States and the role of black youth in it all. Furthermore, they strike at the core of some key concerns involving the supposedly discrete and usually ahistorical boundaries drawn around this dichotomy. The sentiment behind statements such as "Jazz is serious," "Jazz is not popular or commercial," or even the now politically correct assertion—one that has been soundly refuted about western art music—that jazz possesses an "implicit universal intelligibility" begs rethinking.[23]

The idea that some music by its nature can transcend the commercial world and can thus become high art is an accepted tenet of the western art music tradition, particularly in its American context. But art music, in fact, has a commercial history. As William Weber has written: "We must regard the rise of the musical masters [Handel, J. S. Bach, Haydn, Mozart, Beethoven, Schubert] as an early form of mass culture—just early forms, of course, and therefore somewhat limited, but nonetheless clever, profit-seeking mass culture." In other words, he argues that the "commercial exploitation of the masters was a major starting point of the modern music business."[24] These insights are not lost when considering Powell's career in jazz. For example, every composition from Powell's first leader session—with the exception of the two originals and "Indiana"—was considered a hit in the popular music industry at one time or another.[25]

The aesthetic, and therefore political, challenge leveled by this primarily black male youth culture went public in a highly visible and impacting way. The well-known story of bebop's move from Harlem jook spaces to the wider commercial world of 52nd Street is, among other things, shot through with the politics of gendered language: commercial conquest, cultural territorialism, violence, and musical "cutting contests" are among the terminologies we encounter in various accounts. Bebop's move to a "whiter" downtown geographic space represents more than simply a broadening of available venues for the music's presentation. A huge aspect of bebop's revolutionary, heroic status should be attributed to its ability to do precisely that: move "out of its place" geographically. As Katherine McKittrick has argued, "The 'where' of black geographies and black subjectivity . . . is often aligned with spatial processes that *apparently* fall back on seemingly predetermined stabilities, such as boundaries, color-lines, 'proper' places, fixed and settled infrastructures and streets, oceanic boundaries."[26] Following McKittrick's model, I believe that bebop's geographical journey, such as it was, altered the social processes of marginalization, concealment, and boundary making by revealing them as hegemonic strategies that organized race, gender, and class differentiation. In other words, it upset the "traditional geography," an assumption pertaining to the ways in which we "view, assess, and ethically organize the world from a stable (white, patriarchal, Eurocentric, heterosexual, classed) vantage point."[27]

New York in the 1940s was a hotbed of activity for all manner of black artists, but musicians seemed to be in the forefront of what might be called an after-hours renaissance. (We will see later that the emergence of new possibilities in artistic experimentation and black identities was not confined to the jazz world.) Bebop, like any commercially presented music, needed a venue, and Harlem's nightlife in the early '40s provided just that. Pianist Mary Lou Williams claims to know exactly how and why bebop got started. According to her, young black musicians often complained about not receiving enough credit for their contributions. Eventually, Thelonious Monk tried to start a big band to "create something that they can't steal because they can't play it." Monk wrote difficult arrangements and began rehearsing in a basement. However, the group disbanded shortly thereafter because "the guys got hungry" and out of economic necessity had to seek employment with other bands: "Monk started as house pianist at Minton's—the house that built bop—and after work the cats fell in to jam, and pretty soon you couldn't get in Minton's for musicians and instruments."[28]

The story of how young maverick musicians congregated in after-hours jam sessions at Minton's Playhouse (and later at Clark Monroe's Uptown House) is legendary.[29] Jam sessions such those that took place at Minton's and Monroe's were "a mixture of recreation and business . . .

musicians made contacts for future employment, held competitive 'cutting contests' to establish a pecking order, and took advantage of the isolation from public scrutiny to experiment with new techniques."[30] A crucial step in bebop's progression toward economic viability was finding a place that would (1) give the musicians the freedom required to explore new musical territory, and (2) attract an open-minded and supportive clientele, a fan base. For several reasons, Minton's created a suitable atmosphere for bebop's early life. The club's owner, Henry Minton, was a former musician who had, in the 1920s, run the Rhythm Club, an informal clearinghouse for black musicians.[31] When Minton's opened for business, musicians made it theirs. As the first African American delegate of Local 802 of the American Federation of Musicians, Minton was sensitive to the financial and artistic needs of jazz musicians: he was generous with loans, he was fond of food, and, as an old acquaintance recalled, he "loved to put a pot on the range to share with unemployed friends."[32] As Ralph Ellison writes, Minton's policy "provided a retreat, a homogeneous community where a collectivity of experience could find continuity and meaningful expression. Thus the stage was set for the birth of bop."[33]

In January 1940, Minton hired musician Teddy Hill to replace Dewey Vanderburg as manager of his club. Hill, in turn, hired musicians whom he knew and encouraged jam sessions on the small bandstand.[34] According to Kenny Clarke, arguably the first modern jazz drummer, Hill "never tried to tell us how to play. We played just as we felt."[35] Musicians' eyewitness accounts provide valuable evidence of the cultural, and even musical, importance of the after-hours establishment to jazz life. Williams stresses that Minton maintained a down-to-earth atmosphere, believed in keeping the place up, and was constantly redecorating. "And the food was good. Lindsay Steele had the kitchen at one time. He cooked wonderful meals and was a good mixer, who could sing awhile during the intermission."[36] Miles Davis remembers that it did not cost anything to get into Minton's unless you sat a table, and that cost around two dollars. He describes Minton's as a supper club with neat white linen cloth tables complemented with little vases, where the clientele was well dressed. And Davis recalls that a great black woman cook named Adelle prepared the food.[37] Another attraction of Minton's was the "Monday night down home dinners" for the cast of current shows at the Apollo Theater.[38] To away-from-home musicians such as Davis, the Minton's milieu exemplified good food, music, atmosphere, stylish dress, and remembering the cook's name. It was the communal sharing of urban African American culture.

The atmosphere of clubs such as Minton's made Harlem a hothouse for early bebop and other forms of entertainment aimed at local black audiences. Harlem offered these musicians "a rediscovered community of things they had left behind: feasts, talk, home."[39] And, as Malcolm X observed, Harlem's nightlife appealed to many who did not live there when he arrived in the early 1940s: "Up and down along and between Lenox and Seventh and Eighth Avenues, Harlem was like some technicolor bazaar. Hundreds of Negro soldiers and sailors, gawking and young like me, passed by. Harlem by now was officially off limits to white servicemen. There had already been some muggings and robberies, and several white servicemen had been found murdered. The police were also trying to discourage white civilians from coming uptown, but those who wanted to still did."[40] Fifty-Second Street, bebop's new "home" after 1945, was starkly different. Leonard Feather once described the clubs there as having no identity, sleazy, discriminatory, with very small tables and watered-down drinks: "There was nothing to them except the music."[41] Perhaps candid observations by Davis and Gillespie, respectively, comparing Harlem and 52nd Street sum up best the tenor of each space: "It was a wonderful time. But 52d St. was better. Uptown we were just experimenting. By the time we came down[town] our ideas were beginning to be accepted. Oh, it took some time, but 52d St. gave us the rooms to play and the audiences."[42] Gillespie's statement contrasts strongly with Davis's:

> It was Minton's where a musician *really* cut his teeth and *then* went downtown to The Street. Fifty-second Street was easy compared to what was happening up at Minton's. You went to 52nd to make money and be seen by the white music critics and white people. But you came uptown to Minton's if you wanted to make a reputation among the musicians . . . After bebop became the rage, white music critics tried to act like they discovered it—and us—down on 52nd Street. . . . But the musicians and the people who really loved and respected bebop and the truth know that the *real* thing happened up in Harlem, at Minton's.[43]

Wonderful times with rooms and audiences, compared to respect among peers and the *real* thing—a distinct dichotomy produced in two very different cultural spaces. Harlem was a woodshed. It was a rite-of-passage experience in which bebop musicians came of age. Fifty-Second Street, on the other hand, represented the larger marketplace, the media, and commercial industry. With proper exposure on the

Street, an artist could gain access to record contracts and prestigious concert bookings in halls that previously had been off-limits. A bebop musician's career soon depended on having others manage or navigate this move. Thus, bebop's journey to 52nd Street represented another important rite of passage: it became a mainstream business. The economic reality that bebop musicians could not sustain careers in Harlem is an important point to keep in mind while reevaluating the notion that bebop was somehow exclusively anticommercial.

Bebop musicians found themselves turning to audiences outside Harlem for wider recognition. They could not achieve lucrative careers away from the white publications or from downtown audiences. Furthermore, they could not help but care what critics wrote about their music, nor could they thrive economically without them. Miles Davis noted that critics became keenly interested in bebop only after musicians began playing on the Street, which provided them with money and media exposure. Nightclubs such as the Three Deuces, Kelley's Stables, the Onyx, and the Downbeat Club became more important to bebop's survival than Harlem clubs because of the economic opportunities available in midtown Manhattan.

Patrick Burke's study of the Street's social history represents it as a complex, contradictory space where one could find "the most conventional forms of racial discrimination and stereotyping" existing side by side with "a radical trend toward racial integration." These clubs were among the first to feature integrated bands and audiences, and by the 1940s some of them had become the city's first black-owned nightclubs.[44] This social frontier in race relations highlighted the fear of miscegenation as once segregated audiences began to fill with black (and white) hipsters (or "zombies," as they were also called). Zoot-suited, long-haired, and reefer-smoking, these black hipsters quite publicly undermined the Street's entrenched "white bachelor subculture" by openly dating and showing authority over white women. As Burke points out, not all blacks and bebop musicians were hipsters on the Street, and some of the musicians were white. But the bebop movement was closely associated with this hipster subculture, and as Burke, Ingrid Monson, Robin D. G. Kelley, and other observers have noted, its reputation turned on troubling primitivist notions of black masculinity.[45]

As real or imagined sexual threats to white superiority, black bebop musicians became embroiled in a battle of subcultures, sometimes marked by violent episodes. Miles Davis, for example, recalls a specific kind of racial tension surrounding bebop's Midtown move—one that was an age-old and volatile reason for Jim Crow in the first place. For him, the increased visibility of black male musicians dating white women in Midtown, together with the insider's dress code and colorful vocabulary, fanned the flame of intolerance: "[Whites] thought that they were being invaded by niggers from Harlem."[46] Uptown invaded Midtown with a dissonant, polyrhythmic, and uncompromising vengeance. Indeed, bebop's beginnings in Harlem's insular woodsheds and heroic cutting contests, together with the language of conquest used to characterize its move to the commercial and sexual territories of the Street, sharpened the music's experimental, masculinist edges. But bebop was only one side of a multifaceted world of black artistic experimentation at midcentury.

CRITICAL INQUIRY:
JAZZ CRITICISM AT THE CROSSROADS

Although scholars have been among its most ardent advocates, the idea that jazz is an art music did not first emerge in the plodding pages of academic journals, but rather in a messy, noisy, free-for-all atmosphere in which musicians, critics, entrepreneurs, club owners, and publicists battled for cultural turf, prestige, and a slice of the commercial pie. Motivated to varying degrees by self-interest, artistic experimentation, and the politics of American social life, these historical actors established the jazz-as-art idea in what Bernard Gendron has called an "aesthetic discursive formation."[47]

Jazz critics were especially dominant forces in these discourses—many of which borrowed from the western art music world—that laid the groundwork for jazz becoming serious art and, with that, a genre separate from other popular music styles. It should be noted that jazz criticism was a primarily white enterprise in the 1940s, and the bebop musicians themselves primarily African American.[48] The amalgamation of social worlds is only part of the story's complexity, however. Other aspects include primarily journalistic debates in which key ideas—usually oppositional—established a conceptual framework in which jazz would transform its pedigree from folk and mass culture into art. Such debates investigated genres and brand names; art and commerce; folklore and European high culture; progress and the new; standards, techniques, and schooling; affect and antics; and fascists and communists.[49] Many of these ideas formed binary constructions that galvanized the debates. (As we learned above, even the early cultural spaces in which bebop could be heard can be viewed as a dichotomy between the after-hours Harlem and 52nd Street nightspots.)

As Gendron points out, two literary factional wars in the 1940s, the first between swing and the revivalist Dixieland movement, and the second pitting bebop against the two former styles, created a new way to look at jazz. What emerged from this war of words was "a set of agreed-upon claims about the aesthetic merit of various jazz styles . . . [and] a grouping of concepts, distinctions, oppositions, rhetorical ploys, and allowable inferences, which as a whole fixed the limits within which inquiries concerning the aesthetics of jazz could take place and without which the claim that jazz is an art form would be merely an abstraction or an incantation."[50]

Thus a language developed for valuing jazz as art, a strategy contingent upon the notion of the music's organic growth and development.[51] In this framework, a boundary between jazz and other popular forms was drawn. For Gendron, bebop represents an early form of postmodernism because its emergence marked the first time that "popular culture abandoned its previously passive, almost unwitting, engagement with high culture, to become an initiator and even an aggressor."[52] This claim is instructive, especially in its implications for a gendered reading of bebop and jazz's generic shift, as we shall witness below.

The musicians in this saga negotiated this emerging, contentious art world primarily through their sonic experimentations, although Charlie Parker and Dizzy Gillespie, the two iconic figures of early bebop, issued public statements in interviews that critics used to validate one position or another. How can we interpret and understand their cultural work—indeed, their insurrection—as masculinist, aggressive, and transformative? The following commentary identifies some of the ground on which these meanings were fought out.

The journalists who wrote about bebop left behind a trail of print in the popular and trade press documenting a colorful and instructive controversy. With titles such as "How Deaf Can You Get?" (1948) and "Do You Get It?" (1949), many of these articles range in tone from bewilderment to hostility to outrage at bebop. In a record review, Charles Miller writes as if peer pressure had forced him to deal with the new music: "Although I'm less than enthusiastic about a style of jazz called bebop, I feel that it's worth writing about because it's attracting an increasing number of listeners and because it might some day make more sense than it does now."[53] His description below, particularly his choice of such words as "weird," "neurotic," and "foreign," allows us to experience a bit of the distancing effect bebop had on some contemporaneous listeners. Interestingly, these terms function—perhaps unwittingly—to emasculate the work of bebop musicians, especially the embedded innuendo that they were not involved in serious creative acts and seemed to be just "fooling around": "Bebop isn't easy to define, but I think it's safe to call it highly experimental. Bebop musicians like to fool around with weird sounding chord effects and unusually complex melodic and rhythmic patterns, producing stuff that's comparatively foreign to many ears. For my money, it's an intensely neurotic style, and except for occasional passages that show imagination and beauty, I want no part of it." Miller goes on to rehearse a wisecrack about the style: "Bebop is just a bunch of guys covering up their mistakes."[54] Wilder Hobson adopts a similar tone when reviewing a Dizzy Gillespie recording, using the opportunity to expound on the virtues of earlier jazz and to ridicule bebop. While generally dismissive, he compliments bebop musicians for being "incredibly agile" and reluctantly admits that the recording has a certain arresting and eerie quality.[55] In his listening experience, bebop was "a miss."

The mainstream press also took note of the controversy. A *Time* article from 1948, "Bopera on Broadway," about the Royal Roost, a New York club that was among the first to feature bebop exclusively, notes: "Bebop has been around for seven or eight years, and something of a fad for two, but experts still disagree as to what it is, and whether it will last." To this writer, the music was "shrill cacophony" and "anarchistic."[56] The article also mentions that clubs featuring bebop customarily maintained a no-dancing policy, which forced audiences either to listen to or ignore the music. A *Newsweek* article of the same year, "B. G. and Bebop," responding to Benny Goodman's experimentation with bebop in his group, polls several of Manhattan's leading jazz critics. The most negative comment comes from the influential jazz critic and entrepreneur John Hammond, then vice-president of Mercury Records: "To me bop is a collection of nauseating clichés, repeated ad infinitum."[57]

By 1949, the public recognized Gillespie and Parker as leading figures in bebop, and the musicians issued public statements about the music in the press. When he was asked the question "What is bebop?" Dizzy Gillespie answered that it is "just the way I and a few of my fellow musicians feel about jazz. It's our means of expressing ourselves in music just as, years ago, the Chicagoans and the Dixielanders expressed themselves."[58] At face value, his words seem to defend his artistic right to experiment, to achieve artistic manhood. But he was probably also connecting bebop to earlier, more popular styles because he was fighting to keep his career afloat and his bank account in the black. Gillespie, known for his demonstrative, antic-filled stage manner, had a modernism that was an unabashedly commercial endeavor.

For his part in the "debate," Charlie Parker chose another tactic. In Oedipal fashion, he claimed that bebop had developed apart from the older styles of jazz, stressing his music's distance from the musical past.[59] Bebop, for Parker, was rhythmically radical, and he wanted to wear that distinction on his sleeve. Gillespie countered in the October 7, 1949, issue of *Down Beat* that Parker was wrong: Bebop was an interpretation of jazz and certainly a part of its tradition.[60] This debate was about more than a casual exchange of abstract ideas for these musicians. They were engaged in a public struggle for their commercial lives and, by extension, their social lives, in a context in which they exercised little control over the public meaning and discursive dissemination of their work. The critics, although not culturally powerful outside of the jazz community, ruled over these domains.[61]

Like jazz criticism, photographs of jazz musicians became an expressive domain that informed the ways in which bebop's pedigree circulated in the public sphere. The diligence and artful sensibilities with which photographers began to frame jazz musicians had political as well as commercial implications. As Benjamin Cawthra argues: "Jazz photography . . . did its best to bring jazz into a mainstream of American culture. In this mainstream, jazz could function as an ambassador for American values while subtly—but with increasing intensity over time and in the eyes of particular photographers—offering a critique of those values via the presentation of African American virtuosity. Jazz itself existed as a kind of critique of a society divided racially, and its photographers made that critique visible while publicizing and selling the music."[62] The photographs of Bud Powell in this book allow us to see an influential modality in which the idea of his genius—and, by extension, bebop's artistic constitution—was consumed by his public and in history. Indeed, the photographs, Cawthra insists, "shaped that history, making arguments through visual means for the significance of African American musical culture, the meaning of jazz in American history, and the moral necessity of a politics of equality, even though these goals themselves were complicated by the racial dynamics of jazz itself."[63] Bebop visuality, it seems, asserted just as much force in American culture as the music's sonic aspects.

Bebop has certainly traveled considerable critical distance since the days when it was described as "a bunch of guys covering up mistakes" and as "shrill cacophony" and "nauseating clichés." While certainly rooted in the bodily excesses of the dance floor, Powell's music has risen to the lofty status of "head" music. Even the hip dress and speech patterns of bebop musicians, treated routinely in sensationalist terms by the contemporaneous press, seem benign and safe by today's standards.

RACE, COMPLEXITY, AND "THE" JAZZ AUDIENCE

A standard axiom of the western art music tradition is the sheer effort it takes for audiences to comprehend the best of its works. In an article published during bebop's early years (1941), Theodor Adorno compares the cultural work of "popular" and "serious" audiences, especially as they relate to the notions of simplicity and complexity:

> Listening to popular music is manipulated not only by its promoters but, as it were, by the inherent nature of this music itself, into a system of response mechanisms wholly antagonistic to the ideal of individuality in a free, liberal society. This has nothing to do with simplicity and complexity. In serious music, each musical element, even the simplest one, is "itself," and the more highly organized the work is, the less possibility there is of substitution among the details. In hit music, however, the structure underlying the piece is abstract, existing independent of the specific course of the music. This is basic to the illusion that certain complex harmonies are more easily understandable in popular music than the same harmonies in serious music.[64]

Jazz, in Adorno's mind, belongs to the popular realm. He does recognize, however, that it possesses qualities not found in other popular genres. But to him these qualities only camouflage jazz's inherent banality: "In jazz the amateur listener is capable of replacing complicated rhythmical [sic] or harmonic formulas by the schematic ones which they represent and which they still suggest, however adventurous they appear."[65] (If what Adorno says is true, it seems to suggest a certain level of sophistication on behalf of jazz audiences that largely goes unnoticed.)

Establishing the point that jazz is *not* popular has composed an important part of the jazz studies agenda over the last thirty years. In doing so, jazz scholars have ignored or usurped the varied nature of the jazz audience. One strategy has been to make the jazz audience appear to have the same goals and tastes that western art music audiences do. This strategy invariably attempts to place jazz in the realm of high art.

In the fifth edition of his *Jazz Styles,* a popular "jazz appreciation" textbook, Mark Gridley's didactic explanation of why jazz is not "popular music" shows some of the problems implicit in attempts to reify the perceived boundaries between high and low culture: (1) "jazz musicians represent a highly versatile and specially trained elite whose level of sophistication is not common to the population at large"; (2) jazz "is appreciated for its esthetic and intellectual rewards, and it is approached with some effort"; and (3) jazz "requires a cultivated taste."[66] All of Gridley's statements are true. But they rub against his other ideas, designed to put the undergraduate music appreciation student at ease: "Jazz can be a lot of fun to listen to. But some people miss that fun because they let themselves be intimidated."[67] In my view, however, jazz audiences are dynamic entities that defy static representation, and they invite a reconfiguration of terms such as *sophistication, taste, intellectual, cultivation,* and even *fun* as they concern the reception of jazz.

Naturally, this suggests that a history of "the" jazz audience begs to be written.[68] Such a study could help to clear up some commonly held misconceptions, among them that after the advent of bebop, black citizens shunned jazz in favor of rhythm and blues. Such sentiments fail to acknowledge the diversity and complexity of African American audiences, especially in the postwar period. Black audiences have continually demanded that musicians be *avant-garde* with regard to their treatment of *traditional* musical materials.

Moreover, history also proves that for many reasons, African Americans have generally shown little interest in preserving idioms for posterity's sake. That attitude toward music making has produced a huge body of music, some of it among the most influential and widely appreciated music of the twentieth century. Susan McClary has coined the term *terminal prestige* to explain the results of certain contemporary, academic composers' view that audience approval is a symbol of artistic compromise.[69] Some writers have suggested that bebop musicians' temperaments resulted in the same terminal prestige for modern jazz—especially among African American audiences. What these accounts fail to acknowledge, however, is that the black audience's continual demand for an avant-garde necessarily positions *every* musical idiom, artist, and genre as a candidate for supplanting. Such was the case with swing at the appearance of bebop, and with bebop at the advent of rhythm and blues.

There also remains a huge misunderstanding about how black audiences "take music seriously." For many scholars, critics, and other observers, this confusion has led to the assumption that whites are better caretakers of black music making than blacks themselves could be. Martin Williams wrote the following passage in 1964, a racially contentious moment indeed, as a challenge "to the next man who does a sociological study of jazz":

> Now everyone knows, musicians themselves aside, that it had been white men, by and large, who have taken jazz seriously, written its history, cataloged its records, criticized its players, and called it an "art." One might easily say that the mode of the white man's education prepared him to treat this musical activity called jazz in that manner, since he had been trained to treat painting, architecture, literature, and music in a similar manner. Whereas fewer Negroes have been exposed to that sort of education, to that sort of treatment of artistic endeavor, and therefore did not think in those terms. Or those who had been, again, were brainwashed against jazz by middle-class standards.

Williams notes that even black jazz musicians agreed with him: "Louis Armstrong often said that, throughout his musical life, his work was better attended and better appreciated by white men than by members of his own race. And Duke Ellington did not even begin to discover the size of his talent until he started to play at the Cotton Club for audiences that were predominantly white and where Negroes knew they were not welcome."[70]

Williams's argument raises two points worth pursuing here. First, his two examples highlight the need to understand the impact of black jazz audiences on jazz musicians' careers. In that light, Williams's conclusions raise important questions. Was Armstrong far past his vogue, at least as far as black audiences were concerned, when he expressed the sentiments above? In which ways did whites demonstrate their "appreciation"? Could the fact that white audiences at the Cotton Club were able to provide the *financial* support necessary for Ellington's musical growth be a factor in his "epiphany"? If so, then Williams's concerns are more economically based than they are racial. Can the same patterns be seen in the bebop audience?

The second point concerns the role of cultural values and hierarchies. During her tenure in the Billy Eckstine Orchestra, Sarah Vaughan witnessed bebop's impact on audiences. Her comments imply that black audiences paid their highest compliments by dancing: "We tried to educate people. We used to play dances, and there were just a very few who understood who would be in a corner, jitterbugging forever, while the rest just stood staring at us."[71] Mary Lou Williams also recalls that bebop, for a time, pleased dancers where the space allowed: "Right from the start, musical reactionaries have said the worst about bop. But after seeing the Savoy Ballroom kids fit dances to this kind of music, I felt it was destined to become the new era of music, though not taking anything away from Dixieland or swing or any of the great stars of jazz."[72] These examples show the necessity of *historizing* statements about the tastes and reactions of African American audiences (or *any* audience), because these sentiments are dynamic ones that constantly shift. In fact, Lawrence Levine shows that jazz generally enjoys an audience in much the same way that opera in mid-nineteenth-century America did: "Like Shakespearean drama, then, opera was an art form that was simultaneously popular and elite. That is, it was attended both by large numbers of people who derived great pleasure from it and experienced it in the context of their normal everyday culture, and smaller socially and economically elite groups who derived both pleasure and social confirmation from it."[73] In other words, whether one writes histories, catalogues records, founds archives, or "jitterbug[s] forever," there are many ways to get at the *meaning* and the history of cultural expressions.

The tensions surrounding any simplistic view of these points can be illustrated by a recent visit I made to Jazz at Lincoln Center. Situated atop an upscale mall in midtown Manhattan, its stunning facilities have become symbolic of jazz's century-long trek from brothel Muzak to artistic artifact. An in-house repertory ensemble keeps the flame of previous jazz styles alive while a pristine, smokeless nightclub provides current jazz stars an unusually plush and inviting setting in which to share their music before a breathtaking backdrop of Manhattan's skyline. Clearly, the boundaries between art and commerce are laid bare here, in relaxed splendor. Even the most cynical "pro-folk" cultural critic is grateful to witness jazz's ascent to such auspicious surroundings.

We find similar tensions in discussions about the nature of the jazz sound itself. Martin Williams, for example, believes that Charlie Parker was not "a great composer." Parker's best composition, he asserts, is "Confirmation," primarily because of one quality it possesses: "a continuous linear invention," or, in other words, its complexity.[74] (Williams has plenty of distinguished company who share his preferences.) Whenever jazz seemed to stray from certain ideals held in western music, critics have responded hastily. The history of jazz has seen more than its share of calls for greater motivic unity in solos, praise for longer forms in composition, denunciations of repetition, and appeals for formalized concert decorum. Of course, it has seen calls for "back to the basics"/"down-with-elitism" movements as well.

The suggestion that jazz needed a transfusion from the western art music tradition is curious, considering the music's debt to European traditions in the first place. Certainly Powell's early training in classical music provides an obvious case in point. Yet on a deeper level this privileging of the "West" points to the need to understand the complexity of the relationship between African American culture and modernism. Elsewhere, I have employed the term *Afro-modernism* to describe a specifically African American response to modernity, especially in the United States. Its concerns are not just aesthetic, but also social, political, and economic. Expressive practices such as music, photography, visual art, poetry, and literature both reflect and shape these domains. All these factors intersect in the world of one musician: Powell.

SCHOOLING BEBOP

In the 1990s, during jazz's new academic surge, Scott DeVeaux summed up the prevailing view of bebop's new modernist pose:

> The transition from swing to bebop is more than the passage from one style to another. Bebop is the keystone in the grand historical arch, the crucial link between the early stage of jazz and modernity. Indeed, it is only with bebop that the essential nature of jazz is unmistakably revealed. There is an implicit entelechy in the progression from early jazz to bebop: the gradual shedding of utilitarian associations with dance music, popular song, and entertainment, as both musicians and public become aware of what jazz really is, or could be. With bebop, jazz finally became an art music.[75]

I add that with bebop, jazz became a genre separate from other popular music styles, complete with a new social contract with the public, cultural institutions, and musicians.

This perceived change in pedigree has inspired numerous speculations on the art of the politics and on the politics embedded in the art of bebop, with writers coming down on one side or the other of the aesthetics-versus-politics divide. These cultural differences are seen clearly in the language used to argue for this or that position in these debates. If gender is about power, with the ideals of male and female representing different points on a continuum of prestige, then bebop has existed as a slippery, transgendered discourse, at various times being assigned the mantle of great, masculinist art, and at others relegated to "weaker" cultural positions vis-à-vis western art music. Yet certainly one gets the impression from DeVeaux's characterization that, finally, through aesthetic discourse, jazz had "manned up."

Although bebop is recognized as black music, its pedigree has been elevated as the work of an elite class of musicians, akin to modernist composers of the western art music tradition such as Schoenberg, Stravinsky, and Webern. Subsequent musicians who worked in the style known as free jazz inspired similar comparisons to this group of avant-garde, experimental composers. Powell's music (and that of other beboppers) has achieved, in some respects, the status and appeal that cultural critics and theorists desired for black classical musicians such as William Grant Still, whose activities blossomed during the Harlem Renaissance. In fact, African American composers of classical music still do not receive the attention they deserve in the broad scheme of American music studies. Jazz musicians, on the other hand, have become crucial figures in these histories.

The popularity of jazz in the curricula of American colleges and universities is a reliable measure of the respect it now attracts. Performing ensembles and theory and history courses bring serious study to the music once thought unworthy of sustained consideration. Universities bestow honorary doctorates on jazz musicians in this new "jazz age," and their names are cited among the same cadre of honorees as prominent scientists, physicians, educators, artists, and scholars. Yet for all of its sonic riches and rewards, the music alone accounts for only part of this pedigree shift. Writers—both critics and scholars—have played a key role in establishing the music's new and improved social profile.

Jazz criticism as an enterprise has appeared in many guises. Truly international in scope, its expressions are myriad, ranging from publicists' ravings in trade journals to freelancers' rants about the latest pressing controversy. From the French critic Andre Hodeir to the black nationalist Amiri Baraka, from the southern new criticism of Martin Williams to the Big Apple poetics of Gary Giddins, from the staunch and testy prose of Stanley Crouch to the leftist politics of Nat Hentoff, jazz criticism has constituted an eclectic bundle of journalistic impulses. Taken together, these writings brought to the American public a sustained level of critical and aesthetic discourse about a music that had at one time struggled for widespread aesthetic legitimacy.[76]

For its part, jazz scholarship—its most current iteration is dubbed "the new jazz studies"—is now a bona fide area of the music subdisciplines and appears across an interdisciplinary spectrum of humanities fields, including English, history, and American studies. Partly as a result of the deconstruction of the canon and partly inspired by the 1980s jazz renaissance (replete with "young lions" dressed in business suits, new recording deals, and historical classics reissued on compact disc), the 1990s surge in dissertations, scholarly monographs, and articles changed forever how the music was perceived: as a serious artistic pursuit on par with other fine arts. The new jazz studies insists that jazz music is much more than an abstract set of technical principles, chord changes, rhythms, and organizations; it is also a cultural phenomenon whose scope of influence can be experienced in the visual arts, literature, dance, and film.[77]

Since the 1990s, jazz historians have moved beyond the aesthetics of universalism that once ruled jazz academic discourse and led us into richer readings of the topic. A number of scholars (the work presented below is merely suggestive of the available studies) have taken on the challenge of bebop specifically, producing nuanced interpretations of the musicians, the music, its audiences, and the historical contexts that produced them. The most broadly conceived and sweeping of these bebop studies is Scott DeVeaux's blockbuster study *The Birth of Bebop* (1997). DeVeaux writes about the emergence of bebop style by attending to musical analysis and to the political economy of the jazz world during the years that bridged the swing and bebop eras. When the book won the American Musicological Society's best book award in 1998, it sent a resounding signal to this corner of the academic world that jazz studies was viable, attractive, and rigorous. Other scholars tightened their focus around more specific topics. Ingrid Monson's *Saying Something* (1996) penetrates and explains the social meanings generated within the improvisatory setting of the typical rhythm sections of modern jazz ensembles. Her ethnographic work weds the social theories of anthropology to musical analysis and the broader field of cultural studies, the latter of which had rambled through the humanities during the 1980s and 1990s. In *What Is This Thing Called Jazz?* (2002), Eric Porter takes a discerning look at modern jazz musicians as bona fide intellectuals—not as naturally gifted noble savages, but as self-conscious participants in both their creative work and the critical discourses that surround it. Porter's American studies–styled readings of a multiplicity of texts illuminate how bebop opened a space in the popular sphere for aesthetically challenging black music, serious black audiences, and virtuoso black musicians. In two of its chapters, Bernard Gendron's *Between Montmartre and the Mudd Club* (2002) focuses on critical discourses during the bebop era and argues that modern jazz represents a postmodern turn in the historical relationship between high and low culture. By this argument, Gendron means that, in his view, postmodernism emerged when popular culture (in this case, bebop) became the unprecedented aggressor in the historical high and low cultural exchanges that had occurred throughout the twentieth century. Eddie Meadows's *Bebop to Cool* (2003) contextualizes bebop within the black liberation struggles in all its stripes—from Marcus Garvey to Islam. Also narrowly focused on African American reception, my *Race Music* (2003) discusses the social energies that were exchanged between musical cultures such as bebop and historical African American audiences to determine the extent to which each symbolizes specific responses to modernism. Works by David Ake, Ingrid Monson, Farah Griffin and Salim Washington emphasize cultural studies informed readings of bebop—what the music teaches us about the larger social world in which it circulated. And Robin D. G. Kelley's majestic biography of Thelonius Monk is a model for understanding how the historical bebop musician impacted the entire American musical landscape.[78]

All things told, jazz criticism and scholarship have helped to usher the music into a new age of quasi-respectability. Coupled with corporate interest in promoting this new profile, it would seem that we are in the sway of a new orthodoxy that might be called Jazz, Inc. With respectability as one of its core impulses, Jazz, Inc., embodies all of the tensions and contradictions of late capitalism, a state in which a discourse attempts to marshal and stabilize styles, critiques, and theories into something manageable and consumable even as it exploits its perceived marginal status. The emergence of jazz studies in the academy developed in the context of the larger movement of multiculturalism. This leftist-inspired 1990s shift allowed "people of color culture" to gain ground as subjects and objects of study in the academy. And, of course, commerce has played an important role here. Institutional support, in particular funding from foundations, provides financial backing for symposia, endowed chairs, publications, concert series, and artist-in-residence posts—all the trimmings and trappings of an established art form.

This new jazz orthodoxy is reminiscent of similar moves in other areas. The late painter Jean-Michel Basquiat, for example, rose to prominence in the 1980s. He burst onto the scene first as a marginal, self-styled graffiti artist. Later, by virtue of his outsized talent, growth, and ambition, he quickly became an art star whose works today command "some of the highest prices of any African American artist in United States history." Basquiat's important 2005 touring retrospective at the Brooklyn Museum, the Museum of Contemporary Art, Los Angeles, and the Museum of Fine Arts, Houston, was sponsored by none other than JPMorgan Chase.[79]

Closer to jazz's home, Wynton Marsalis, a gifted jazz musician who emerged as a young titan in the early 1980s, has become a notable ambassador of Jazz, Inc., in his highly visible roles as the artistic director and philanthropic pitchman for Jazz at Lincoln Center, a powerful institution with a reported $31 million operating budget, supported by both sponsors and ticket sales. A newcomer to the Lincoln Center complex, jazz first became a strong presence there in 1987 when it took its place next to opera and concert music, genres with much longer American histories of philanthropic backing.[80] These "from margins to center" narratives—be they about specific artists or entire genres— did not occur in vacuums, but within a political economy that is constituted by the obvious suspects of race, class, gender, commerce, and other discourses that always mediate interactions between the powerless and the powerful.

Now we can begin to examine the relationship between the historic figure (Powell) and the "historiographic," the world of histories of and ideas about expressive culture. I seek to understand Powell and his music from many perspectives and interpretive positions and with many tools, an exercise that is in sync with other recent examples of contemporary jazz scholarship. These studies, as John Gennari notes, investigate how "jazz has been imagined, defined, managed, and shaped within particular cultural contexts. [They consider] how jazz as an experience of sounds, movements, and states of feeling has always been mediated and complicated by peculiarly American cultural patterns, especially those of race and sexuality."[81] With an ambitious model of investigation in mind, this study of Powell illuminates his life's work, but also takes this opportunity to address larger issues in African American music.

2

Something Else

The Tests and Triumphs of a Modernist

He was what you call a real genius. . . . He was something
else in his young age.

Cootie Williams, Institute of Jazz Studies Oral History interview

When the contemporary pianist Marcus Roberts presented the music
of Bud Powell and Earl Hines in the opulent splendor of Jazz at Lincoln
Center's Rose Theater in the spring of 2011, the event boasted all the
trappings of fine-art celebration. The repertory-styled ensemble performed Powell's compositions in a way that intended to showcase the
music's enduring artistic appeal, beyond its moment of inception, a
characterization that always accompanies "art" status. There, in the
bosom of one of New York City's premiere sanctuaries for high culture, the inventive Roberts explored Powell's unmistakable melodies
and clever harmonic turns in a way that pleased the knowing audience
and would have certainly thrilled the composer himself. Who could
have known that the work of a child born in black uptown New York
would be contemplated and revisited in the most prestigious circles
some eighty-plus years after his birth?

Any version of Powell's short life, the contours of which are traced in
this chapter, must attempt to make sense of it in relationship to a number of narratives, some dominant and others downplayed in existing
accounts. I imbed and interpret his biography's major elements in several contexts: his family and friends; the sonic worlds that he engaged;
the rough-and-tumble, mostly exploitative, emerging business of modern jazz in which he made his reputation; the close network of musicians and members of other art movements who rocked 1940s and '50s
culture in America and beyond; and the difficulties that ravaged the

lives of many young African American men of Powell's ilk: drug and alcohol abuse (or, in his case, self-medication), psychiatric (mis)treatment, and the criminal (in)justice system.

The story begins modestly. Earl "Bud" Powell was born on September 27, 1924, to Pearl and William Powell, Sr., in Harlem Hospital, in the heart of a neighborhood that was rapidly becoming an enclave of diverse black ethnic groups. In the realm of race politics, times were indeed changing, and Harlem figured prominently in those changes. Harlem Hospital, established in 1887 to provide medical care to poor residents of Manhattan's growing population north of Central Park, became the first hospital in the city to employ a black physician on its staff in 1920.[1] Beyond this and many other firsts, the neighborhood ultimately would become well known throughout the world as an incubator of some of the most dynamic cultural activities, institutions, and artists of its era, one that shaped African American cultural production for decades to come.

The 1936 Harlem Hospital mural project certainly was one symbol of the neighborhood's progressive attitude. Featuring images of black physicians and backed by the Works Progress Administration, it became controversial among white doctors employed at the hospital for being too "Negro." The mural shows that Harlem's air was thickening with social change and artistic energy during the early decades of the century. One must appreciate, however, that notions of black empowerment were juxtaposed with another sensibility in Harlem. In this reality, one in which age-old ideas about race and sexuality were rehearsed and reified, well-heeled whites safaried the nightlife "in search of supposedly more authentic black entertainment, cross-racial sexual encounters, and the anonymity necessary to allow themselves to indulge in the 'primitive' behaviors and desires they associated with blacks."[2] When Powell's parents moved to Harlem while Pearl was pregnant with Bud, they could not have chosen a more exciting place.[3] How could the young Powell not soak up all the dynamic and contradictory elements of this atmosphere? Certainly he did, for a few short years later, he would be part of the network of important musicians who extended (and, in some cases, upended) all these social energies into new conceptions of art for a new time and the next generation.

A family tradition of music making rooted Powell's muse. His paternal grandfather, Zachary Gregory, it has been reported, learned flamenco guitar in Cuba during the Spanish-American War and fought "side by side" with Theodore Roosevelt.[4] When he began classical piano study at the age of six, Powell was taught by a Mr. William Rawlins.[5] Rawlins, reportedly of West Indian heritage, apparently introduced Powell to classical piano literature. Bebop saxophonist Jackie McLean, a family friend of the Powells', recalls Rawlins as a diligent pedagogue, "a hidden genius" whose quick raps with a ruler to Powell's hands encouraged strict observance of the "proper fingerings."[6]

As a classical musician of African descent, Rawlins was part of a growing rank and file of black musicians who aspired to the highest level of performance in western art music. This group could trace their existence to the earliest years of the nineteenth century through musicians such as the Philadelphian Francis Johnson (1792–1844), and when the National Association of Negro Musicians formed in 1919, black classical musicians organized themselves and became evangelists for their work among African Americans. Despite the long history of discriminatory practices in the classical world, many black musicians dedicated themselves to the repertoire and its associated decorum, and Powell himself intended to become a concert musician in this ritualized world.[7]

Powell's father appears to have been the first guiding force in his musical life. Powell once stated, in a rare interview with Sharon Pease, a writer for *Down Beat,* that he had received "much advice, inspiration, and encouragement" from his father, whom he identified as a professional stride pianist.[8] McLean says that the senior Powell was still playing in the early 1960s, and also working as a building superintendent in Harlem.[9] According to William Sr., his son was an exceptional and gifted pianist, and by age seven, Bud was being chauffeured from place to place to perform for older musicians.[10] William Sr.'s, circle of friends included musicians who had significant influence on the younger Powell's musical development. In his father's report, by age ten Powell was reproducing with ease what he heard, including some of the music of Art Tatum and Fats Waller, a friend and frequent visitor to the Powell home. William Sr., took great pride in his son's musicianship and supposedly preserved some of his performances for posterity. Francis Paudras claims to have heard in 1964 William Sr.'s homemade recordings, made between 1934 and 1939, which featured Bud as a young virtuoso playing Bach, Chopin, and Debussy, as well as jazz interpretations of "Tea for Two," "How High the Moon," and "Honeysuckle Rose."[11]

Powell's musical activities eventually expanded into his church, school, and social life. In the mid- to late 1930s, Powell served as an acolyte at Harlem's St. Charles Roman Catholic Church, at 211 West 143rd Street.[12] Reverend Monsignor Owen J. Scanlon remembers Powell singing in the choir and playing the organ for services. He also recalls that while Powell was still in school, the church hired a band that Powell played in for what Scanlon describes as "teen-age dances."[13] Bob Doerschuk notes that during this period Powell "tried his hand at playing written pieces on the organ, and with his boyhood friend, Elmo Hope . . . he would pass the hours listening to classical records."[14] In fact, Hope had begun to win medals for his solo recitals by 1938.[15] Both Hope and Powell would eventually devote themselves to full-time careers in jazz and popular music, perhaps because very little opportunity existed for blacks to work in classical music.

In his early teens, Powell became more interested in jazz, and according to pianist Walter Davis, a friend of Powell's, his parents and teacher were let down: "They had been working on him like a Frankenstein monster, perfecting, perfecting, perfecting. They wanted him to be the best classical pianist in the country. That's why they made him learn all of that music. But Bud broke their hearts going another way."[16] Powell became enchanted with the work of pianist Billy Kyle (1914–66).[17] Kyle is best known for playing in the John Kirby Sextet, billed as "The Biggest Little Band in the Land." He performed with the group from February 1938 until he was drafted into the armed services in late 1942. It was probably during these years that Kyle first caught Powell's attention. Born in Philadelphia, he studied classical piano and organ in childhood and then branched out into various local bands. Among his earliest influences were Teddy Wilson, Earl Hines, and the tradition of classical piano he learned as a child.[18] Powell's attraction to Kyle's abilities can be understood in the context of his own eclectic musical background: Kyle possessed a sure technical command of the piano, a light touch, and an ample musical imagination. The repertoire of his sextet—mainly arrangements by Kyle himself and the group's trumpeter, Charlie Shavers—included pieces by such composers as Grieg ("Anitra's Dance"), Chopin ("Minute Waltz," "Fantaisie-Impromptu"), and Beethoven ("Beethoven Riffs On," based on the second movement of *Symphony No. 7*), all of whom would have been familiar to Powell from his classical training.

William "Skeets" Powell, Jr., Bud's older brother and a trumpeter and violinist, provided him with his first real taste of playing music professionally. William, Jr., led his own band around 1938 and 1939, and Bud joined the group as they began working in small clubs around

Coney Island and greater New York. Although he had matriculated to the DeWitt Clinton High School in the Bronx, the all-boys' institution that produced writer Countee Cullen, James Baldwin, and artist Charles Alston (the director of the Harlem Hospital mural project), school could not compete with the lure and excitement of show business. Some days Bud probably never made it to the Bronx, instead cutting classes to see shows at the Apollo Theater, which began its rolling itinerary at ten in the morning.[19] When Powell dropped out at age fifteen, music became the dominant force in his life, and he joined the ranks of professional musicians. In these early years, Powell is known to have taken solo piano jobs at the Place (later known as the Limelight Coffee Shop) in Greenwich Village, and he also worked at Canada Lee's Chicken Coop in Harlem. But he remained interested in classical music as well, continuing his piano lessons and possibly still clinging to his childhood dream of becoming a recitalist—at least part-time.

Throughout the early to mid-1940s, Powell gradually secured new connections in the New York music world. Soon his path crossed with that of another pianist who would deeply influence both his musical outlook and his professional life: Thelonious Monk. They met at an uptown bar sometime in late 1942, when Powell was not yet eighteen. Together with his close friend Elmo Hope, Powell grew to idolize Monk, an older musician who taught him some of bebop's idiosyncratic approaches to the harmonic parameters of American popular song that he had been developing. And some of these lessons probably involved learning harmony through the study of Monk's growing list of original compositions. Although Powell had been studying classical piano since he was six, that kind of training doesn't always translate directly into a deep knowledge of how harmony works. Such insight, for many, is earned through the kind of specific attention which Monk paid to harmony, and he obviously shared his insight freely with the admiring younger musician.[20]

Powell's and Monk's backgrounds were probably the basis for their fast friendship. Monk had also studied classical piano in childhood, beginning at age eleven. As his biographer Robin D. G. Kelley points out, despite the lore to the contrary, Monk "possessed an impressive knowledge of, and appreciation for, western classical music, not to mention an encyclopedic knowledge of hymns and gospel music, American popular songs, and a variety of obscure art songs that defy easy categorization."[21] Both came from musical families. Monk's mother could play piano; his father played piano, the "Jew's harp," and harmonica. The

Monk family also formed a singing gospel quartet after they moved to New York City from North Carolina.[22] Both Powell and Monk shared a fascination with and cut their teeth in the dynamic musical universe that was black New York City. And both left high school to become working musicians. Kelley's observation about Monk probably applies to Powell as well: "For a young African-American man in Depression-era New York, any income was welcome."[23] A divergence can be found, however, in Monk's two-year stint with a traveling tent evangelist, through which he saw the country as a teenager, matured as a responsible and focused musician, and may have begun to discover how to work up the Holy Ghost for eager congregants through intensive and exhaustive harmonic explorations of the repetitive forms upon which sanctified church aesthetics thrive. This experience, together with the exposure he obtained in the Baptist hymn tradition through his mother's affiliation with the church, was quite different than Powell's, whose background in Catholicism would have exposed him to another sound world altogether.

Powell and Monk shared personal struggles, too, as each bore the burden of staggering mental and physical health issues. Kelley succinctly captures the difficulties of maintaining a creative life and livelihood while trying to stabilize one's equilibrium:

> Various mental and physical ailments began to take an even greater toll [on Monk], exacerbated by poor medical treatment, an unhealthy lifestyle, the daily stresses of a working jazz musician, and an unending financial and creative battle with the music industry. Some writers romanticize manic depression and/or schizophrenia as characteristics of creative genius, but the story of Monk's physical and mental ailment is essentially a tragedy, a story of his slow decline and the pain it caused to those closest to him. Its manifestations were episodic, so he continued to function and make incredible music up until the day of his retirement in 1976. During these nearly twenty years, his ability to lead a band and to dig out fresh interpretations of compositions he had been playing for decades, in spite of his illness and protracted struggle with the industry, is astonishing.[24]

Though Kelley says this of Monk, it surely describes Powell as well, although the latter's ailments were a more constant specter and played a larger and disruptive role in his life and in the tales surrounding him.

Monk introduced Powell to the jam sessions at Minton's.[25] But Powell was not immediately accepted among the musicians who would soon compose bebop's inner circle. Ira Gitler writes that the shy, young, and apparently a little socially awkward pianist almost managed to get himself put out of Minton's on his first visit to the club: "Powell sat on a chair and put his feet up on the fresh white tablecloth. When a waiter started to throw him out, Monk intervened on behalf of his protégé: 'Don't do that. That kid's got talent.'"[26] As Monk was a respected figure on the scene in Minton's, he took it upon himself to force others to give the young pianist opportunities to play, even going as far as to threaten to quit if his protégé was not allowed to sit in.[27]

Monk and Powell remained close throughout the decade. Jackie McLean recalls that in the late 1940s, Powell "spoke of Monk quite a bit. . . . He would always play Monk for me."[28] Powell was one of the few musicians who played Monk's music publicly at a time when, according to Gitler, it was generally misunderstood. Powell would later introduce Monk's composition "Off Minor" on his first recording date as a leader in 1947. Bebop innovator and drummer Kenny "Klook" Clarke believed that "Monk wrote for Bud. All his music was written for Bud Powell. All this piano music, he deliberately wrote for Bud because he figured Bud was the only one who could play it. He wrote for Bud just like a composer writes for a singer. And when you hear Bud play Monk's music, then you really hear something."[29]

Between 1940 and 1942, Powell made professional connections with musicians other than Monk. He met and played with many who over the next ten years would introduce a new idiom to the jazz world, and he broadened his contacts beyond local musicians. When trumpeter and vocalist Valaida Snow (1900–56) opened at the Apollo Theater in April 1943 with the Sunset Royals, Powell had just joined the group. The American Federation of Musicians (Local 802) Directory shows that Powell joined the union sometime in 1943. The engagement with Snow's band appears to have been his first important job, so he may have joined the union to secure the position in her band.[30] He remained active in the small club scene as well, frequenting "carving sessions" at the Hollywood Club with other pianists, including Clyde Hart, Dorothy Donegan, and Art Tatum.[31]

"A BAD BAND THAT SOUNDED SO GOOD"

Many early bebop musicians began their careers in swing/dance bands. Charlie Parker, Dizzy Gillespie, Kenny Clarke, and Dexter Gordon, among others, all paid their dues in big bands of the late 1930s and early 1940s. Likewise, Powell began his ascent to prominence in the jazz world under the watchful eye of trumpeter Charles Melvin "Cootie"

Williams (1911–85), one of jazz's best-known soloists. Powell joined Cootie sometime in 1943, and this association circulated his name and growing reputation in jazz circles. During his tenure with Williams, Powell toured the country and made studio and live broadcast recordings in a variety of settings. (Porter, Ullman, and Hazell note, for example, that pianist Tommy Flanagan first heard Powell with the Williams band during a riveting live performance in Detroit.)[32] Furthermore, the group's repertoire and musical approach placed Powell in a unique environment where swing, rhythm and blues, and an emerging bebop style intersected.

When Powell joined him, Williams was enjoying popularity with the American public as well as respect among his peers. His star had first risen through an eleven-year association with Duke Ellington. After brief stints with the Chick Webb and Fletcher Henderson bands, Williams joined Ellington in 1929, replacing Bubba Miley during Ellington's long engagement at Harlem's Cotton Club from 1927 to 1930. Williams's initial role was to master the growl and plunger techniques that Miley had made a staple feature of the "Ellington sound." Williams not only mastered these techniques, but extended them into a highly personal style.[33] The fruit of Ellington and Williams's long professional association crystallized in *Concerto for Cootie* (1940), a piece that one writer considers "an ongoing continuity of gradual masterly development" in Ellington's work as a whole.[34]

In addition to the high visibility and quality of his work with Ellington, Williams's association with Benny Goodman, whom history has dubbed "The King of Swing," increased his popularity and raised his stock. In the late 1930s, Williams recorded small group sessions under his own name and also with Goodman, Teddy Wilson, Billie Holiday, and others. Williams's appearance on the bill of Goodman's famous Carnegie Hall concert (January 1938) confirmed his stature in the jazz world.[35] In fact, according to Goodman, the success of the concert, long considered a watershed event in the history of jazz, was due in large part to Williams's participation. In November 1940, Williams left the Ellington Orchestra to join Goodman, who hired him to play primarily in his sextet. After a year with Goodman, Williams's reputation had grown to such a degree that at Ellington's urging, he formed his own permanent band.

Williams's associations with Ellington and Goodman influenced his leadership style and his band's repertory. And his work ethic served him especially well when dealing with both the enormous talent and the impulsive behavior that the young Powell displayed while a member of his group. Like Ellington and Goodman, Williams had a knack for discovering new talent. From time to time during the 1940s, his band featured young musicians who won great respect in jazz. Powell, Charlie Parker, pianist Ken Kersey, and saxophonists Eddie "Cleanhead" Vinson and Eddie "Lockjaw" Davis were all employed by Williams at various times. During his Ellington years, Williams described himself as a surrogate disciplinarian, settling personal and musical disputes among band members such as Sonny Greer, Johnny Hodges, and Barney Bigard: "Duke would never say nothing to them. I'd be the one that had taken over that spot." But Williams tolerated unruly behavior among some of his own band members, including young, reckless ones such as Powell: "Now, like Bud Powell, and those types of people would come in half-high and messed up. I'd overlook it. Because when they would be straight, I would get some great sound."[36] Goodman, in contrast, ran a tight ship—musically and otherwise.

Williams created his own style of leadership, balancing traits from both of his former employers. Charles Holmes, once a member of Williams's band, fondly recalls his days with Cootie: "I've never in all my life played with such a bad band that sounded so good. There were more people in there who couldn't read a note as big as a house, and they had no more conception of music than the man in the moon, but they could play, and they could swing, and it sounded good."[37] Likewise, "Lockjaw" Davis describes Williams as "good to his sidemen" and says that his group was "musically . . . ahead of the others."[38]

At least two stories exist about how Powell first came to Williams's attention. One comes from the bandleader himself. According to Williams, he learned of Powell through one of his former sidemen, trumpeter George Treadwell. Treadwell may have known Powell from Monroe's Uptown House, where the former served as a house band member in the early 1940s. Powell came to one of the band's rehearsals, played for Williams, was hired immediately, and, in the bandleader's words: "He was what you call a real genius. . . . He was something else in his young age."[39]

"Lockjaw" Davis tells another story about Powell's joining Cootie. Davis was working at a club in Greenwich Village in October 1943 with a combo that included Powell. Cootie, according to Davis's recollection, hired five members of the group on the spot. Shortly thereafter they played the Savoy Ballroom: "Now I'm in New York," Davis recalls, "working at the Savoy—earning 42 dollars a week! That was the beginning."[40] Davis considered his tenure with Williams—an established soloist with an international reputation—the beginning of his professional musical life.

One can only speculate that a young, talented high school dropout such as Powell would be equally excited about the prospect of accompanying the great Cootie Williams—no matter which circumstances led to his getting the job. After all, by this time, swing had long since secured its position as a viable style in the music industry, and through campaigns by successful promoters and musicians such as John Hammond and Lionel Hampton, it had shed at least some of its associations with the drug underworld of marijuana (sometimes called tea), which was criminalized in 1937. In other words, post-Prohibition, post-Depression, postsegregationist sensibilities had already begun to position jazz as less subcultural than it had ever been before. Jazz was big business.[41]

At the same time that Powell was making his first recordings and tours with a group that embraced several idioms—blues, swing, and, to a lesser degree, a nascent bebop—other musicians were ushering in the so-called bebop era in earnest. This sonic development would establish many social contracts with listeners, including a turn back toward a subcultural status on many levels.

RE-BOP BE-BOP MOP AND STOP:
THE GENIUS IN BEBOP

When bebop appeared, seemingly out of nowhere, in the early to mid-1940s, the public heard it as something strange, something new. Although the music sounded self-consciously "modern" to many, the creators of bebop crafted, individually and collectively, a musical style that combined the dance impulse of earlier forms of jazz with fresh rhythmic, melodic, and harmonic innovations that turned the jazz world on its ear. Together with changes in the social standing of African Americans in the United States, bebop seemed to open up new avenues of expression for black musicians across the board. The days of the "shucking and jiving Negro" bent on serving up what American audiences demanded—even if that meant engaging in the performance rhetoric of minstrelsy—seemed like a bad memory. Bebop musicians have come to symbolize for many the broader shifts that occurred both in the realm of entertainment and in the larger social world of the 1940s and beyond.

Bebop represented much more than wider artistic avenues to black musicians. These musicians showed the world that the American popular songbook, African American blues and jazz traditions, and various notions of instrumental virtuosity could be stretched, revised, and amplified to maximum creative effect. In fact, the great American melting pot myth played out itself yet again in this unlikely art form: Jewish American songwriters and producers, Italian Americans, Cuban Americans, "White Negroes," and many others participated to varying degrees in the development of bebop style and most certainly in its criticism.

What were bebop's distinctive musical qualities? The size of bebop ensembles was similar to those of the swing style. They typically were small groups (saxophone, trumpet, piano, bass, drums), but eventually they, too, included large ones modeled after swing-era big bands. The smaller ensembles featured a more dynamic, interactive rhythm section. Big-band bebop sounded closer to its swing predecessor, but included bebop's innovative approach to melody and harmony, and of course, its virtuosic solos. Bebop's rhythmic devices were, perhaps, the most dramatic departure from jazz's previous idioms. Tempos were notoriously faster in bebop, although many musicians, such as Charlie Parker, continued to play ballads throughout their careers. The rhythm component emphasized a shimmering wall of syncopation on all levels of the music, in both the solos and the accompaniment. But the heady sense of propulsion—indeed, the playful and sometimes bewildering give and take that listeners experience in bebop—emanated primarily from bebop drummers. The dramatic crashes they provided seemed to shake heaven and earth with the "re-bop be-bop mop and stop" groove, as suggested by the epigraph to chapter 1, taken from Langston Hughes's 1951 poem "Flatted Fifths."

Beboppers composed and improvised dramatic, disjunctive melodies that were more instrumentally conceived than previous jazz styles. That is to say, the typical bebop melody placed demands on listeners that some found deliciously challenging and others experienced as off-putting. Bebop melodies generally covered large ranges and did not depend on the even antecedent-consequent (question-and-answer) phrase structure of popular songs. They were generally not as singable as other styles of popular music, although their innate musicality, together with the sheer virtuosity that it took to perform them at top speed, astounded listeners.

Bebop musicians introduced a rich harmonic vocabulary into black popular music. While the basic chord progressions of most bebop compositions were based on the American popular songbook and twelve-bar blues forms, the musicians continually enriched these standard structures by brushing them with ninth-, eleventh-, and thirteenth-scale degrees in the melodies and supporting accompaniments. Use of the flatted fifth-scale degree became a signature gesture within this new harmonic approach. Timbre in bebop underscored the notion of individuality within the collective. Although earlier idioms of jazz had certainly produced highly individualized approaches to "quality of sound"—Coleman Hawkins, Sidney Bechet, and Bubba Miley come to mind—bebop pushed this aesthetic to the limit. Charlie Parker's acerbic tone and Dizzy Gillespie's streamlined bite became models for similar experimentations in timbre among jazz musicians.

This was a new music for new times. Langston Hughes was among the first cultural critics to connect these musical innovations with the sociopolitical realm of modern African American culture. In the foreword to his *Montage of a Dream Deferred*, Hughes writes: "In terms of current Afro-American popular music and the sources from which it has progressed—jazz, ragtime, swing, blues, boogie-woogie, and bebop—this poem on contemporary Harlem, like bebop, is marked by conflicting changes, sudden nuances, sharp and impudent interjections, broken rhythms, and passages sometimes in the manner of the jam session, sometimes the popular song, punctuated by the riffs, runs, breaks, and distortions of the music of a community in transition."[42] With impressive prescience, Hughes hits the mark. He places bebop at the nexus of musical innovation, local culture, and social change, each factor contributing to the specific language of the music. In the poem, Hughes seeks to capture the nuances of both the music and the moment. He depicts how young black, urban males, who were often treated as enemies of the state, wrested bebop out of the social experience of 1940s black male "cullud"-ness and created a style that ultimately spoke broadly to listeners throughout a world turned upside-down by World War II.

As I have discussed in my book *Race Music*, jazz's change in pedigree indexed other shifts in American culture. I use the term *Afro-modernism* to describe these sociopolitical and economic developments, ones that characterized African American notions of "progress" throughout the twentieth century and which reached an apex in the 1940s. World War II, black mass migration from southern states to northern urban centers, a mounting, urgent sense of black political and social efficacy, and an increased African American presence in all aspects of the cultural media coincided. Jazz, and all other styles of black popular music, wore the traces of these shifting movements and sensibilities. A most salient point here is that despite rigorous efforts by the black intelligentsia to promote African American participation in high culture as the sole avenue to social equity, the realm of mass culture—the one in which bebop was recorded and disseminated—became the most visible site of African American progress. Thus the perceived movement of jazz through the folk, mass, and art categories of cultural hierarchies is a richly layered topic.[43]

The bebop phenomenon continues to fascinate more than seventy years after its practices first began to coalesce in Harlem. Those who have dealt seriously with bebop—musicians, critics, and historians—recognize it as a demanding idiom, a complex crystallization of African American experience during a pivotal period in history. Not solely conceived for a dancing audience or designed specifically for mass consumption or even the traditional highbrow concert audience, bebop presents a challenge to those who contemplate its emergence and rise as the standard language of modern jazz musicians. Was it pop culture gone awry or a new intellectual turn in African American music?

HIPSTERISM ON THE MOVE

We begin with a familiar tale of bebop's industry origins. As the "official" story goes, in late 1943, trumpeter Dizzy Gillespie and bassist Oscar Pettiford searched up and down 52nd Street in midtown Manhattan for work. By January 1944, they were booked in the Onyx Club. Their group, which also included Max Roach, George Wallington, and later Don Byas, is considered by many to be the first commercially viable bebop quintet. Gillespie called the engagement "the birth of the bebop era."[44] Although origins are always complicated matters, his claim is understandable because over the next few years, bebop could be heard at several nightclubs along the Street as well as on recordings.

But, as we've learned, 52nd Street was not the incubator of the first bop ensembles. Most jazz histories acknowledge that the informal collectives of musicians who participated in the musical experiments of the early 1940s after-hours jam sessions, such as those at Minton's Playhouse and Monroe's, played that role. Within this context, Thelonious Monk, Kenny Clarke, and guitarist Charlie Christian, among others, worked out "the language of riff and accent."[45] The jam sessions at Minton's attracted many musicians from 1940 onward, and they provided a space for those who had been working through their ideas independently to come together and build some steam collectively.[46]

Many of the musicians there contributed to the energy of the scene as soloists, accompanists, and composers. Monk was a central figure, but he always maintained, somewhat famously, that nobody was "giving lectures" at Minton's, undoubtedly to counter the axiom that the sessions were self-consciously fashioned as a formal, organized laboratory. Myths are nice like that. Nonetheless, musicians were quite deliberate about experimentation, freedom, and sharing ideas. Although not every single musician present was sympathetic to bebop, like minds were connecting and gelling: something new was being created.

Just consider the results. Parker, Gillespie, Monk, Max Roach, and the composer-arranger Tadd Dameron all built impressive and important careers. Among these pioneering modern jazz musicians, Gillespie and Parker are, perhaps, the best known outside the jazz world. Gillespie's visage in particular gave bebop a distinctive iconic component to accompany the musical style. Some, such as Gillespie and Roach, remained musically active throughout the remainder of the twentieth century, sustaining creative and uninterrupted careers that have been aptly celebrated. Gillespie, Roach, and a few others actively sought out and nurtured young talent along the way. Others, such as Dameron and Parker, succumbed to the lure and devastation of alcohol and narcotics, which shortened their lives. Sarah Vaughan, the most visible female artist to participate in bebop's early years, applied some of the new techniques to her vocal approach. Her contributions cut numerous pathways in jazz, pop, and American vocal artistry in general. Vaughan's presence in this scene remains an underappreciated aspect of the bebop movement.[47]

What remains truly remarkable is that in the face of profound and naturalized bigotry, the toughest economic exploitation, and the crippling effects of substance abuse among their ranks, these musicians as a whole went on to contribute immeasurably to American and international musical life. They were poised to present the sounds of their Harlem-based experiments to the world, and indeed were soon to influence the course of modern music. This is the context in which the young pianist Bud Powell was planted: a sound environment that would over the next decade become financially viable, artistically challenging, and heard around the globe.

The reputation that he built rests chiefly on his ability to solo in the idiom, although he also composed memorable original works known for their delicate intricacy, idiosyncratic style, and, at times, stark emotional clarity. He was a virtuoso titan, a preternatural improviser, and a hero to jazz pianists active during the mid-1940s and beyond. Powell's contributions overshadow those of Al Haig, George Wallington, and Dodo Marmarosa, all fine early pianists in bebop's inner circle. Pianists Lennie Tristano and Thelonious Monk, both contemporaries of Powell's, crafted bebop voices that rivaled his in originality, but Powell's ingenious technical presence in the bebop idiom was surpassed by few. The next generation of pianists, including Tommy Flanagan, Red Garland, Wynton Kelly, and Horace Silver, among many others, learned Powell's devices well. Because of his enormous influence and the respect he earned among musicians, fans, and aficionados, Blue Note record company producers, on an album released in 1951, dubbed him "the Amazing Bud Powell," a title that has endured through the years.

But by most accounts, Powell's personality and emotional state were notoriously unpredictable. Beginning in 1945, he spent intermittent periods in mental institutions, where his "treatments" included electroshock therapy. When one experiences the beauty and edgy logic of his music, it is difficult to imagine how this musical mind could have endured such abuse. His abundance of musical gifts seemed at odds with the world around him, or at least his view of it.

One might venture that Powell—like the protagonist in Ralph Ellison's novel *Invisible Man*—played the music of his own invisibility; as a difficult-to-know individual, he may have communicated his innermost emotions through his art.[48] (Certainly his experience with the mental health care of his times suggests a connection to the narrator of *Invisible Man*.) Of all the major figures in jazz (excluding, perhaps, Charlie Parker), it is Powell, with his well-known psychological complexity, who has most invited this kind of speculation. But his complex relationship with the social world was only one quality distinguishing Powell from his peers.

Powell's lightning-fast technique was matched only by his powers of invention. While the inner man will probably remain shrouded in mystery (Powell left no memoir), his musical contributions remain with us. Most jazz pianists who have "taken a few choruses" are indebted to

Powell. He played a major role in the creation of a modern jazz piano style that integrated the earlier ones of Earl Hines, Billy Kyle, Teddy Wilson, and Art Tatum. He was very respected in his prime, a known quantity among beboppers.

Powell's classical training, the compelling, almost ecstatic edge he developed in his playing, his youth at the time of his rise to prominence, his eminent position in the development of jazz piano (despite the check-ered brevity of his career), and his alliances with various important fig-ures of the moment in the early years of his work would invite repeated contemplation by his fans. He became a versatile musician, perform-ing expertly in numerous settings—solo piano, trio, small ensemble, and big band. This young man was going to become important in the bebop idiom, the jazz tradition writ large, black music history and crit-icism, and the entire American musical landscape. To understand the structures in which Powell made his ascent, we turn to the activities of a musician who appeared to lead the way with regard to the business.

DIZZY GILLESPIE'S BUSINESS OF BEBOP

Gillespie and Oscar Pettiford led the first bop quartet known to per-form outside of Harlem. As I noted earlier, they appeared at the Onyx Club in January 1944, the same month that young Powell began his recording career.[49] According to pianist and author Billy Taylor, the combo began the gig without a piano player. Gillespie originally wanted Powell to fill the spot, but Cootie, who was reportedly an informal guardian to the impetuous Powell, refused to allow him to play with the quintet.[50] Nonetheless, the Gillespie/Pettiford combo's appearance on the Street began a series of events that brought bebop greater recognition.

When Gillespie and Pettiford split and formed their own groups in mid-1944, 52nd Street customers could hear two bebop bands in dif-ferent clubs.[51] Although this was not the first time that black musi-cians had performed on the Street, the transition from swing to bebop brought certain racial and economic tensions to the new style and sensibility. Black musicians routinely earned lower wages than their white counterparts. It was Taylor's perception that although one could hear interracial groups on the Street, there were "of course differ-ent pay scales. White musicians often earned more than comparable black men. Even though famous musicians such as Basie and Ellington earned more downtown than they did uptown, downtown clubs usually paid black musicians less than white."[52] Second, according to Miles Davis, Gillespie, and others, violent racial clashes were commonplace in Midtown.[53] Discriminatory compensation patterns and violence poignantly exemplify the kinds of obstacles confronting black jazz musicians, even those courting stardom and enjoying celebrated careers.

Despite these challenges, the Street gradually provided wider recognition for bebop. During the Onyx Club stint, Coleman Hawkins was leading a group at a nearby nightclub. After hearing Gillespie, he quickly arranged a record date on February 16, 1944, that featured Gillespie's group as well as musicians from his own combo. Many regard these recordings—the first for the Apollo label—as the first bebop recording session, primarily because of Gillespie's contributions. His composition "Woody 'n You" appears on the date; his solos on that piece, and another composition, "Disorder at the Border," are unmistakably bebop in character. Max Roach, who made his recording debut on the date, considered it "the beginning of a whole new world for me, musically and also creatively."[54]

Other events marked 1944 as significant in the history of bebop. In the spring, vocalist-trombonist Billy Eckstine formed an orchestra that included Gillespie (as music director), Parker, Gene Ammons, and Dexter Gordon, among others. The group proved to be an important space for bebop's rise. Eckstine's live performances, as well as his recordings on the Deluxe label, helped to disseminate the new sound. Parker made his first small-group recordings for the Savoy label in guitarist Tiny Grimes's group in September of the same year.[55] Although bebop was gaining a larger audience, bebop historian Scott DeVeaux reminds us that "for the most part, recordings played a minor role in spreading bebop in 1944, simply because they were virtually unobtainable. With restrictions on shellac and manpower shortages at pressing plants, the independent recording companies were unable to produce enough records to meet the growing demand."[56] In spite of these limitations, Gillespie grew in popularity. He resigned from Eckstine's band in December 1944, and soon thereafter recorded for the Continental, Manor, Black and White, and Guild labels, including his first session as a leader in January 1945.[57]

Powell's fortunes took a downward turn at the beginning of 1945. In January, during a one-night stand in Philadelphia with Williams and His Orchestra, Powell was arrested for disorderly conduct. As Williams recalled some forty years later, Powell arrived late for the job: "He was full of something. He jumped up on the bandstand, and jumped up on the piano while the band was playing. And after the date, he didn't go back with us on the bus. And . . . the police called me here in New York and told me they had one of my men locked up over there in jail. They didn't know what was wrong with him, so they had beat him on his head, with this blackjack or something. And I told them to call his mother."[58]

Powell was fined and released the next day into the custody of his mother, who took him home to convalesce. Williams speculates that Powell's reckless behavior and his weakness for alcohol—and above all the severe beating he received on that eventful night—were the beginning of the difficulties he would face throughout his adult life.[59] Williams could not have known that Powell's lot, from that night until the end of his life, would be a cycle of triumph and trouble. Nor could he have known that his behavior hinted at deeper, more serious issues. In February 1945, Powell entered Pilgrim State Hospital, Long Island, New York, where a psychiatrist commented on his hyperactivity and how his "thoughts were flying away with him." After ten weeks, he was stabilized and released "in convalescent care," and one year later the hospital officially discharged him.[60]

On May 2, 1945, Powell made his first recording after his hospitalization on a session led by tenor saxophonist Frank Socolow. The Duke label session reflects Socolow's swing-based style, which was heavily influenced by Lester Young. Of the four recordings made that day, two were released: the standard "The Man I Love" and a simple swing tune, "Reverse the Charges." (Some sources list the tune as "Reverse the Changes.") On the latter, Powell solos for sixteen bars. His playing, although certainly proficient, lacks the momentum, spirit, and drive of his recorded work with Cootie. This may be the first musical evidence—however slight—that Powell's output would become erratic at various times throughout his career, a point highlighted in every account of his life.

If Powell's recorded work still evidenced a music that embodied qualities of both swing and bebop styles, Gillespie had begun to record full-fledged bebop. Nine days after Powell's swing session with Socolow, on May 11, 1945, the Manor/Guild record company recorded the Dizzy Gillespie Sextet, featuring Parker. The group's recordings, including Tadd Dameron's composition "Hot House" and Gillespie's "Salt Peanuts" and "Shaw Nuff," show many stylistic properties of the new bebop idiom. (I discuss the procedures and practices that compose the bebop style in detail in chapter 5.) Shortly after the recording session, Monte Kay, Dameron's manager, took a risk and arranged a bebop concert at Town Hall. At the suggestion of *Down Beat's* owner, Kay first went to see Symphony Sid, who had a rhythm and blues show on radio station WHOM, but who also "really dug jazz." Kay offered Sid half the profits if he would plug the concert on his show. Sid complied, and as Kay recalls, bebop found "a market" and expanded its audience beyond its relatively small 52nd Street fans: "As soon as he began playing the Guild recordings by Dizzy and Bird, tickets began selling. And the concert was almost a sell-out. It gave both of us so much confidence that we ran another a month later, also at Town Hall. . . . We found a college-age audience that was ready for the new music, also a black audience."[61]

Shortly thereafter, also in the spring of 1945, Gillespie, perhaps full of optimism because of bebop's relative commercial success on the Street, decided to organize his first big band. He hired Milt Shaw as his manager and planned a tour of the South with a diverse road show. Dubbed the "Hepsations 1945," the tour looked very much like the aggregation that had traveled with Williams and Powell a year earlier. It included the Nicholas Brothers, dancers featured in the 1943 motion picture *Stormy Weather*, comedians Patterson and Jackson, vocalist June Eckstine, a shake dancer, and some chorus girls. In addition, Gillespie made, in his words, "a major effort to gather the best modern jazz talent available and to organize the band well so everybody could hear exactly how hip the cream of the crop sounded."[62] Many of the arrangements, stands, uniforms, and microphones—and even band members—were garnered directly from the disbanded Billy Eckstine Orchestra. In this particular context, bebop remained connected to other styles of black popular music.

At the helm of a big band, Gillespie was obviously concerned with revenue and the commercial aspects of the business. His touring aggregation was aimed squarely at the masses. Furthermore, he collaborated on the arrangements with Walter "Gil" Fuller, who recalls contriving inexpensive strategies to reap as rich as possible a commercial reward from the tour:

> We took all of Dizzy's records, and he and I sat down and wrote them out. My argument was, why give them the royalties off of "Bebop" when we don't control the publishing, and give them everything, and they don't pay you anyhow. So let's write something new, another melody on top of it.
> Dizzy and I sat down, and Dizzy, basically, did most of it. The lines on

"Bebop" were his. We changed the line, reversed the line on, "This Is The Way," and I made the arrangement for the band. We did that on the basis of Woody Herman playing "Caldonia." Because they had the hottest band out there, and everything that Woody Herman was playing was in Dizzy's style. They were taking Dizzy's licks. . . . People thought Dizzy had made the arrangement.[63]

Despite Gillespie's and Fuller's efforts, audiences in the South showed little interest in bebop, demanding instead to hear the blues and other dance music. The tour ended in late fall. When Gillespie returned to New York, he formed a combo that he later described as "the height of the perfection of our music." The group included Parker, Roach, Curley Russell, and Powell. Later, Ray Brown, who had moved to New York, replaced Russell, and pianist Al Haig and drummer Stan Levy replaced Powell and Roach.[64] Brown recalls vividly his excitement at meeting Gillespie at the Spotlite Club on 52nd Street and receiving an invitation to join the group: "So he gave me a card that says, 'Come to my house tomorrow night at 1 o'clock for rehearsal,' you know just like that. And I got there the next night, and it was Bud Powell, Max Roach, Dizzy and Bird, wow! Outta sight, just like that."[65] Brown's description of his first rehearsal with the premier bebop ensemble shows something about how they played, how they learned tunes, and which kinds of musical issues were central in the bebop "school":

It was mind blowing. These guys were playing something entirely differ- ent from what I'd ever played, you know. But the one thing, I guess, I had going besides enthusiasm was a lot of stamina. You see, they liked to play fast and it didn't bother me to play fast. I can play fast all night, that wasn't my problem. It was just a matter of learning the way they played changes. Because Dizzy played—he voiced his chords differently, and he wanted a different bassist. That's what I had to learn, you know, what notes to play, things like that. It was like going to school. That's one thing about Dizzy, if you don't understand something, he'll take you to the piano and show it to you. That's how all of us learned a lot, you know.[66]

When the combo played the Three Deuces on the Street, they were so well received that the owner nearly doubled their salaries after one week.[67] The emergence of an audience for bebop on records and in New York's small clubs and concert halls, the engagement of disc jock- eys, personal managers, and promoters, and the bebop style's crystal- lization among a growing circle of practitioners made one fact clear: bebop was no longer Harlem's after-hours secret. But that is not to sug- gest that it was big business, either, or that it had eclipsed other styles of jazz. Gillespie points out that in 1945, the Street boasted numerous groups and performers, or, in his words, "different sets." On any given night one could hear "Coleman Hawkins, Art Tatum, Billie Holiday, Al Casey, Benny Carter—all of these great musicians playing at the clubs."[68] Despite the presence of many "sets" in the New York scene, however, bebop's influence grew steadily throughout 1945.

As a definitive and recognizable bebop style emerged, entrepreneurs began to seek out the musicians behind the sounds. Herman Lubinsky owned the small record company named Savoy, and he, as one observer notes, "possessed a special talent for producing great jazz records at minimum expense to himself." Initially, Lubinsky proceeded with caution when it came to recording modern jazz. "I needed a lot of convincing," he once explained, "before I went into it. . . . I didn't think it would be commercial."[69] In a 1978 interview, Teddy Reig, a producer at Savoy in the mid-1940s, states that Lubinsky "was known up and down The Street as a cheap bum! He'd come into a joint like The White Rose, spread out his contracts and have an office!"[70] Most of the independent labels founded in the mid-1940s operated with low budgets and relatively low returns on their investments. The key to commercial success was simple: secure a large number of diverse artists. Lubinsky, at Reig's prompting, saw commercial potential in bebop and sought to record its most outstanding practitioners.

On November 26, 1945, Reig arranged a recording date of bebop's finest, which was Parker's first session as a leader. The date was scheduled as a "standard three hour/four side session."[71] The planned roster carried promise for great success: Parker and Miles Davis on the front line, and Powell, Roach, and bassist Curley Russell in the rhythm section. Historically important, the Savoy session produced several Parker compositions, including "Billie's Bounce," "Warming Up a Riff," "Now's the Time," "Thriving on a Riff," and "Ko-Ko." Numerous accounts exist about the exact circumstances of the event that Savoy later called "the Greatest Recording Session in Modern Jazz History."[72] Although Powell was slated for the session—a union contract had been arranged the preceding week—he chose instead to accompany his mother to the Philadelphia area, where she was buying a house. Upon learning this, Parker secured the services of Gillespie and Argonne Thornton (later known as Sadik Hakim), who shared the piano duties.[73]

In two short years, bebop had traveled far from the days when Pettiford and Gillespie "went looking up and down" 52nd Street for work. It was even farther removed from its original cultural context:

down-home dinners and tooth-cutting jam sessions in Harlem's wee morning hours. Bebop and its practitioners were now bona fide commodities. Gillespie and Parker headed to Los Angeles to test the waters for bebop on the West Coast. As for Powell, it became increasingly clear throughout 1946 that his musical activities would put him in an almost exclusive position within the emerging bebop world, in spite of his unpredictable temperament. In fact, both his prowess and his pathos would soon be strongly identified with the art.

"THE AUDIENCE WASN'T HIP": GO WEST, BEBOP

In December 1945, bebop moved westward when Gillespie, with the help of agent Billy Shaw, booked an extended engagement at Billy Berg's club in Hollywood, California. In Los Angeles at that time, as entrepreneur Ross Russell puts it, there was a small, "almost clandestine market in more serious music . . . the new style [of jazz] that went by the once derisive name of bebop."[74] But in many ways, as Gillespie's experiences would prove, bebop was still a New York phenomenon. The music first reached the West Coast primarily via the recordings that Gillespie and Parker had cut earlier that year. They were disseminated through underground networks such as the shoeshine stand of local drug dealer Emery Byrd (a.k.a. Moose the Mooche) and by a man known simply as "Bebop." These recordings, together with a semi-bop ensemble led by Coleman Hawkins (and including trumpeter Howard McGhee) that had toured and recorded in Los Angeles in early 1945, represented bebop's arrival on the West Coast.[75] But the Gillespie engagement promised to be, for those in the know, the initiation of the real article on the West Coast: bebop at its best, featuring its most prominent practitioners.

Gillespie, perhaps sensing the importance of the engagement, carefully assembled bebop's most competent players. His combo was integrated, still an uncommon practice, and included Parker, Al Haig, Stan Levy, vibraphonist Milt Jackson, and bassist Ray Brown. But despite Gillespie's efforts, the group's reception fell flat, though it generated interest among jazz musicians. "Opening night was big," Ira Gitler reports, "but as the week went on the crowds diminished, and the hip minority did not order drinks often enough to make the cash register ring with any consistency."[76] No one was more keenly aware of bebop's tenuous commercial status than Billy Berg, the club's owner.

The fact that Gillespie's group shared the bill with novelty vocalists Slim Gaillard and Harry "the Hipster" Gibson, both popular on the West Coast, probably highlighted the combo's struggles. Ray Brown and Gillespie recall that Berg insisted that the group "sing or something" to draw a larger audience.[77]

As he did with the unsuccessful Hepsations tour of the South, Gillespie interpreted California's lack of interest in bebop as an audience problem, not one with the music itself: "We hit some grooves on the bandstand at Billy Berg's that I'll always remember, but the audience wasn't hip."[78] Brown concurs that despite the negative reaction, the music was outstanding there: "Where Diz and Bird were compatible was on the bandstand, musically. I mean it was like one guy with two heads was playing together. . . . And such fantastic soloists."[79] Years later, Gillespie would recall the California experience with his typical resolve, a quality that probably fostered the remarkable longevity of his career: "Sea to sea, America in 1945 was as backward a country musically as it was racially. Those of us who tried to push it forward had to suffer."[80]

There was, however, a keen interest in bebop on the West Coast in certain limited circles. Progressive-minded musicians such as Howard McGhee, Sonny Criss, and Hampton Hawes, among others, loved bebop and played in the style. Furthermore, entrepreneurs such as Ross Russell; his partner, attorney Marvin Freeman; and impresario Norman Granz eagerly sought to record and feature new bebop talent. But when the Billy Berg job ended on February 3, the group (except for Parker) headed back to New York, where, as *Down Beat* reported in late January, Gillespie had already decided to "build another large band."[81] Parker remained in California, living hard: working with his own groups in small clubs, nursing his voracious narcotics addiction, recording for Russell's Dial label, and ultimately finding himself criminally indicted and committed to Camarillo State Mental Hospital.

"A BOOST OF PRESTIGE"

In many ways, 1946, the first year after the Second World War, proved to be a watershed for Powell and the bebop movement. Dizzy Gillespie maintains that in 1946 "bebop took a great leap in popularity," a judgment that, as we shall see, reflects the trajectory of his own career.[82] The trade press, such as *Down Beat*, began to diligently report Gillespie's activities to its national audience. In fact, a February 1946 *Down Beat* advertisement by the New York–based company Notes Inc. announced the publication of a collection of Gillespie's transcribed solos: "A folio of five groovy originals by the great jazz stylist."[83] (Other collections in the series included those of Roy Eldridge, Harry James, and Cootie Williams.) Gillespie recalls of that period: "My name hit the billboards as a great trumpeter before I knew it. . . . Two clubs on Fifty-second Street, the Spotlite and the Three Deuces, were begging me to accept extended engagements when I returned to New York from California in 1946, and we went into the Spotlite Club, a bigger club, instead of the Three Deuces."[84]

During and perhaps even because of Gillespie's extended engagement there (February to July 1946), Leonard Feather, a critic, musician, and champion of the music, convinced RCA Victor to record a bebop group. Until the Spotlite appearance, bebop had been available only on "offbeat labels such as Savoy, Guild, Manor, Musicraft, Roost, Three Deuces, Blue Note, Apollo, Continental and Black and White."[85] Victor required Feather to use some of the year's *Esquire* Award winners on the session to ensure name recognition. Having *Esquire* involved gave bebop, in Feather's opinion, a boost of prestige: "To read about jazz, you had to go to *Down Beat* or *Metronome*. There was nothing in *The New Yorker, Saturday Review* or even the *New York Times*."[86] The album was released as *New 52nd Street Jazz;* the term *bebop* (not to mention *Harlem*) was consciously avoided in the title and the music's new "home," 52nd Street, was prominently displayed. Feather's efforts paid off. The public—at least the New York public—changed its attitude toward bebop. *New 52nd Street Jazz* was successful: it eventually finished as the best-selling jazz album of 1946. Its acceptance led to a June recording date with a sixteen-piece big band on Musicraft and a successful tour with Ella Fitzgerald.[87]

A STAR IS BORN:
PRESENTING THE BUD POWELL TRIO

Between January and September 1946, the twenty-one-year-old Powell recorded with an impressive cadre of musicians, all closely associated with the bebop style. Leaders of these sessions included Dexter Gordon, J.J. Johnson, Sarah Vaughan, Sonny Stitt, Kenny Clarke, and Fats Navarro. By 1946, the bebop era was undeniably underway.[88] Gillespie and his band settled in for their long engagement on 52nd Street, and the Savoy label began its historically important recordings, which were among bebop's finest up to that time. Powell's career gathered steam. On January 29, 1946, he made the first of the recordings that would soon secure his position as one of the most sought-after sidemen in bebop and as the paragon of modern jazz piano.

On the Savoy recordings, Powell reveals the virtuoso style of soloing and accompanying that made him the most influential pianist among the rising young stars of modern jazz. And young they were: Of the seven studio sessions on which Powell appeared, all the leaders (except Clarke) were twenty-two or twenty-three. Taken together, these recordings allow a specific look at not only Powell's development, but also at bebop repertory, performance practice, and compositional procedures. The recordings document how throughout the year, he and his colleagues established themselves as the avant-garde of jazz, further crystallizing and expanding their techniques seemingly with each recording.

Powell made his first recording as a leader on January 10, 1947. The session features eight trio performances, with Powell accompanied by Roach and Russell. On these recordings, Powell proves himself the equal of any of the other beboppers in technique, versatility, and feeling. The session is composed of a mix of standards and original compositions, including "I'll Remember April," "Indiana," "Somebody Loves Me," "I Should Care," "Nice Work If You Can Get It," and "Everything Happens to Me." The originals are "Bud's Bubble" and Monk's "Off Minor." When considered as a whole, the repertory alone on this session is instructive about bebop in 1947. Its breadth suggests that the term *bebop* tends to limit the rather broad range of personalities and musical approaches represented in the movement.

Powell's first leader session was obviously rehearsed well. From the introductions to the unison accents and gestures within the tunes to their tight codas, these recordings possess a polish that was still somewhat unusual for early bebop sessions (they were certainly more polished than those on the Savoy label). Since Claude Schlouch's discography shows no alternate takes, we can assume that Powell, Roach, and Russell were well prepared for the date.[89] Whether Deluxe (the company for which these recordings were made) paid for the rehearsals is difficult to determine. But since the label had begun only in 1944, one can guess that resources were limited, and it is therefore unlikely that musicians were paid for rehearsal time.[90] These sides were not available to the public until the early 1950s, when Teddy Reig founded Roost Records and purchased the masters from Deluxe, which had liquidated its inventory.

This sketch of Powell's journey from apprentice to sideman to leader outlines the early years of his professional development. During these years, Powell laid a solid foundation for his subsequent musical contributions—the memorable solos and live performances, the important collaborations with Gillespie, Roach, and Parker, and the innovative compositions. In the broader world of bebop, as Gillespie continued to champion the style, a wider audience took notice. Gillespie's Carnegie Hall appearance in September 1947 and *Metronome*'s "best trumpet" and "Band of the Year" awards boosted both his confidence and his profile.[91] Gillespie emerged as the media icon of the bebop movement; he was the subject of many articles, and for much of the public, he symbolized the bebop "image." His most ardent admirers—across racial lines—mimicked even the most casual and incidental aspects of his personal demeanor and dress. In October 1947, Gilbert S. McKean noted in *Esquire:* "The Savoy Ballroom clique copy his walk, clothes, glasses, mustache and goatee, his laugh, his bizarre voice which often sounds off-pitch. It is startling to go to Harlem of late because you see a reasonably accurate facsimile of Dizzy everywhere."[92] Photographed with the bottom of his shirt inadvertently unbuttoned, Gillespie started a fad among his young fans, who began to leave their shirts partly unbuttoned. And in Paris, when Gillespie played a borrowed, beat-up old horn, young French bebop trumpet players mutilated their own horns to resemble his.[93] A new era in jazz had begun.

EXPERIMENTATION IN OTHER ART WORLDS

At the same time that early bebop musicians were forging their new musical language, a community of black visual artists and writers thrived in New York. Black artists experimented across mediums and manipulated the forms, vocabularies, and scope of their work, and in the process they expanded, questioned, and challenged the range of acceptable representations of "blackness" in the artistic realm. Music proved to be a central theme and, perhaps, a preoccupation among these disparate artistic movements.

Romare Bearden (1911–88) gave his first solo exhibition in the spring of 1940 under the auspices of Harlem's "306," a diverse and informal circle of artists, writers, and musicians. Headquartered at 306 West 141st Street in upper Manhattan, the group offered a community of support and a cross-fertilization of ideas. Painter William H. Johnson (1901–70) and writers Langston Hughes, Ralph Ellison, Richard

Wright, and Alain Locke were among the regular visitors to the decidedly male artistic collective.[94] Bearden, once described as "an Omni-
American . . . part urbane Harlemite and part blues-idiom hero,"
used music as a recurring theme in his art. He absorbed the sights and
sounds of Harlem and compared the structure and process of his art
to jazz improvisation. Bearden was very much aware of the presence of
Charlie Parker, Dizzy Gillespie, and Bud Powell during bebop's early
years.[95] After moving to Harlem in 1939, following twelve years living in Europe, William H. Johnson abandoned the landscapes and still
lifes he had painted overseas and directed his focus toward African
American culture.[96] By doing so, he captured the imagination, rhythm,
and spirit of black America in the 1940s. His use of sharp angles and
vivid splashes of color seem to visually represent some of bebop's musical traits. But, in my view, other painters captured the spirit of the
music more directly.

Indeed, for black visual artists of this time and place, the air was
heavy with the possibilities embedded in experimentation. Some
African American artists, such as Norman Lewis (1909–79), sought to
break through the boundaries of racial representation in the their work
altogether. For Lewis, this meant a move toward abstraction, although
as art historian Kellie Jones points out, his work in the early 1940s
oscillated "between representational and purely abstract styles for a
number of years."[97] This back-and-forth move between representation
and abstraction I find analogous to Powell's moves among bebop and
other, less experimental musical styles early in his career.

In 1946, Lewis grew concerned with what he saw as the limitations
of having his work labeled with terms such as "African Idiom," "Negro
Idiom," and "Social Painting."[98] Lewis's resentment of the social pressure to produce paintings considered "black" resounds with bebop
musicians' resistance of the label *bebop* in lieu of the more expansive
term *modern*. Lewis believed that by moving away from social realism
and figuration and into the realm of abstraction he could not only free
himself from the burden of mimetic representation, but also grow as a
human being. As art historian Ann Gibson has shown, Lewis's refusal
to play the role of noble savage, his self-conscious articulation of his
artistic inner life, the stylistic flexibility and deliberate mutability of
his work, and his somewhat uneasy relationship with the artistic critical establishment are evidence that his art was drenched in the cultural
politics of the 1940s.

While Lewis intentionally distanced his paintings from the social

NORMAN LEWIS, *TWILIGHT SOUNDS,* **1947.** Oil on canvas. 23½ × 28 in. Saint Louis Art Museum, Funds given by Mr. and Mrs. John Peters MacCarthy, Mr. and Mrs. Havey Saligman, Billy E. Hodges, and the Art Enrichment Fund.

protest and realism of previous generations, they were praised for their connections to jazz. Critics use musical metaphors to describe his painterly technique, referring to it as "pure eye music" and noting his "lyrical touch." One writer stresses the musical qualities of a painting as it unfolds in real time: "He starts softly on the blank page like a musician improvising, and as he sees a suitable motif taking shape, swings into it with confidence, plays it for what it is worth, and then, satisfied he has gone the whole way with it, permits it to fade softly out."[99]

The move toward abstraction by black artists has other affinities to jazz. Lowery Stokes Sims has argued that during the early twentieth century black visual artists had developed what she calls an "aesthetic system of figuration" that sought to visually express the notion of black identity.[100] For the most part, it drew on African aesthetic sensibilities and leaned heavily on realist figuration, and thus could be easily identified as "black." Musicians also forged a musical language—a schema of gestures, forms, and techniques historically associated with the social experience of black Americans—that expressed, for many, black subjectivity and the "collective unconscious," as artist Jack Whitten once put it, following Jung.[101]

The styles that essentially constituted an aesthetic system of black musical figuration were marketed in the "race music" category by the industry. Easily identifiable (or so it was believed) as black, race music was promoted to target African American audiences, although it was well known that its fan base had swelled beyond this narrow demographic. Nonetheless, African Americans did invest their own meanings in black music, and powerfully so. Thus, when bebop musicians began to gradually move beyond the conventions of black figuration and toward abstraction, a turn that would ultimately culminate in the free jazz movement, some grew uncomfortable with the development. If diatonic melodic and harmonic structures, pentatonic scales, danceable isorhythmic patterns, and American popular song formed an important structural basis for black music, bebop and free jazz challenged these boundaries and, by extension, the social structures that had been built alongside of this music.

Visual artists' bold experimentations with color, form, symbolism, and abstraction found a suitable musical analogy in the disjunctive melodies, dramatic rhythmic conceptions, chromaticism, and harmonic experimentations of bebop. In both the visual and musical realms, abstraction's practitioners equated it with artistic and social freedom. Furthermore, with the elevated role of virtuoso improvisation at the heart of both bebop practice and the idea that visual abstraction allowed viewers access to the painter's unconscious interiority, we see in each the "making" of complex black subjectivities in the public sphere.

Poets also probed the relationship between the written word and jazz and found that experimentation suited a social moment that seemed pregnant with possibilities. When writer Langston Hughes returned to Harlem in late 1941 after spending two years in California, he heard bebop for the first time. Hughes considered bebop a signal of a growing fragmentation in African American culture, with the myth of integration and America's "social harmony jarred by a message of deep discord."[102]

During World War II, Hughes explored his politics through a fictional character, Jesse B. Semple. "Simple," as he was later known, first appeared in his *Chicago Defender* column, called "Here to Yonder." To Simple's scores of fans among the *Defender*'s faithful readership, he represented the quintessential Harlemite—a talkative "everyblackman" always ready to share his audacious, homespun, and politically charged views. To one observer, he was a significant literary symbol of modern political efficacy, "the very hipped, race-conscious, fighting-back, city-bred, great grandson of Uncle Remus."[103] One Sunday afternoon, Simple explains to a passerby the circumstances of bebop's birth:

> "You must not know where Bop comes from," said Simple, astonished at my ignorance.
> "I do not know," I said. "Where?"
> "From the police," said Simple.
> "What do you mean from the police?"
> "From the police beating Negroes' heads," said Simple.
> "Every time a cop hits a Negro with his billy club, that old club says, 'BOP! BOP! . . . BE-COP! . . . MOP! . . . BOP!' . . . That's where Be-Bop came from, beaten right out of some Negro's head into them horns and saxophones and piano keys that plays it."[104]

Another literary contribution by Hughes from this period was a collection of poems titled *Montage of a Dream Deferred*. Arnold Rampersad, Hughes's biographer, characterizes the eclectic *Montage* as "vignettes of Harlem life, discrete and sometimes clashing fragments of culture . . . unified thematically by the notion of the dream denied; and unified technically, in Hughes's art, by a centripetal appeal to the rhythms of the new, 'bebop' jazz."[105] Hughes seems to mirror the asymmetrical rhythms of bebop in the excerpt below:

> Listen to it closely:
> Ain't you heard
> something underneath
> like a—
>
> *What did I say?*
>
> Sure,
> I'm happy!
> Take it away!
>
> *Hey, pop!*
> *Re-bop!*
> *Mop!*
>
> *Y-e-a-h!*[106]

Hughes's poetry, with its evocative language about music, provides a way to access some of the affective power bebop might have conveyed to African Americans, since there was a paucity of black jazz critics during the postwar years. Hughes, a longtime observer and champion of black vernacular music, offers a unique perspective, for his work embodies the heartbeat of the black community, where he "listened in the bars and jazz joints as no other writers listened." In bebop, Hughes "heard the unmistakable sounds of cultural change."[107]

Another poet, Gwendolyn Brooks, responded to the wave of mid-century Afro-modernism sweeping across America's black urban archipelago. Born in 1917, the same year as Dizzy Gillespie, Brooks found inspiration in Harlem's midwestern counterpart: the rambling black neighborhoods of Chicago's Southside. Affectionately nicknamed "Bronzeville" by its residents, the area became an artistic hub for a cross-section of writers, painters, dancers, musicians, and photographers. In her autobiography, Brooks recalls a world in which art, politics, and hope came together at the buffet table:

> My husband and I knew writers, knew painters, knew pianists and dancers and actresses, knew photographers galore. There were always weekend parties to be attended where we merry Bronzevillians could find each other and earnestly philosophise sometimes on into the dawn, over martinis and Scotch and coffee and an ample buffet. Great social decisions were reached. Great solutions for great problems were provided. . . . Of course, in that time, it was believed, still, that the society could be prettied, quieted, cradled, sweetened, if only people talked enough, glared at each other yearningly enough, waited enough.[108]

Poet and literary scholar Elizabeth Alexander comments on both the subject matter and formal structure of Brooks's poetry, arguing that "her formal range is most impressive, as she experiments with sonnets, ballads, spirituals, blues, full and off-rhymes. She is nothing short of a virtuoso."[109] A sensibility of virtuoso experimentation ruled the day among musicians, artists, and poets: rich polyrhythms and disjunctive melodic contours, explosive and defiant nonfigurative abstraction, and offbeat prose that plowed and cultivated the black American experience in ways that voiced the concerns of a people—concerns that would have otherwise been known simply as "Negro problems."

BUD POWELL'S GLASS ENCLOSURES AND INSTITUTIONS

Powell's leader session marks an important crest in his career. He made only one other recording in 1947, a May 8 Parker-led date that produced four classics in bebop's repertory: "Donna Lee," "Chasing the Bird," "Cheryl," and "Buzzy." This date was the only time that Powell and Parker appeared together on a studio session. With Miles Davis, age twenty-one, on trumpet, bassist Tommy Potter, and drummer Max Roach, this stellar lineup affirmed Powell's position on the front line of the musical style, one that fit the progressive, experimental attitude of black arts at this historical moment. The young virtuoso was poised for greatness. Unfortunately, his drinking (and probably drug use) had picked up quite a bit by now as well. Like most young mental patients, particularly one trying to make it in the 1940s jazz world, Powell probably could not accept that he would have to restrict his substance use. With his appetites unchecked, the unthinkable now became reality to those around him, and his precious talent always found its expression in the midst of his personal storms.

Spiraling out of control, he became combative and abusive and was paranoid that he would be attacked whenever he had left the house. In November 1948, he suffered a breakdown. Unable to cope, he was committed to Creedmore Hospital for an extended stay; released at the end of 1948, Powell had to return ten weeks later. His treatment there included electroshock therapy, a relatively new procedure used at the time to treat patients with depression, various forms of mania, bipolar disorders, schizophrenia, and even homosexuality. However, with the development of chemical treatments for mental illness during the 1950s, the use of antipsychotic medicines expanded in the field, "rendering calm seemingly uncontrollable patients, thereby eliminating the need for such hospital-based treatments as electroshock therapy, insulin coma, and psychosurgery."[110]

While institutionalized at Creedmore, he was allowed to play piano enough to "keep his fingers supple and his mind [musically] active."[111] During his ten-week break between his two stays at Creedmore, Powell managed to play lucidly on a recorded Royal Roost (soon to be named the Metropolitan Bopera House) club date on December 19, 1948. He was also composing, as evidenced by his piece "Celia," recorded in early 1949 on the Clef label. But not even music could soothe his illness or stop the foreboding voices in his head. Powell, the shining experimentalist in art, was no match for the experiments being conducted in the mental health field, particularly in the state institutions, whose patients were overwhelmingly poor and African American. For all his impeccable sense of rhythm, Powell, as an institutionalized, underemployed young black man, had very bad timing. Apart from his music, most of his life was beyond his control: he toggled between recording brilliant original music and performing in the hospital's annual minstrel show.

This downturn surely caused sadness, fear, and disappointment for all those in his circles. Bright futures were not the typical lot of even the most earnest urban African American men at this time. But Powell had everything in place for a successful run in the music business. He was young, dashing, a brilliant technician, a fast learner, and he was moving up the ranks as a professional musician on the New York scene. How far he had come: from being Thelonious Monk's awkward and sometimes argumentative protégé to creating a standard for pianism in the new modern jazz style. He had developed a personal voice that highlighted the piano's ability to range from streamlined and percussive to robust and orchestral. At the height of his creative virility, right at the point where his potential would likely have morphed into international recognition, his once-tolerated youthful belligerence began to be perceived by others as unusual and unmanageable.

This period set the tone for the rest of his life: his years would be marked by various institutions, mental and otherwise. For this reason— his checkered and somewhat cloistered presence on the scene—Powell has not attracted the level of literary attention of his more famous bebop colleagues. Leonard Feather's *Inside Jazz* (1949), the first book with specific information about Powell, has a brief biographical note about the pianist.[112] To date, three book-length treatments on Powell exist. The first to appear was *La Danse des infidèles* (1986) by Francis Paudras, the French commercial artist who befriended and cared for Powell in the final years of his life while Powell lived in Europe. The book is a touching treatment but does not discuss Powell's music—his most important legacy—in any detail. *La Danse des infidèles* inspired the script for Bertrand Tavernier's 1986 film *Round Midnight*. Starring the legendary bebop saxophonist Dexter Gordon and featuring a score by pianist Herbie Hancock, the film tells the story of an expatriate black jazz musician, who, like Powell, lived in Paris in the early 1960s. Gordon was nominated for an Oscar for his understated performance—the same understatement that has been attributed to Powell in his various states of physical and mental oppression. Since Gordon was a contemporary of Powell, he obviously had his experiences with the pianist to guide him. Peter Pullman's e-book *Wail: The Life of Bud Powell* appeared while the present book was close to production.

In 1993, British journalists Alan Groves and Alyn Shipton published *The Glass Enclosure: The Life of Bud Powell,* a concise and chronologically organized biography of the musician. The authors lead readers through the major events of his life, detailing his musical exploits and personal journey. Through their discussion of Powell's recordings, activities, hospitalizations, arrests, concerts, and important club dates, one gets a clear sense of an unusually complex life in a book that admirably attempts to sort it all out. Several broad themes work together in this compressed narrative that together paint Powell as a tragic historical figure, one whose musical abilities and triumphs—when he managed a great recording or a live performance of the kind that got him the titles "genius" and "amazing"—ebbed and flowed in direct correlation to his mental state and factors beyond his control. The book details this complex dance with careful attention to available evidence.

In a remarkably succinct paragraph, Groves and Shipton sum up the stark reality of the mental and physical challenges to Powell's career; the restrictions these challenges seem to have imposed on his mobility; and the disappointing, for many, artistic output from one so deeply and uniquely gifted, yet so challenged in his thought life and social relationships:

> His unstable mental condition meant that, from the mid-1940s onwards until he settled in Paris in 1959, he rarely left the New York area to work. Until about 1950, he worked or recorded with other leaders (these included Miles Davis, Dizzy Gillespie, Charlie Parker, John Kirby, Don Byas, J.J. Johnson, Dexter Gordon, Allen Edgar, Sonny Stitt and Sid Catlett amongst others). Working for others, he could be difficult, defying bandleaders' choice and conception of music. After 1950 he usually worked only with his own trio; rarely was he part of other groups, and these were generally organised all-star ensembles, such as the Quintet of the Year in 1953. Apart from a visit to Europe with the "Birdland" concert package in 1956 and an appearance at the Essen Jazz Festival in 1960, Powell was largely absent from the international touring circuit (which became staple employment to many of his contemporaries). He was to return from Paris to New York in August 1964 to play at Birdland, and his last important performance was at a Town Hall concert the following spring. He died in 1966.[113]

Indeed, after Powell had entered his vicious cycle in the criminal justice and mental health systems, his life seemed to contain a comparatively narrow set of experiences. He did not seem to have a robust social life to speak of; rather, he had a short list of significant companions, guardians, escorts, and overseers. Beyond Elmo Hope and Thelonious Monk, they included bandleader Cootie Williams; musicians Al Tinney and Jackie McClean; Oscar Goodstein, manager of the nightclub Birdland; Alfred Lion, a friend of Powell's and founder of the Blue Note record label; Paudras; and various bandmates—each self-appointed at various times to monitor the pianist and ensure that he was mending from his latest mental breakdown or that he'd show up to the gig or recording session sober and with his faculties present. Or that he wouldn't simply wander off into the night. Other figures also appear throughout the book: well-wishing fans and unintentional enablers who provided Powell with alcohol or other substances that would, according to report, instantly change his demeanor from friendly or lethargic to agitated, erratic, and sometimes violent.

Women in Groves and Shipton's narrative fit a range of predictable roles in the life of a black musician: first there was his devoted mother, Pearl Powell, whose clash of pride and anguish one can approach only with speculation. Then there was his surrogate mother/big sister of sorts, pianist Mary Lou Williams, who mentored and advised both Powell and Monk. An experienced musician, Williams obviously appreciated what she heard in Powell enough to overlook his personal eccentricities, and the respect was mutual: "We became friends right away. I thought his playing was terrific. Fantastic. He used to come to the house and play, play, play. And I was the only one who could do things for Bud. Bud had a tendency to go overboard; I'd make him take a bath or go to sleep."[114]

His significant romantic interests seemed to be few. Nor did he have a reputation, as many jazzmen do, of being a relentless womanizer. His first significant relationship appears to have been with Frances Barnes, eighteen at the time of his first brush with the law and the Philadelphia police beating. She helped Pearl Powell with his care and was the mother of his daughter, Celia, for whom he named one of his best-loved tunes in 1949, when she was five years old. Eventually their care was not enough, and, as noted earlier, Powell went to Pilgrim State Hospital for ten weeks—the first of three hospital confinements in the 1940s alone.

His marriage in 1953 to Audrey Hill, who is described in an *Ebony* magazine exposé as "a buxom music-loving white girl from Los Angeles," is a curious episode.[115] The article reports that she, mysteriously connected to Oscar Goodstein, manager of the nightclub Birdland and Powell's guardian and manager for a time, knew Powell as early as 1949, presumably during his relationship with Frances Barnes. Shortly after Powell was released from his latest stint in Creedmore on February 5, 1953, they "got real tight," as Powell said, and were married on March 9. *Ebony*'s "middle-class and respectable" makeover for the couple included the observation that "since getting married Bud has become neater and cleaner in his appearance and appears to be moving through life with a little more purpose."[116] Asked for her opinion of their romance, Hill—further described in the article as a "fervent devotee of the bebop school"—said: "He's just the greatest, that's all." The marriage didn't last very long, for some reason, and Groves and Shipton add—perhaps to affirm how right this relationship was for Powell—that "the marriage does not seem to have disrupted" his work life.[117]

And, finally there was Altevia Edwards (a.k.a. Buttercup), his common-law wife, who, with her young son, Johnny, moved with Powell to Paris in 1959, where she managed his career and served as an all-around caretaker up to the final months of his life. Buttercup does not fare well in Groves and Shipton's narrative. She comes across as overbearing, parsimonious, pill-pushing, mercenary, and domineering. In fact, Paudras is credited with getting Powell away from both Buttercup's "grip" and the drug Largactyl, an antipsychotic that she was thought to be providing him inappropriately. The authors describe how "she used it to keep the man she referred to as her 'breadwinner' in a docile condition in which she found it easy to control him." The book also accuses Buttercup of gradually increasing the doses to the point that they impaired his ability to musically perform.[118]

Clearly, Buttercup and Powell's relationship was frustrating to those invested in the heroic genius narrative that provided the pianist his fame. In fact, I find this pointed critique of her symbolic of many elements in Powell's historic treatment. In these narratives, the dominating woman, the police beating that many claimed caused his initial mental spiral, racism, and the brutish yet commonplace mental health treatment he endured are used to explain Powell's frequent inability to live up to the flashes of artistic brilliance that he showed in his lifetime. As we shall see in the next chapter, the genius title depends on a conception of masculinity in which one is pitted in battle against various societal structures to make great art. Unfortunately, the brazen, "emasculating" black female (a familiar stereotype in literature and film) who "controlled" Powell cannot be seen as a sympathetic figure in this setup: in fact, I argue that some of the resonance of his genius narrative is dependent on her strong-willed reputation (over which he had to triumph) and on the perception of their supposedly dysfunctional relationship (from which he had to escape).[119] Tellingly, a structural factor in Powell's life that rarely receives such strong critique is the jazz industry itself. The business of jazz in the 1940s and 1950s was notoriously pitted against the financial and emotional well-being of black musicians, yet this pattern is naturalized in lots of jazz literature as benign and transparent.[120] This structural reality, however, was ever-present, and it certainly impacted Powell's life and work in many ways.

In a phone interview in 1994, Celia Powell stressed two sentiments: music was her father's life; it was the driving force of his existence, in her opinion. And she thought the music industry had very much taken advantage of him.[121] Indeed, the most accurate record we have of his relationship with the industry, of some of his comings and goings, is his history of recordings. They are reliable sources for knowing where he was on a given date, and perhaps yield some indication of his inner thought life as evidenced by the music he made. Carl Smith's *Bouncing with Bud: All the Recordings of Bud Powell* (1997), Claude Schlouch's *Once upon a Time: Bud Powell: A Discography* (1983), and Alyn Shipton's "Recording Chronology" in Groves and Shipton's *The Glass Enclosure* are wonderful guides to Powell's recording history.[122] They each show that between his initial release and recommitment to Creedmore in late 1948, Powell was back in the studio, leading a session for Norman Grantz's Clef label in either January or February 1949. Peter Pullman's gorgeous CD compilation *The Complete Bud Powell on Verve* (1994) has accurately set the date of this important recording, against previous sources that stated it took place in May. This correction makes Powell even more impressive: he recorded such an excellent record *between* institutionalizations.

The session was his first as a leader since January 1947. Billed simply as the Bud Powell Trio and featuring Ray Brown (bass) and Max Roach (drums), it certainly counts as a triumph for the pianist, especially given the artistic success of his first recording as a leader. Powell was prepared to make a statement, as evidenced by his catalogue of original compositions: "Tempus Fugit," "Celia," and "Strictly Confidential" appear for the first time on this record.

Powell made two other history-making studio recordings to close out the 1940s. In early August 1949, he recorded a session for the Blue Note label, supervised by none other than Alfred Lion. It featured a quintet that included Fats Navarro on trumpets, Sonny Rollins on tenor sax, and Tommy Potter and Louis Haynes on bass and drums, respectively. Of the six songs on the session, three are Powell originals: "Bouncin' with Bud," "Wail," and "Dance of the Infidels." One, "52nd Street Theme," was composed by his good friend Monk. The remaining two songs are the bebop standard "Ornithology" and a popular ballad, "You Go to My Head," both performed in a trio setting.

In December, Bob Weinstock's new label, Prestige, on its mission to record the new modernists, released the Sonny Stitt/Bud Powell Quartet (with Curley Russell and Max Roach). The four-song release is an excellent example of how crystallized bebop convention had become since Powell first started to record. The pianist's introductions, accompaniment, and solos seem picture perfect—clear, logical statements that show the influence of all his musical forebears: Monk, Teddy Wilson, Art Tatum, Earl Hines, and Billy Kyle. Powell and Stitt were the same age; both had come up through the ranks of the 1940s jazz scene as bebop messengers, and both had struggled with substance abuse and with trying to eke out a living as a professional jazz musician. Each piece—"All God's Chillun Got Rhythm," "Sonny Side," "Bud's Blues," and "Sunset"—displays the professionalism and commitment to musical excellence they had internalized and mastered on the scene.

Between 1943 and 1947, Powell began the stage of his career that would ultimately position him as one of the most influential pianists in jazz history. During this time, Powell landed his first important job with an established bandleader and shortly thereafter made his first commercial and live recordings. These events shifted Powell's career into high gear by disseminating his talent and reputation beyond the tight circle of jazz musicians in the greater New York area. As one jazz historian has noted, a musician's first recordings are "always a crucial mark of recognition, equivalent to a classical performer's favorable review in the *New York Times* or a composer's première by a major orchestra."[123]

Powell's early recordings show a crucial stage in bebop's development, offering a snapshot of the revolution from the vantage point of a single musician. His career took the familiar pattern of many others before and after him: "a stage of apprenticeship and learning is clear, a time of growth and development follows, and a period of mature artistic creation at the highest level is attained."[124] These recordings document the remarkable speed with which Powell moved toward the realization of his mature style. And, most important, in them we experience his own highly personalized synthesis of bebop convention, his own style: a blistering palimpsest consisting of Tin Pan Alley structure overlaid with virtuoso melodic, harmonic, and rhythmic intensities. It became a new language and, indeed, one of the most influential styles in jazz history.

In the context of the wide array of experimental production by black artists in the 1940s, Powell was positioned to exceed expectation. And he did so in many ways. Yet at the close of the decade, Powell's identity was uneasily triangulated: a technically brilliant musician working in recording studios and jazz clubs, a domestic recluse, and an intermittent patient in mental hospitals. He would experience some version of this triangulation for the next sixteen years of his life—the time considered by many to be the prime of life. There would be many more triumphs and tests for the pianist throughout the 1950s and 1960s. Through them all, the amazing Bud Powell remained committed to the highest standards of artistry, even when his state of mind would not allow for his usual level of technical heroics. The kid with talent was in a fight to overcome his appetites, to play beautiful music in the midst of an otherwise uncontrolled thought life, and to make a living doing the thing he knew best.

3

Notes and Tones

Black Genius in the Social Order

A group of radical young black American improvisers,
for the most part lacking access to economic and political
resources often taken for granted in high-culture musical
circles, nonetheless posed challenges to Western notions
of structure, form, communication, and expression. These
improvisers, while cognizant of Western musical tradition,
located and centered their modes of musical expression
within a stream emanating largely from African and
African-American culture and social history.

George E. Lewis, "Improvised Music after 1950"

Bud Powell recorded "Bud on Bach" in 1957 on Alfred Lion's Blue Note label. The composition is made up of two large structures: a rendition of C. P. E. Bach's "Solfeggietto" and a hard-bop vamp in C-minor. Compressed into two minutes and thirty-one seconds, the recording traverses a couple of sound worlds and, for many, is evidence of Powell's dual pedigree in classical music and black popular music. The recording begins with a breakneck rendering of Bach's tune in which the pianist seems to scramble to keep up with the tempo that presumably he himself had set. Following this dramatic presentation, Powell settles into a groove framed by a single-note passage played with both hands outlining the dominant C-minor. The meat of the groove is primarily a vamp that toys with the tonal center by circling in and around harmonic turnarounds in the minor mode. Rhythmically, the piece swings deep in the pocket, propelled forward by Powell's left-hand syncopated chords. Powell's solo, played with his right hand, sings above it all, exploiting the semantics of Bach and bop with sinewy melody. "Bud on Bach" signals more than a juxtaposition of different musical styles. Powell's collapsing of his primary musical tributaries demonstrates for his audience the inner workings of a facile and flexible musical mind. The best musicians have always found such mixing and matching an attractive creative process. Interpretations of this kind of musical play, however, are always a tricky matter.

In a brilliant essay dealing with the idea of "difference," Ruth Solie reminds us that power is central and is precisely what is at stake in debates about difference and the cultural politics of interpretation. She writes: "Whether the issue is gender, sexuality, race, social class, or a complex combination of these and other factors, interpretive controversies swirl around the legitimacy of labeling groups 'different' from one another and, conversely, the legitimacy of claims of 'difference' those same groups may make for their own purposes—for instance, to assert authority and control over their history or the interpretation of their own texts."[1] Thus, in my view, Powell's inclination to signif(y) on the classical tradition, to play in the "musical dark," and to stomp some pop demonstrates more than musical mastery. It can be interpreted as a way for him to creatively lay claim to a complex social identity as well.

Bebop musicians such as Powell participated in a process of self-fashioning, described provocatively by Ingrid Monson as "aesthetic agency." They, and other jazz musicians of the 1940s and 1950s, drew from a rich sonic palette composed of five major streams: (1) African American vernacular musics such as jazz and blues; (2) the language of American popular song; (3) western art music; (4) music of the African diaspora; and (5) other nonwestern music such as that of India. Their eclectic aesthetic mixing participated in an "alternate aesthetics of modernism," indeed, an Afro-modernism that Monson and other writers argue "blackened modernist aesthetics" and coded their work with powerful meanings. Their particular brand of modernism seemed to create a kind of middle ground—"at once more populist than its European counterpart, yet committed to articulating its elite position relative to the more commercial genres of R&B and rock and roll."[2] The notion of blackening musical modernism at this point in American music history can be traced to certain perceptions of jazz since its inception, especially its associations with the idea of "Africa"—both real and imagined.

Throughout the 1950s, the aesthetic agency outlined by Monson and exercised by musicians such as Powell existed and indeed was interpreted in the context of a changing world in which various social orders—both large and small—were abandoned, some maintained, and others newly established. Powell's life and work during this decade intersected with important societal structures: the mental health and criminal justice systems, America's race politics, the jazz industry and the various critical positions of its developing profile, and the cosmopolitan internationalization of jazz. Even as Powell continued to record a mix of high-quality and less-respected work, perform in nightclub and concert settings, and shuttle in and out of mental hospitals, jazz continued to thrive as an art form and as a subject of critical focus. His artistic pedigree rose on the wings of the lore and ritual associated with his genius status. At the same time, the jazz industry worked overtime in a complex dance to secure the music as a discrete art world in and of itself and to come to terms with the racial implications of the music.

By the 1950s, within the communities of critics, musicians, scholars, and aficionados, Powell had earned the label "genius."[3] The social category of musical genius is connected to a powerful set of ideals that are in turn connected to the idea of the autonomy of art. The word *autonomy* here presumes that certain categories of cultural production (and the people involved in them) can and do transcend the limits of the political, social, and everyday world.[4] It has been an enduring (and uniquely populist) theory of art. But Powell's connection to this notion is anything but easy and self-evident. His social status as a young, male African American jazz musician, his engagement with the western art music tradition, the specifics of African American culture, the particularities of the American social milieu—and, of course, the riff, run, and rapture of his solo flights over, under, and through bebop harmonic substitutions—all factor prominently into his genius distinction. And I submit that these elements anchor him in, rather than lift him out of, his specific time, place, and social circumstance. To understand the significance of his genius label we have to scratch below its façade of artistic autonomy, its universal claims, and its transcendent patina.

My argument here doesn't question the reality of genius, because the concept describes an accepted social fact, an idea rich in signifying and meaningful affect. People believe that musical genius exists, and they invest lots of cultural capital in those who fit the bill.[5] Many African American artists have earned the title: Blind Tom, Louis Armstrong, Duke Ellington, Billie Holiday, Ray Charles, Stevie Wonder, Charlie Parker, and Art Tatum. More jazz musicians have been granted genius status than those in perhaps any other genre of black music, including those who have composed and performed in the western art music tradition. Blind musicians populate this list in outsized proportion. Women are scarce.[6] Genius—as the case of Bud Powell shows—is a historically situated designation, a social process best illuminated by exploring the interactions among specific social identities, cultural structures, and social orders.

Powell's musical genius, like that of others, is the product of a complex bundle of historically specific, culturally determined discourses that are passed off as "natural." Audiences recognize it as a dynamic and compelling concept that performs important cultural work.[7] Genius is a powerful idea, marshaling its strengths, privileges, and curses from a number of cultural and social antecedents. A question, then, is raised: How does genius work, and where does it get its power in musical discourse? Which structural narratives worked together to make the idea of Bud Powell's genius possible?

The idea of musical genius in jazz gets its logic from a number of cultural configurations. Indeed, the very notion of Bud Powell's genius designation unites several sometimes contradictory forces, including the act of projecting current ideas about genius onto the past, contemporaneous notions of African Americans' abilities that circulated during bebop's popularity in the 1940s and 1950s, and western culture's historical beliefs about blacks' intellectual and physical capacities.

Underpinning the black musical genius notion are historical patterns that situate musical talent on a continuum between literacy and athletic ability. Literary production is, of course, the most prestigious of the three; after all, this activity reflects the kind of cultural capital most closely linked to western cultural dominance. The physical labor associated with the legacies of slavery, sharecropping, and the institutionalization of a black service class continues to shape how black achievements in other spheres are interpreted. Toiling black bodies became distanced from associations with intellectual pursuits. Musical ability seems to occupy a middle ground in this configuration. It requires a combination of physical and intellectual activity, and depictions of Powell's genius are always cast as a public, almost voyeuristic, drama involving either a tug-of-war or a temporary truce between the two types of activity. Thus, the proclamation of Powell's astounding musical abilities cannot be understood as simply an acknowledgment of a virtuoso's creative work, but must be thought of as part of a larger complex of ideas.

Over the years, the "genius industry" has involved both demythologizing and venerating genius. Museums, archives, and tourist traps vigilantly collect ephemera associated with geniuses and obsess over them so that the lesser among us can touch and possess their greatness.[8] (The compilation box sets and the accompanying liner notes of well-respected performers also serve this purpose.) At the same time, scholars have sought to turn over the very myths that have helped to establish genius in the first place. These scholarly activities have begun to spill out of the ivory tower and into the mainstream.

Consider a *New York Times* article detailing "Mozart-mania" that examines the mixture of fact and fiction that has constructed our modern-day view of the musician. Writing in July 2005, Nicholas Kenyon observes that following his death, Mozart's biography was transformed and romanticized. He writes: "The workmanlike composer became the inspired artist; the servant-artisan became the free-spirited creator."[9] Under the scrutiny of ever-unfolding research, many of the ideals that we have traditionally associated with the term *genius* have begun to unravel around the composer's legacy, revealing a prodigious talent, but also a gift that must be understood in relationship to the local cultures with which Mozart interacted, to the financial dealings of a freelance composer and teacher, and to a musician who desired to be appreciated in his own time. In other words, he has become a contextualized genius. It is striking, however, that Kenyon concludes his article by reestablishing key aspects of the genius myth (i.e., timeless universalism and autonomy), writing that Mozart's "music continues to speak with unrivaled force across more than two centuries, and that, we might guess, would satisfy a man who knew the supreme worth of what he was creating."[10]

But given that Powell's reputation as a virtuoso was established in a context far removed from eighteenth-century Austria, which cultural configurations—both local and historical—close to home helped to shape our contemporary views of his genius? After all, bebop musicians such as Powell earned their reputations not by simply composing and learning difficult themes, but also by spontaneously creating technically impressive and emotionally moving solos within the parameters of the bebop style. The emphasis on improvisation earned bebop musicians a certain prestige and cultural capital. In fact, it might be argued that bebop solo techniques cleared the way for the study of jazz improvisation within academic circles. Perhaps the most important reason for this shift was that academic music study already had a paradigm in place for the appreciation of individual virtuosity.

Musicologist Robert Walser has labeled this category of musical excellence "the rhetoric of the virtuoso."[11] He explains that the term *virtuoso* was used in fifteenth- and sixteenth-century Italian aristocratic courts to designate "a type of individual excellence. . . . As applied to art, it reflected the relationship of art to power, as larger-than-life images and performers celebrated the wealth and power of the elite." In the nineteenth century, the idea "attained broader social relevance," as demonstrated in public concerts by Paganini, Liszt, Chopin, and others.[12] Virtuosos' performances were often spectacles in themselves; the mysterious aura surrounding these artists often inspired conjecture that their extraordinary gifts were supernatural or the result of a Faustian pact. "Like all musical techniques," Walser argues, "virtuosity functions socially." While some find virtuosos' technical acrobatics "distancing," for others the powers embedded in their performances "are the most effective articulators of a variety of social fantasies and musical pleasures."[13]

As a site of such fantasies, bebop drew out strong feelings and deep identifications from its followers, who connected with the covert political message that they perceived in almost every aspect of the music. Quincy Jones, for example, writes that bebop "was more than a style— it was a wavelength, a network of common interests with adherents worldwide. The bebop world signaled such a change just with the song titles. Instead of 'Has Anybody Seen My Gal?' [there was] Charlie Parker coming up with 'Ornithology,' and Thelonious Monk writing 'Epistrophy.'"[14] Obviously, bebop, with its astounding displays of virtuosity, established a dynamic compact with its fans.

The power of these fantasies and pleasures is an important source of music's attraction. But there's another side to these virtuoso geniuses creating fanciful sound flights. Take Miles Davis, for example, who remains both revered and reviled among jazz musicians of his age. Robin D. G. Kelley demythologizes Davis's genius as a way to face head-on our sometimes challenging task of "liking" our musical heroes. On the one hand, his large body of awe-inspiring work—one of sweeping stylistic changes and preciously conceived beauty—has stood the test of time, critical scrutiny, and commercial viability. On the other hand, his self-disclosed violence toward women, his stage deportment, and so on have caused their share of dissent in the jazz audience.[15]

Kelley intervenes in this aesthetic dilemma by contextualizing Davis's genius. He asks us to think about his work in another cultural framework: the inner-city pimp aesthetic. Kelley takes each parameter of Davis's life and work—the numerous photographs, his musical rhetoric, his treatment of women, his attitudes toward whites, and his stage management—and analyzes it vis-à-vis the mythic hustler-pimp of ghetto lore. Kelley mounts a convincing argument, and the end result is more than just another way to interpret Miles. Perhaps unconsciously, Kelley shows how Davis's genius may, in fact, be *dependent* on his imperfections.

Between May 1949 and July 1950, Powell recorded for three labels: Blue Note, Prestige, and Clef. He also performed at Carnegie Hall, Birdland, and other New York clubs such as Café Society between recordings. He even took a rare trip out of New York to play in Chicago on a June 1950 date arranged by local DJ Al Benson.[16] Groves and Shipton's *The Glass Enclosure* provides vivid snapshots of Powell during this period, a time when the word *genius* was used with increasing frequency to describe him.

Onstage, he cut an intriguing figure, a "highly individual stage persona," adopting an intense facial expression with tight lips, accompanied by a "guttural grunting" heard on many of his recordings because it was picked up through the piano mic: "He would generally sit sideways at the keyboard. . . . His right leg would be twisted out, his foot stabbing the floor. His trouser legs had a tendency to ride up over his calves, and he would hunch his shoulders, giving a sense to the onlooker of his great physical involvement in the music."[17] The physical involvement he displayed on the stand, as scholar and musician David Ake reminds us, could be read by his audiences as his way to communicate "a sense of artistic and personal depth (profundity, sensitivity, seriousness)."[18] And this artistic depth, in Powell's case, might easily tip the scale toward the slightly bizarre, as when, for example, he behaved garishly: playing a great solo and then getting up, walking off the bandstand midsong, "and applauding himself as he went."[19] Now here was a genius who knew his worth!—or another such conclusion could be drawn.

And what heroic genius narrative would be complete without an Oedipal challenge to a venerable elder? One night, as one report goes, Powell, billed opposite Art Tatum, audaciously pointed out some mistakes in his rival's performance of a Chopin prelude. Tatum countered by criticizing one of Powell's most obvious artistic signatures: his right-hand dominance. Powell answered the critique the next night (perhaps first woodshedding a bit to get it perfect) by playing one of his chestnuts, the standard "Sometimes I'm Happy," reportedly at a mercurial tempo, with only his left hand.[20] But the lore of such grandiose musical exploits was increasingly juxtaposed with his bandstand deportment, which consisted of an unsettling, taciturn, emotionless glare at a fixed point in the audience or at fellow performers for long periods of time.[21] Or even this alternate, unthinkable version of the Art Tatum confrontation: Powell cut his left hand with a pocketknife, "bandaged it up and went on playing with the self-inflicted handicap. He showed such virtuosity in both hands that Tatum was dumbfounded." His point proven, Powell's actions nonetheless upset all those around him, including his manager at the time, Oscar Goodstein, who implored the pianist to not play the next set. Powell ignored him.[22]

At his family's home in Harlem, Powell withdrew from the world into a cloak of eccentricities and debilitating memory loss that was perhaps exacerbated by mind-altering drugs: "Bud was quiet, saying little, perhaps laughing to himself, getting up to eat or play the piano. Friends remember that he was already starting to be silent in the company of strangers, and from time to time, when the names of fellow musicians were mentioned, Powell asked about them as if they were strangers. He also had to be told about events in which he had participated and what he had done."[23] His health challenges, together with the substandard wages of a black jazz musician, probably made it very difficult for him to live on his own. So this was Powell's ostensible existence in his uneasy nexus: a rising "star" recognized for his astounding skill set in a marginalized art world, but also a young man living a sequestered life in his parents' apartment, and a prime statistical target for both the underground drug culture of New York and a criminal justice system primed to overcriminalize his coping mechanisms. With all these factors guiding his trajectory, more trouble was likely to follow. And it did.

The year 1951 was a momentous one in Powell's life. He made studio recordings for the Clef (February) and Blue Note (May) labels that solidified his reputation as a superior pianist and composer, laying down what many believe to be his finest representations of his own music. Among the songs are the solo numbers "Parisian Thoroughfare," "Oblivion," and "Hallucinations" for Clef and "Un Poco Loco" for Blue Note. Together with his recording of his classic versions of standards such as "Just One of Those Things" and "Somewhere over the Rainbow," these works, varied and executed with command, remain at the heart of his aesthetic output. In March, Powell appeared with Charlie Parker, Dizzy Gillespie, Tommy Potter, and Roy Haynes at Birdland in a concert memorialized in a recording that features the bebop chestnuts "Anthropology," "'Round Midnight," and "A Night in Tunisia." While all these recordings don't necessarily amount to a prolific output, they are among his most important work.

Then the unthinkable happened. In early August 1951, almost two years to the day after Powell had recorded his first Bud Powell Modernists/Trio date for Blue Note, the pianist caused his good friend Thelonious Monk to get arrested and jailed. Powell and two friends had met Monk to socialize one evening. When narcotics police officers advanced toward the car in which the four were sitting, Powell, no doubt stunned and afraid, tossed a translucent envelope containing a small amount of heroin to the ground near Monk. The officers arrested all four, charging them with possession, and they were sent to the Tombs, an infamous detention center in Manhattan. Monk, essentially an innocent bystander, could not make the fifteen-hundred-dollar bail and spent sixty days incarcerated because he refused to snitch on his friend.[24] The stress of the episode, together with the fact that he had begun to drink heavily again, caused Powell to crash emotionally. His baseline paranoia ratcheted up; he "went berserk," as he believed he was going to be killed. Authorities poured ammoniated water on their emotionally fragile prisoner, after which he was sent first to Bellevue for examination, then to another commitment at Pilgrim State, and then to Creedmore, hospitalized, broken, electroshocked, and taken off the scene.[25]

Although Powell's troubles removed him from the day-to-day happenings of the jazz world, his reputation had by now moved overseas to France, where a young jazz fan scoured the press for any news of the pianist whose music had moved him greatly. Francis Paudras read the following notice, published in October 1951 in the French magazine *Jazz Hot*: "If you believe what you hear, two news items in rapid succession have caused a wind of panic among modern pianists—Thelonious Monk has been arrested for drug dealing and Bud Powell is hospitalized in a rest home." Paudras characterized the report, which he details in his book on Powell, as "a drop of poison eating away at my imagination."[26]

A classically trained pianist himself, Paudras first learned of Powell when he was fifteen years old. When he heard Powell's music on radio broadcasts, he describes it as transformative and revelatory, inspiring a feeling that he would spend the rest of his life honoring Powell through the promotion and protection of the pianist's physical and mental well-being and artistic legacy. In Paudras's telling, his first hearing of Powell's music had an almost palpably mystic power over the modern jazz acolyte: "The experience was like a lightning bolt, a sublime and blinding revelation. I was filled with bliss. . . . I couldn't explain why, but I knew at once that for me this music was the most important in the universe. As this certainty grew, the course of my life was transformed. The power of the music became part of my everyday gestures, my everyday acts."[27] Through radio broadcasts and the magazines *Jazz News* and *Jazz Hot,* Paudras diligently watched for any news—good, bad, or indifferent—about Powell, whom he now considered his "master."

Indeed, Paudras's attitude quickly crossed from that of a mere fan to a devotee of what he apparently understood to be Powell's divinely inspired genius. *Dance of the Infidels,* first published in 1986 in French, twenty years after Powell died, is Paudras's testament of his commitment to the pianist's life and art. He leads his readers through his efforts to learn any tidbit he could about Powell, mostly by gleaning reports of his comings and goings in the jazz press. As he pieces together knowledge of his hero, one can get a keen sense of the spell Paudras fell under during his teen years and into adulthood. But neither Powell nor Paudras could have known in the early 1950s what an integral role they would play in each other's life in the near future.

Yet even the devoted fan Paudras confesses that "as a white European," he could probably never really know "all the facets of Bud's interior world because of the complexity of his genius." Nonetheless, despite the differences in their social backgrounds, Paudras believes that there was something in Powell's art—"this great exponent of black American culture"—that was so profound it could speak to people around the world as a universal "message of great beauty, hope, and peace."[28] Many fans believed this to be true of the entire jazz genre itself. In fact, the tradition of jazz criticism (through which Paudras tracked Powell's every reported move), readers' polls, and reviews became a crucial lens through which a wide variety of people came to understand the music, and a space to rehearse and debate what it all meant in the larger scheme of things. Thus, even as the troubled Powell languished in and out of confinements, jazz criticism was steadily extending its role as a global community theater animated by, among many other notions, two important ideals: that jazz was the perfect place to understand the long history of race relations and "raced" expressions, and that because of American racism, Europe was better suited to provide black American musicians with the proper support structures for their art. Each of these beliefs would profoundly impact Powell's life and music.

THE "AFROLOGICAL" IDEA IN JAZZ CRITICISM

Charlie Parker and I played benefits for the African students in New
York and the African Academy of Arts and Research which was
headed by Kingsley Azumba Mbadiwe. . . . Just me, Bird, and Max
Roach, with African drummers and Cuban drummers; no bass,
nothing else. . . . Those concerts for the African Academy of Arts
and Research turned out to be tremendous. Through that experience,
Charlie Parker and I found the connections between Afro-Cuban and
African music and discovered the identity of our music with theirs.
Those concerts should definitely have been recorded, because we had
a ball, discovering our identity.

Dizzy Gillespie and Al Fraser, *To Be or Not to Bop*

I've been writing about Powell's music, and jazz in general, as if it fits
naturally under the rubric of "black" or African American music. Is
this a reductive characterization? The question, of course, taps into
a long history of controversy, cultural politics, and debates about
American musical culture. Jazz itself has been interpreted as a cultural
activity in which Americans of many different backgrounds have participated as performers, composers, and businesspeople. And because
jazz, like many other forms of American popular music, has been a
global phenomenon since at least the 1920s, one must carefully unpack
any "racial character" it may possess, especially if such a depiction
informs the music's analysis and interpretation. Since Powell himself,
to cite just one complex example, was musically shaped by his experiences in popular music and his childhood studies of western art music,
then the "African" in the term *African American music* here requires
discussion.

Here I move my discussion to explore one way in which the "black
difference" described by Paudras and others has played out in jazz discourse by tracing its treatment in selected critical works. Jazz's road to
artistic autonomy, a major theme in this book, has rarely been linked
purposefully to Africa and its cultural influences in the New World.
It's quite remarkable, in fact, to consider the degree to which Africa
has provided jazz with a sizable portion of its "history" despite the
West's denial of a history to its darker brothers and sisters. Ironically,
we find in this discussion that the jostling over jazz's Africanness denies
the music the disconnection from the social world that the concept of
autonomy seems to require.

Two points are important to keep in mind. Ingrid Monson has
noted that the 1960s are generally viewed as the time when the populist notion of what might be called African identification reached its

apex. The idea's historical trajectory reaches from the critical engagements of W.E.B. Du Bois and Marcus Garvey up through those of Malcolm X. The historiographical survey below highlights how discussions of Africa's relationship to jazz aesthetics were formative in jazz criticism. Writing in 1996, George E. Lewis argues, and I concur, that any construction of "blackness" (or "whiteness," for that matter) in jazz discourse should not suggest essentialist, biological connections, but social and practical ones. To this end, he forwards models that he calls "Afrological" and "Eurological," critical frames that "refer metaphorically to musical belief systems and behavior which . . . exemplify particular kinds of musical 'logic.' At the same time," he writes, "these terms are intended to historicize the particularity of perspective characteristic of two systems that have evolved in such divergent cultural environments."[29]

While some of the historical writings discussed below slip in and out of essentialist perspectives—they are, after all, anchored in their various historical moments—it is crucial to keep in mind that the writers are attempting to explain "a socio-musical belief system that differs in critical respects from that which has emerged from the dominant culture itself." But difference itself does not exclude the possibility of cultural sharing or exchange. As Lewis further argues: "My construction of 'Afrological' and 'Eurological' systems of improvisative musicality refers to social and cultural location and is theorized here as historically emergent rather than ethnically essential, thereby accounting for the reality of transcultural and transracial communication among improvisers. For example, African-American music, like any music, can be performed by a person of any 'race' without losing its character as historically Afrological, just as performance of Karnatic vocal music by Terry Riley does not transform the raga into a Eurological music form."[30]

Predating the politically charged Black Arts Movement notions of Pan-Africanism in the 1970s, the discussion about blackness in jazz letters is far from mundane, pedestrian, or uninformed. Rather, it has all the trappings of literary high drama: hard-core identity politics, social theory debates, and aesthetic brush clearing. It is a feisty and fraught discourse, one thoroughly grounded in a rapidly changing social world. The discussion below, then, provides what might be called an archaeology of jazz autonomy—a narrative that shows that the idea of jazz as art has been dependent on a very black, orally driven history. This topic is rich and influential enough to merit extended attention, as its insights form a useful framing for my discussion of Bud Powell's aesthetic palette.

WHAT'S THE DIFFERENCE?

American music historian Charles Hamm writes that "the most characteristic and dynamic music to emerge from American culture over the past two centuries invariably resulted from interaction among musicians of several different cultural, racial, national, and ethnic backgrounds."[31] Indeed, scores of musicians have self-consciously crossed these real and imagined boundaries of lived experience to slake their insatiable thirst for enticing and sometimes forbidden musical materials. The idea of difference provides power to many of these acts of homage, inspiration, love, and theft. And beyond its role in the creation of music, difference can also inform the interpretation of a musical work. Difference, it seems, imbues music with signifying qualities, charms that allow it to express something tangible to listeners, especially to those who are keenly aware that some kind of boundary has been crossed.

African American music discussions have, since the nineteenth century, included many debates about cultural difference, what it means, and the extent to which we invest in its claims of cultural authenticity. At the center of this discourse has been the relevance of historical Africa in the creation and interpretation of music, from the spirituals to jazz to hip-hop. Throughout the late nineteenth and twentieth centuries—and into the millennium—writers, musicians, artists, and activists have found in "Africa" contested truths, a constructed past, a dynamic present, and a utopian future.

These activities have taken many forms, but in music study specifically, they have manifested in debates over the degree to which African sensibilities exist in cultural forms in the Americas and the Caribbean. On the one hand are those who believe that the evidence is obvious: qualities, traits, or artifacts known as "retentions" or "survivals" exist and unite the African Diaspora culturally and spiritually. Views from this camp are anything but unified—they include a range of thought, from the most crudely essentialist and reductive to the most thoroughly researched, provocative, and theoretically sophisticated. On the other hand, some believe that the commonsense notion of "black music" is so fraught with ideologies and myths from its origins in outmoded nineteenth-century racialism that the term does not reflect its multicultural, syncretic character.

Let's consider two influential works from each of these intellectual camps: Samuel Floyd's *The Power of Black Music* (1995) and Ronald Radano's *Lying Up a Nation* (2003). It's probably not entirely fair to ask these ambitious, highly nuanced studies to be representative of any single intellectual position, but we can tease out and compare each of their basic premises about African retentions and survivals in African American music. We will see that the debate is really about other issues: cultural identity, cultural ownership, the contested nature of origins, and the importance of visible evidence.[32]

Floyd provides a theoretical framework for analyzing black music that draws on the fields of history and postmodern literary theory. From history, he draws the idea of the slave culture's ring shout as providing African American music history with a foundational sonic template. Floyd argues that the sounds and conceptual qualities of the ring shout were passed along through oral and written culture—the shouts, cries, hollers, improvisation impulse, calls and responses, hand clapping, dancing, and so forth developed into modern forms such as blues, jazz, and gospel, and they even became musical tropes embedded in art music.

Floyd interprets the relationship of the music's African past to a modern American present—indeed, the connections between Africa's rituals and American slave shouts—through the spyglass of esoteric black literary theory. He wants to show how "African survivals exist not merely in the sense that African-American music has the same characteristics as its African counterparts, but also that the musical tendencies, the mythological beliefs and assumptions, and the interpretive strategies of African-Americans are the same as those that underlie the music of the African homeland, that these tendencies and beliefs continue to exist as African cultural memory, and that they continue to inform the elaboration of African-American music."[33] Floyd's summary represents a preciously held view about the relationship between Africa and African American cultural production, one maintained by writers such as anthropologist Melville Herskovits, art music composer Olly Wilson, and ethnomusicologists Portia Maultsby and Ingrid Monson.[34]

Radano begs to differ. He writes that the term *retentions* misleads, that it cannot "explain the phenomenal complexities of performative experience across the history of America. It cannot do so because it is an abstraction based on the extraction of a hypothesized African purity that had been recast within North American racial discourse."[35] Working against the idea of what he calls "cultural absolutes and authenticities" and following the insights of black cultural studies of the 1990s, Radano argues for a more malleable blackness, a less historically stable idea of black music, and a theoretical profile in African American musicology that interrogates any "simplistic determinations of culture."[36]

All told, Radano proposes "in no uncertain terms to challenge . . . those strategies of containment that uphold the racial binaries informing the interpretation of black music. It goes against the grain of a pervasive, yet remarkably underanalyzed assumption that correlates an enduring black musical presence with the myth of a consistent and stable socio-racial position of 'blackness.'"[37] The questions of cultural identity, ownership, and the nature of African American music will not be settled here (or, perhaps, ever). Yet I think it is useful to ask a question of these somewhat competing theories of African American music: What cultural work are they doing, especially as it concerns the interpretation of styles such as bebop and jazz more generally?

I place Floyd's proposition in a legacy of writing that can be traced back to what we know as the beginnings of the African American literary tradition in the Anglophone world. The idea of "becoming African" predates any of the modern forms of the notion, and it has always been, I might add, difficult cultural and social work. The idea of being an "African" is entirely a product of a violent encounter in which chattel slavery flattened out ethnic and cultural differences in the service of making the social practice of human commodity an efficient one. As James Sidbury has argued, the idea that black peoples on the African continent formed "a unified cultural and/or 'racial' unit" was a European invention that flourished between 1650 and 1750 as plantation slavery and its cultures shaped race ideology, trade economies, and social practices on both sides of the Atlantic.[38] As a necessary function of the dehumanizing act of race-based enslavement and as a casualty of the growth of the Enlightenment notion of human progress, the new "Africans" were relegated to positions outside of progress, outside of humanity.

But, as Sidbury reports, early acts of literary resistance from writers such as Phillis Wheatley and Ignatius Sancho turned Africa into inspiration—into a conscious symbol of unity and black pride. In their influential writings, they developed "a language of African identity," and they wrote against the empire, using the master's own tools to do so. They and subsequent black writers used literature to create a discursive space for the making of the African subject, to facilitate the heroic journey from "thing to human being" in the Anglophone world.[39] This construction of African identity occurred not only among writers, but among all manner of black people as they founded "a wide range of churches, schools, and fraternal organizations during the decades surrounding 1800, and many included the term 'African' within their titles."[40] As intellectuals who understood full well the diversity of black people, Wheatley and Sancho wrote into existence a black kinship based on common interests and suffering, and not necessarily on mystical blood ties. Thus we see that the pressure to become African was exerted from two sides: as a result of structural racism and as an act of self-fashioning with the goal of sociopolitical uplift.

It is fascinating to consider the extensive cultural ramifications of these dual notions of Africa on America's cultural history. For art historian Gerardo Mosquera, in order for us to understand these new cultural forms, we must think first about the language we use in our descriptions. Rejecting terms such as *impact* and *influence,* he would rather we speak of an African "presence" because the term seems, on the conceptual and ideological level, not to capture an cultural encounter from the outside in, but to depict an Atlantic culture that would not exist in its modern form without the new Africa. Mosquera draws on provocative food metaphors from Fernando Ortiz, a writer on Cuban culture, who "proposed the felicitous paradigm of *ajiaco,* a rich stew or soup of different ingredients cooked until it makes a broth of synthesis. . . . The hybridized African proves to be the key to many of America's cultural expressions, not [as an] intertextuality but as a constitutive presence; not as inspiring element, and not even as something added, but as a Promethean ingredient in the formation of the new culture."[41]

What about the relationship between cultural identity and this African presence? How does it correlate to Radano's provocative idea of "the myth of a consistent and stable socioracial position of 'blackness'"? Once the African background that was invented on both sides of the racial power struggle became a social reality, how was it experienced, used, and transformed through the years? Cultural critic Stuart Hall writes that "cultural identities come from somewhere, have histories. But, like everything which is historical, they undergo constant transformation. Far from being eternally fixed in some essentialized past, they are subject to the continuous 'play' of history, culture, and power."[42] Thus, whatever the answer is, it is clear that black cultural identity will be on the move, constantly adapting to structures of inequality and pressed into the service of those who are identified as black.

This play of which Hall speaks results in two kinds of cultural identities. The first is a collective one, based on what people believe are common historical experiences that provide "stable, unchanging and continuous frames of reference and meaning, beneath the shifting divisions and vicissitudes of our actual history."[43] The other cultural identity is marked by a sense of "becoming," a divergence from the larger cultural identity of Africanness, especially in the context of Caribbean identity, which is Hall's subject. Cultural identities are thus dynamic cultural processes, and the identities that develop are ultimately informed by lived experiences and perspectives. These perspectives constitute "reality as perceived, conceptualized, and evaluated by individuals who are stigmatized and discriminated against because they are designated as 'Negroes' or 'Blacks.'"[44] Far from representing a narrow frame, these perspectives are cross-pollinated with multiple identities, social positions, and experiences. Far from being monolithic, cultural identity always takes into account "that social class, nationality, ethnicity, tribal affiliation, and/or religious orientation all make the experience different from person to person."[45]

Modern jazz's growing status as art music, together with the argument that jazz is America's "classical music," has richly complicated the issues surrounding the black aesthetic or perspective in jazz. Jazz's artistic profile has either emphasized its heritage in European musical practice or been a powerful symbol of *difference* created by "Africanisms," which have sparked controversy since the early days of jazz criticism. Jazz critics either stressed or downplayed the idea of African influence, depending on which political or aesthetic point they wanted to make about the music they loved or the marginalized people they perceived to be the creators of the music.

WRITING THE JAZZ-RACE-ART COMPLEX

In America during the 1920s, writers of various stripes—composers, journalists, music critics, musicians—published many books and articles on jazz.[46] Among these early writers were Gilbert Seldes, R.D. Darrell, Paul Whiteman, Virgil Thomson, George Antheil, Carl Van Vechten, and Henry Osborne Osgood. Jazz impressed these writers in a variety of ways, some favorably, others not. Moreover, since the word *jazz* in the 1920s represented what we now consider to be a range of styles, these writers were not always referring to the same thing when they wrote about jazz. With their personal biases worn on their sleeves, writers of the 1920s made it their business to grapple openly with what they believed to be the aesthetic underpinnings of this music. Most important, Africanisms were discussed in early jazz literature in an unselfconscious way, but often from an essentialist perspective.[47] These writings are important to understanding a style such as bebop because they form the historical grounding for the idea of blackness in jazz, in the same way that Wheatley's and Sancho's writings form a foundation for the literary black Anglophone tradition.

Henry O. Osgood claims, in his foreword to *So This Is Jazz* (1926), to have written "the first attempt to set down a connected account of the origin, history, and development of jazz music." Although other writers were thinking about jazz in the late 1920s, Osgood provides a telling bird's-eye view of the discourse. He saw himself as part of a "little group of serious thinkers" taking up "jazz in a serious way," and Africa figured prominently in his concerns. On the kinetic aspects of black jazz players' performances (he called them "contortions"), he writes: "They are purely Negrotic in themselves and come directly from the 'ring shout,' the dances of religious frenzy or ecstasy, without question of African origin."[48] Osgood also believes that the word *jazz* itself came from Africa. Despite his interest in jazz's roots in black culture, Osgood gives considerable attention to George Gershwin, Ferde Grofé, and the merits of symphonic jazz.

In Europe, and especially in the France of the 1930s, jazz captured the imagination of writers. This enthusiasm, in fact, led to the establishment of the important periodical *Jazz Hot: La Revue internationale de la musique de jazz* in 1935. Some have connected French interest in jazz to the primitivist movement there during the first two decades of the twentieth century, which included a strain of essentialism present in early French jazz writing that would later influence perceptions of the music.[49] French writers—especially Hughes Panassié and Charles Delaunay—sought to come to terms with what they believed to be an essential quality of jazz: its African heritage. As the title *Jazz Hot* suggests (there was also a Hot Club of France), these enthusiasts saw "hotness," an illusive spirit in the music (in particular in its rhythm), as crucial to its character.

At the same time, interest in jazz produced the first generation of important American critics, including Marshall Stearns, John Hammond, Paul Eduard Miller, and George Hoefer, among others.

By the end of the 1930s, literary treatments of jazz had escalated and booklength studies by American authors had begun to appear. As with the French literature, these writers referred to Africanisms, but with varying degrees of essentialism, cultural insight, methodology, and philosophical motivations.

Winthrop Sargeant's *Jazz, Hot and Hybrid* (1938) stressed the mixed pedigree of jazz. Sargeant writes in the third edition's preface that when his book first appeared, it was "the only serious musicological study of its type," a departure from previous, "mostly ecstatic," personal-ity- and discographical-centered jazz writings.[50] For Sargeant, jazz is neither strictly European ("completely lacking in the intellectual and structural features that sustain the interest of a cultivated 'highbrow' musical audience") nor African ("very few influences can be given doc-umentary proof").[51] Jazz was something unique, and he sets out to explain why through detailed musical analysis.

Sargeant leads his reader through twelve chapters of scalar, rhyth-mic, harmonic, and melodic analysis of jazz, complete with musical examples. In chapter 12, "Influences from the Dark Continent," he answers an important question he posed at the beginning of his book: "Did the Negroes invent jazz?" He responds: "When one examines the musical structure of these arts in detail . . . it becomes apparent that they represent a fusion of musical idioms in which both White and 'African' contributions play indisputable roles. It is safe to say that vir-tually no Afro-American music today is wholly without White influ-ence; and it is obvious that all jazz, from the most primitive hot variety to the most sophisticated, is heavily influenced by Negro musical hab-its."[52] In *Jazzmen*, published a year later, authors Frederick Ramsey, Jr., and Charles Edward Smith make very little of the Africanisms issue. For them, the distinctiveness of jazz, especially during the New Orleans period, was achieved through musical illiteracy, a condition these authors considered a virtue, one that enabled musicians to retain "much of the African material in their playing."[53]

But in the 1940s, Africa became something of a controversy in American jazz writing. Research on African American culture by social scientists such as Melville Herskovits and Gunnar Myrdal, together with dramatic wartime shifts in American racial politics, found their way into jazz writing.[54] The idea of "racial purity," a version of essen-tialism, was still present in this literature, but jazz writers began to think more about the idea of culture and the acculturation processes that are at the heart of African American culture.

Rudi Blesh's *Shining Trumpets* (1946) provides a good example of this development.[55] Blesh's introduction reveals his eclectic approach to the subject. The book, which grew out of a 1943 lecture series at the San Francisco Museum of Art, begins with acknowledgments to anthropologists Herskovits and Dr. Richard A. Waterman for "great and generous assistance," as well as to the curators of archives of African American culture and a host of black and white jazz musicians.[56] Blesh, unlike Sargeant before him, has no problem locating jazz's origins on the African continent: "African music is the key that unlocks the secrets of jazz. For jazz, regardless of the origins of its melodies, is a *manner* of playing derived directly from the music of the West African Coast. . . . Jazz is no musical hybrid; it is a miracle of synthesis," he writes, disagreeing with Sergeant.[57] Blesh's work stands as a response to Sargeant's call in *Jazz,* and seems written to correct the perceived shortcomings in Sargeant's approach.

A singular and fascinating aspect of *Shining Trumpets* is the tension created by Blesh's "outsider" social scientist positioning, the personal satisfaction he obviously experienced from jazz, and the role he believed jazz could play in racial and cultural politics. Throughout the book, Blesh reminds his readers (inferred to be white) of the social and morally edifying rewards gained by jazz appreciation:

> The understanding of jazz, as opposed to the mere emotional reaction to it, requires effort. This is even more true than with our own serious, or classical music, for the latter, unlike jazz, represents a continuous development in our own native culture. Yet never was understanding more richly rewarded. Jazz has widened our artistic horizons immeasurably; subtly but unmistakably it has influenced our own musical practice. . . . A music, improvised freely by blacks and whites together, it sounds a summons to free, communal, creative living. A music of vital and forward motion, jazz is a symbol of that improvisational process, guided by the instinct for freedom, which all social progress essentially is.[58]

Echoing the sentiments of late-nineteenth-century black nationalist politics and the "New Negroism" of the 1920s, Blesh believes that the appreciation and recognition of jazz as an art form would ultimately lead to "an increasing awareness of the Negro's stature and integrity as a man [*sic*]."[59] To support his argument, Blesh advances the notion that African music should be viewed as far more than a primitive urtext for African American folk expression: "African, particularly West African, music has been a complex and highly developed art for centuries. Its origins are perhaps more remote in the past, its continuum of development perhaps of longer span, than those of European music."[60]

Blesh's copious listing of what he calls "African survivals in Negro jazz" is deeply indebted to Herskovits's work on African American culture. His suggestions that jazz criticism combine methodologies from African music study and European art music and take into account the American milieu also reveal more than a faint trace of Herskovits's idea of cultural syncretism and transformation. Anthropology (and sociology) provided jazz writers with what many thinkers on African American culture appear to have been waiting for: research on the African past and a way to talk about difference without propagating negative racial stereotypes.

Blesh uses these tools handily. But at the same time he is unable to abandon the notion of "pure Negro-ness." Blesh's chapter on his "fieldwork" (conducted primarily in libraries and archives) praises the stubbornness of Africanisms and is quoted at length here because of its remarkable synthesis of liberal intention; penetrating, if somewhat undeveloped, cultural observations; and essentialism:

> This is the stubbornness of the African character, not only in Africa but on alien soil, and through racial dilution even to the evolution of a new physical type. This character persists in spite of the unusual adaptability of the Negro to foreign influences. It is at its purest, the most *Negro*, where the transplanted black man is kept ignorant and isolated from surrounding society, as in slavery. It becomes less purely *Negro* in proportion to the degree of his assimilation. It will, perhaps retain a Negroid character, not only because the art of the Negro is different in character from other arts, but more basically still, because a strong case may be made out for the belief that the Negro is different physically and psychologically, from other peoples. Anyone who has watched the Negro in athletics or in ballet is aware of the different quality of his movements. Psychologically, too, he is different in a great many of his reactions. Where he speaks characteristically in ellipsis, for example, and with double meanings, he is not evading the issue. Instead, he is presenting it, more complexly than we, in various meanings and from various points of view, simultaneously as it were. And his power of *direct communication beyond the spoken word* is vital and unatrophied.[61]

During the next twenty years, the debate on Africanisms intensified, providing jazz writers with numerous flashpoints, depending on their political and musical persuasions. Marxist critic Sidney Finkelstein, author of *Jazz: A People's Music* (1948), blasts writers such as Blesh for carrying the Africanisms idea (he calls it "folk," "subconscious," "African," and "primitive" theory) to the extreme. Finkelstein views them as a harmful extension of the primitivist-influenced writings of Panassié and other French critics. He defends his stance vehemently: "Jazz is not African music, as anyone can tell who compares Johnny

Dodds' 'Joe Turner Blues,' Louis Armstrong's 'Knocking a Jug' or Kid Ory's 'High Society' to an African drum or vocal performance. Jazz is not even 'Afro-American.' . . . To use such a hyphenated term implies that there are two Americas."[62]

Barry Ulanov's *A History of Jazz in America* (1952) continues Finkelstein's line of thinking on Africanisms. Ulanov, a longtime critic at Metronome and a bebop enthusiast, credits the French critics for teaching him that there was "order,and meaning" in jazz. He continues, "The European devotees . . . demonstrated to me that the abandon of the jazz audience could also be creative and discerning."[63] Ulanov rails against the work of "industrious anthropologists and social scientists" who champion the idea that blacks created jazz "by imposing a heavy layer of [their] native jungle chants and rhythms upon . . . European materials." Like Finkelstein, Ulanov believes that such a story "confirms the average man's impression of the Negro as a jungle-formed primitive whose basic expression is inevitably savage." Labeled by Ulanov as chief spokesman for the Africanisms theory is "the highly placed and indefatigable" Melville J. Herskovits.[64]

Ulanov rejects the notion of long cultural memory except when it serves to argue for jazz's "universal" appeal. While admitting that "the African background of the first jazz musicians played some part in their music," Ulanov writes that a researcher must also understand "the music of the English and Scottish settlers in the Atlantic states in the seventeenth and eighteenth centuries, of the Irish and German in the nineteenth, of the French who preceded the Negroes to the Louisiana Territory."[65] His argument is reasonable. But his desire to argue for the universality (read the "European-ness") of jazz prevents Ulanov from realizing that he invokes the same cultural memory model he has vehemently rejected. He writes: "Without any awareness of what he has done, the jazzman may have gone back to some of the beginnings of music, tapping once more the creative roots which nourished Greek music, the plain chant, the musical baroque and its immediate successors and predecessors."[66]

Jazz enjoyed more visibility and status in the mid- to late 1950s, a new standing that was represented in many ways: diligent recording techniques and serious liner notes by jazz record labels such as Blue Note, Riverside, and Prestige; governmental support through State Department–sponsored tours by jazz artists such as Dizzy Gillespie (1956); academic interest, as symbolized by Gunther Schuller's Third Stream movement (1957) and the establishment of the Lenox School of Jazz in Massachusetts (late 1950s); and, finally, an explosion of jazz literature, which extended well into the 1960s, by writers whose work remains central to the study of jazz to this day. Among these writers were Stearns, Nat Shapiro, Nat Hentoff, André Hodeir, Francis Newton, Whitney Balliett, Gunther Schuller, Martin Williams, and especially LeRoi Jones (Amiri Baraka).[67]

The critical debates concerning jazz's aesthetics, racial qualities and conceptual origins, while eventually impacting the reception of Powell's work, could not have been further from the pianist's mind when he was enduring his latest hospitalization. His discography tells the bleak story: he did not make a studio recording between May 1951 and August 1953, although about a dozen live performances were caught during this period. For most of his nearly year-and-a-half confinement, Powell was allowed to play the piano only once a week because hospital staff noticed how agitated he would become on his instrument.[68] It was probably frustrating to feel some rust. About a year after his arrest, sometime around September 1952, pianists Thelonious Monk and Marian McPartland visited Powell in Creedmore. McPartland says she coaxed Powell to play in this setting, after which he hesitantly obliged: "After a while Bud did play the piano. Notwithstanding the defective keys he seemed to get wonderful tonality out of the piano and seemed to be able to play around the defective keys."[69] Elmo Hope reports Powell's overall physical decline and says that he had even drawn a keyboard on the wall at some point, perhaps out of desperation to play.[70]

Inside the mental health system, Powell was not considered an amazing artist revered for his startling technique and sophisticated compositions. He was just another delusional African American man in his late twenties—a statistic. Not that there existed a huge statistical literature on mental health and African American men at this time. As one scholar notes, it was not until the aftermath of World War II, when the need to serve a large black male population who were returning home from their experiences in a Jim Crow armed services arose, did mental health care for minorities began to uncouple itself from age-old stereotypes that linked blackness to mental illness. About the period when Powell was beginning his string of hospitalizations, Ellen Dwyer observes the following: "Psychiatrists increasingly attributed psychiatric disorders to social and economic factors, but a number remained unwilling to abandon altogether the notion of biologically based racial difference. These two very different perspectives would continue to coexist, albeit uneasily, in mainstream medical writings and practice through the long, hard years of the war and well into the 1950s."[71] In other words, mental health treatment for African American populations was an in-flux practice dictated by broader racial biases in the society at large.

In a book that shows how mainstream American society has equated race with insanity, Jonathan Metzl notes that African American men receive a diagnosis of schizophrenia at a rate four times greater than whites do. Moreover, for Metzl, the language of "insanity" has often been used to couch racial relations in American society: any threat to the "racial order" is described "as a form of madness that is, still, overwhelmingly located in the minds and bodies of black men. At other times, members of minority communities use the language of insanity to describe the psychical effects of living in racist societies."[72] At the core of his argument, Metzl teaches us that clinical symptoms are real—their impact on families, careers, and the material existence of patients is devastating. But the diagnosis of such illness has been an evolving process, open to interpretation at best and, at worst, dictated (often unconsciously) by the underlying racial attitudes of the psychiatric community. The diagnosis of schizophrenia, for example, at one time described a primarily white woman's disease of mood swings, but it was subsequently considered a black man's disease of rage, volatility, and aggression. As Metzl observes, "In the worst cases, psychiatric authors conflated the schizophrenic symptoms of African American patients with the perceived schizophrenia of civil rights protest, particularly those organized by Black Power, Black Panthers, Nation of Islam, or other activist groups."[73] In a close precursor to the Civil Rights movement, historical actors could sense the paramount changes in the air in the 1950s, ones that with little doubt shaped how a young black male psychiatric patient would have been evaluated.

Given these circumstances, Powell's experience with the early-1950s mental health system stood little chance of rising above the level of horrific. Fortunately, the inner circle of bebop musicians and enthusiasts had not forgotten him, as is often the case with many mental health patients. His family still loved him, their precocious and gifted treasure. And certainly the Parisian superfan and future caretaker Francis Paudras's eyes remained trained on the jazz press for any new developments about his hero. The lore of Powell's musical exploits still seemed to be fresh and bankable in the minds of nightclub and record-label owners. With this support, and despite the odds, Powell would begin to function again, to the point where he was allowed to leave the hospital on one-day passes to perform at Oscar Goodstein's Birdland, but only with supervision. This was deemed a successful experiment; Goodstein then posted a thousand-dollar bond and, with the help of Powell's mother, Pearl, secured legal rights and governorship over his financial affairs, accounting "for all monies received and spent."[74]

In Paris, Paudras caught the news, reading a report in a January 1953 *Jazz Hot* issue that "Bud Powell will soon be back at work. He played Birdland on December 11 with Max Roach and Curley Russell replacing George Shearing, who was off that night conducting a symphony orchestra."[75] Indeed, on February 5, 1953, Powell left the hospital, free again to pursue his career, although it was clear by now to all who cared about him that he would always require a certain level of supervision when he wasn't executing some awe-inspiring feat at his natural station: a piano, "thrivin' on a riff," to quote the title of a bebop song. Powell's discography shows that two days later, on February 7, he was back playing at the Royal Roost, as documented in "airshot" recordings made with a trio consisting of Oscar Pettiford on bass and Roy Haynes on drums. He played throughout March as well, and even took a road trip for a gig at Club Kavakos in Washington, DC, presumably his first out-of-town date since Chicago in 1951. Powell was back.

Powell as a genius, as a black man, as a musician of Afrological and Eurological traditions, as a lawbreaker, as an experimental modernist, as a laborer in the modern jazz industry, as a subject in jazz criticism and history, and as a mental health patient: for such a young man, he had occupied and negotiated many social orders, many notes and tones. And there would be more to come. One thing was sure: in his newfound freedom, he clearly needed to stay away from self-medicating substances because, as his track record affirmed, they always rocked his emotional stability.

Avoiding illegal substances in New York's early-1950s jazz scene, however, was a very tall order, particularly for someone who did not have the personal fortitude to withstand an environment saturated with temptations. Bebop had trekked from Harlem to 52nd Street, and by the late 1940s it had landed in its latest "home": Times Square. This geographic space, an intense entertainment district teeming with young people and many others in search of good times, demonstrates the importance of spatial logic in understanding drug use in subcultures such as bebop. Urban studies scholar Eric Schneider makes one thing clear regarding Times Square, the location of professional opportunities waiting for Powell upon his discharge: "Heroin permeated the entertainment district." There was not, in Schneider's view, an inevitable link between drugs and jazz. He argues, rather, that "there was a spatiality to drug use and to the transmission of 'drug knowledge' that occurred in places where interested novices could interact with experienced users. In the immediate postwar years, these were fairly few—specific jazz and after-hours clubs, bars, and cafeterias that catered to a crowd of pimps, hookers, drug dealers, jazz musicians, and their hangers-on."[76] This subcultural element of the jazz scene had precedents in the 52nd Street clubs (whose predecessors were the clubs catering to marijuana users when using the drug became illegal). Indeed, 52nd Street clubs such as "the Onyx, the Downbeat, the Three Deuces, and the Spotlight—all lost their cabaret licenses for a time in 1945 because of narcotics trafficking on the premises."[77] The jazz occupation took place in an atmosphere rife with opportunities to abuse alcohol, marijuana, and more.

When heroin became a part of the scene in the late 1940s, the structural elements to foster and support a conducive environment already existed: a combustible mix of "musicians, hustlers, dealers, and fans; a hipster subculture based in this social setting that valorized heroin as part of its rejection of square America; and the music itself (with the related influence of Charlie Parker) together account for the spread of heroin among bebop-playing musicians."[78] Musicians and fans were drawn into the circle. For their part, musicians lived lives that were structurally different than those of the "square" world; they belonged to a select group whose lifestyles, work conditions, and values diverged from the "norm."[79] Unfortunately, some of the musicians believed that heroin would enhance their playing abilities, an aphorism particularly strong among Charlie Parker devotees, who thought that his habit composed an important source of his power.

Fans also bought into this idea. Young, impressionable, and looking for peer-approved thrills, teenagers flocked to Times Square, and bebop, the hippest music around, was a sufficient attraction for this crowd. When Bop City, Birdland, and the Royal Roost opened in the late 1940s, their bleacher seats, installed for underage patrons, facilitated an easy social exchange among fans, drug users, their dealers, and, of course, musicians.[80] This was the cultural space into which the still-convalescing Powell returned. Maybe he could make up the musical ground he had lost while away, or at the very least use his firebrand version of the bebop trio—a form that he himself had helped to codify—to help pacify his mind, body, and soul.

Anyone with an interest in Powell's well-being understood the challenges he'd face in the underbelly of the jazz scene. How do you control an unpredictable musician whose professional life put him in the direct line of what might be called friendly fire? Powell was determined legally incompetent in 1953 (a status that would last for three years), with Oscar Goodstein appointed the guardian of his affairs. Things moved fast under Goodstein's control. As discussed in chapter 2, Powell married Audrey Hill a little over a month after leaving Creedmore. In August 1953, *Ebony* magazine reported that he would soon demand a thousand dollars per week from "clubs from San Francisco to Toronto . . . [that] want to present him as a genius who was rescued from oblivion." Though this was obviously a marketing ploy to maximize Powell's earning potential, Goodstein insisted to the interviewer for the article that even Powell's disconcerting habit of giggling for no cause was not a symptom of his condition, but "happiness welling up inside him and bursting into expression."[81]

Johnny Powell, son of Buttercup, told writer Eugene Holley that he believed Goodstein had cooked up the idea of Hill marrying his father in order to secure more control over the pianist.[82] If this is true, it seems to have worked, particularly from a public relations angle. Powell's domestic and professional lives looked picture perfect: he wasn't drinking at this time, he was prompt to gigs, and he sat around his apartment on 45th Street listening to "classical" records and satisfying his sweet tooth by consuming large quantities of soda per day. Black genius now involved a legally sanctioned guardian who also doubled as an employer and a personal manager—Goodstein probably had sway over all matters, both professional and personal.

All of Powell's documented work activity over the next three years seems to have been in the business orbits of several men: Morris Levy, owner of the Royal Roost, Birdland and a publishing house that owned Powell's original music; Goodstein, manager of Birdland; the Moe Gale Agency for bookings; Norman Granz, owner of Norgran and later Verve Records; and Alfred Lion, founder of Blue Note Records, a company with which Powell recorded some of his most expertly produced work. The quality of Powell's business relationships during this period appears to be varied; in most cases he was just trying to play without lots of demands. But clearly he was an extraordinary commodity.

Writing in her column "The Sound of Truth," Maely Daniele Dufty, a Jewish jazz fan who had fled World War II–era persecution in Czechoslovakia and who became a fierce defender of jazz musicians' rights, critiqued Powell's labor status. She believed that Powell's problems stemmed from "the damages of oversize talent trying to function in a wholly materialistic society riddled with prejudice." Dufty expressed skepticism at Goodstein's appointment as a "committee of one" over the pianist's affairs. She complained about the exploitation of modern jazz performers on the Street and in the Times Square district, describing the musicians as "overanxious to work" and "overabundant." She found it incredible that, as far as she knew, Charlie Parker was never paid for the use of his name on the club Birdland, but the management still had eventually "barred him from the joint." She reserved specific criticism for Goodstein's dealings with Powell. Together with Morris Levy, Goodstein had say-so in all three revenue streams in the music business: recording, publishing, and live performance.

As Dufty put it, commenting on Goodstein's ambitions to manage musicians, he was positioned to monopolize—"All he needed was some real talented 'boys' he could sell to himself and his boss and/or partner at the price he in his double-function as buyer *and* seller of talent [could set]." Dufty was one of the few who pointed out the asymmetrical power relationships at play in the situation: "Bud Powell was ideally suited to such a set-up. The State said, Bud Powell had no right to handle his own money, his committee was to handle it. He had no right to make decisions about anything concerning him without his committee. The only thing the State didn't say a blessed thing about, was how a man this incompetent in handling his own life could be so desirable an asset to promoters that they should work him 6 nights a week to packed houses and critical acclaim."[83] Despite the facade of domestic and business bliss forwarded in the *Ebony* article, another picture emerges from the international jazz press a few months later. Musically, Powell was solid: the spectacle of his virtuosity was attracting the attention it always had. But beyond this, something else lurked, and many found it unsettling and disturbing:

> Bud is a strange man. He barely speaks and between pieces seems lost in a dream from which he emerges only when one of his sidemen reminds him he has to play. . . . After each set he sits alone in a corner of the room looking exceedingly sad. . . . If you can manage to get a seat up front, your eyes are about eight inches from Bud Powell's hands. Those hands are unforgettable! They are beautiful, with long slim fingers that Bud holds in a surprising way, flat on the keyboard, almost arched backwards from the normal position.[84]

Powell's association with Blue Note Records produced six sessions between 1949 and 1958. Alfred Lion considered the pianist a friend, and many jazz musicians held the producer in high esteem. The company, formed in 1938, carried its statement of purpose in its first brochure: "Blue Note records are designed simply to serve the uncompromising expressions of hot jazz or swing, in general. Any particular style of playing which represents an authentic way of musical feeling is genuine expression. By virtue of its significance in place, time, and circumstance, it possesses its own tradition, artistic standards and audience that keeps [sic] it alive. Hot jazz, therefore, is expression and communication, a musical and social manifestation, and Blue Note records are concerned with identifying its impulse, not its sensational and commercial adornments."[85] Attention to the detail of every level of a recording—engineering, paid rehearsals, the material, the photography and graphics—set Blue Note apart from its contemporaries. Pianist Horace Silver once pointed out that Lion and his partner Francis Wolff "were men of integrity" whose commitment to artists was rare among record labels.[86] Jackie McLean even believed that Lion and Wolff could have made a difference in his life if they had handled him earlier in his career, because they treated him "with the greatest respect."[87]

When Lion was interviewed in 1985, he recalled that during a May 1951 session, he had Powell stay with him overnight so that he wouldn't "get out of sight, you know." Despite his descriptions of Powell's paranoid behavior (e.g., trying to stab his cat) and disappearance before the recording, Lion remained supportive of the pianist. When he visited Powell, during his tenure at Birdland that followed his release from Creedmore in 1953, Lion described Powell's apartment as a form of "house arrest," as he was locked in the place:

> When I wanted to see Bud, I'd go to Oscar Goodstein . . . and tell him. One day, Oscar gave me the key and I went up. There was a piano there and he played me some new things. One piece really stood out. I asked him what he called it. He looked around the apartment and said "Glass Enclosure." I knew that we had to record that. Morris Levy insisted that everything we recorded had to be written out because they had all the publishing rights. So the bass player George Duvivier wrote out Bud's tune. We rehearsed at Birdland that afternoon. And Goodstein was there, making sure that Levy got the written music. That's how that went down.[88]

Other times, Lion recalled, it would be just pleasure, going to movies with Powell, who loved Westerns: "The old railroads, the horses, the rolling hills, everything."[89] With each recollection of Powell, Lion reveals that to be friends with the pianist was to deal in a life of extremes, in adventures of musical profundity, and in personal, heart-wrenching drama. Some of the experiences shook him to the core, such as the time when he found Powell hiding, for no logical reason, under a parked car across the street from a nightclub he was to perform in that evening.

Although Powell's life in music continued its bipolar existence—artistically respected yet personally challenged—jazz's devotees continued their disjunctive campaign to increase the music's prestige and international presence. When the New Jazz Society of Toronto hosted the now famous Massey Hall concert on May 15, 1953, Powell was asked to join via his new representation, the Moe Gale Agency. The event was advertised as a reunion of some of bebop's greatest talents and also featured Charlie Parker, Dizzy Gillespie, Charlie Mingus, and Max Roach. Powell's representation secured him five hundred dollars for the gig, which was a larger fee than the others received. He also performed a trio set of standards plus one original titled "Sure Thing," a piece paying obvious homage to Bach's *Two-Part Inventions,* albeit splayed with whole tone scales.[90]

This concert has gone down in history primary because it united some of the architects of the bebop style. By this time it was clear, however, that the original beboppers were now such an eclectic bunch, with so many different personalities, financial demands, professional goals and profiles, and personal challenges, that it would be difficult to sustain these connections and to hear them all play together often. They weren't kids anymore, but grown men trying to make it in a difficult business. What they still shared was repertoire and performance practice: there was no rehearsal set for this historically important gig. "So it was pure spontaneity," recalls Gillespie. "That's the thing about that date. It wasn't like, 'O.K., we'll rehearse two or three hours.' We just went onstage, and things began to happen."[91] Mingus recorded and released the project on his Debut label.

The reverence with which this concert has been held in the historical memory of jazz symbolizes for many the music's march toward acceptance in the pantheon of America's art world. For its part, increasingly professionalized jazz criticism would continue to grapple with how to talk about musicians such as Powell, about the growing number of idioms beginning to emerge under jazz's stylistic umbrella, and with identifying the best method to argue for the music's power and rights to prestige. A subtle shift occurred in which the explication of individual works began to take priority over discussions about culture in broad strokes. As the Africanisms controversy began to subside, a new critical purview took hold among writers. During the 1950s, the "universal" and academic significance of the music became its new critical profile, together with the canonization of the tradition's "masterpieces."

THE BIRTH OF A MODERN JAZZ CRITICISM

During the 1950s, a point at which ideas about modern jazz and the critical discourses surrounding it were settling into a mutually dependent relationship, musicians and writers alike were absorbing and influencing the grander narratives of the "Jazz-Art" idea. Marshall W. Stearns, a PhD in English (Yale, 1942) living in the New York area, had had an interest in jazz since his student days, when he was president of the Hot Clubs of America at Harvard and Yale. Stearns's *The Story of Jazz* (1956) reflects his background and training, with its academic thoroughness mixed with a familiarity of live jazz performances in New York. His foreword acknowledges his debt to a wide and diverse swath of scholars, journalists, poets, musicians, and entrepreneurs: Gilbert Chase, Harold Courlander, Ralph Ellison, Leonard Feather, Alan Merriam, Richard A. Waterman, Langston Hughes, W. C. Handy, and Norman Granz, among others.

His first three chapters discuss the prehistory of jazz, and African survivals figure prominently. When he poses the question "What are the roots of jazz and how did they take hold in the New World?," he is well prepared to answer: "Many African musical characteristics survived in the New World—adapted, blended, and changed to fit new conditions."[92] This statement sets the tone for the musical, sociological, and anthropological journey through the black Atlantic world on which Stearns leads his readers. His insights were not universally shared among jazz writers. Writers such as André Hodeir still depended on reductive speculations such as the following statement: "As we know, the blue notes resulted from the difficulty experienced by the Negro when the hymns taught him by the missionaries made him sing the third and seventh degrees of the scale used in European music, since these degrees do not occur in the primitive five-tone scale."[93]

There was another important turn in Jazz-Art at this time. Jazz criticism, according to John Gennari, began to look in the late 1950s like the New Criticism of literary studies in tone, aim, and method. The New Criticism approach, which reached its apex in American universities between the 1930s and 1950s, "held that the primary task of criticism is to elucidate individual works of art."[94] Other related tenets of

116 | Notes and Tones

this method include the autonomy of the work of art, close readings that sought to explain organic unity, and the notion that meaning was determined by the structure of the text. This development was an obvious attempt to gain acceptance for "the study of literature as a legitimate way of acquiring knowledge"[95] and as "a way of competing with the hard sciences on its own terms."[96]

The important critic Martin Williams's writings fit in this critical universe.[97] He believed that jazz criticism needed to take the music—and itself—more seriously. In his introduction to his *Art of Jazz* (1959), Williams echoes some of the sentiments Sargeant had expressed two decades earlier: "As they have been telling us for a long time now, jazz is 'America's contribution to the arts,' but, from the way it is most often discussed, one would hardly think so. And if it had inspired only the kind of enthusiasm we are all too familiar with, one might conclude that the 'art' of jazz did not exist but that it was some kind intriguing emotional outburst that happened to be expressed on musical instruments, a pseudo-musical track meet, or a strange bunch of big-time show biz that interests adolescents of all ages."[98] In truth, Williams's philosophy and method differed in some ways from the principles of the New Criticism. "The New Critics," Eagleton writes, insisted "that the author's intentions in writing, even if they could be recovered, were of no relevance to the interpretation of his or her text."[99] Williams's *Jazz Tradition* celebrates jazz's "authors." Nonetheless, jazz critics such as Williams, who rose to prominence in the late 1950s and early 1960s, did prioritize identifying and explicating what they perceived to be the masterpieces of the jazz tradition, and they talked about what made them tick.

This group of jazz critics accepted the idea of Africanisms as a "source of" (as opposed to a presence in) jazz, but did not extend the idea to explain individual works. In "The Future of Form in Jazz," for example, Gunther Schuller's first published jazz essay, from 1957, he argues that jazz had developed over the years toward complexity. "Obviously," Schuller writes, "an art form which is to remain a legitimate expression of its times must grow and develop."[100] For Schuller, the key to understanding development in jazz was western musical analysis. In his much-heralded essay "Sonny Rollins and the Challenge of Thematic Improvisation" (1958), he again stresses the idea of development: "Since the days when pure collective improvisation gave way to the improvised solo, jazz improvisation has traveled a long road of development. . . . Today we have reached another juncture in the constantly unfolding evolution of improvisation, and the central figure of this present renewal is Sonny Rollins." With these words, he sets the stage for his explanation of what makes a particular Rollins recording ("Blue Seven," 1957) "so distinguished and satisfying": the motivic and structural unity in the solo.[101] Such an exercise was central to the aims of the New Critics of jazz: "Such methods of musical procedure as employed here by Sonny and Max [Roach] are symptomatic of the growing concern by an increasing number of jazz musicians for a certain degree of intellectuality. . . . Yet the entire history of the arts shows that intellectual enlightenment goes more or less hand in hand with emotional enrichment, or vice versa. Indeed, the great masterpieces of art—any art—are those in which emotional and intellectual qualities are well balanced and completely integrated—in Mozart, Shakespeare, Rembrandt."[102]

It is telling that Schuller's thesis is devoid of any hint that some of the power of Rollins's performance came from its grounding in an African musical heritage. As Mark Tucker has surmised, this had to do with jazz criticism's cultural politics of the moment. Schuller and others formulated their ideas in a "conservative cultural climate" in which they sought—against the odds—"to demonstrate the importance of jazz to the numerous skeptics and nonbelievers who surrounded them."[103] Pushing an "Africanist" agenda would not have served this purpose at this historical moment.

MAKING ART IN A GLASS ENCLOSURE

As this eclectic group of writers sought to discipline the messiness of jazz discourses, personalities, debates, styles, and so on into a coherent narrative, it's stunning to think about Powell's life at this moment against this ordering. As Grove and Shipton show us, he could be heard live, on the radio, and on recordings. Powell was still actively trying to achieve musically in spite of his many challenges. He would have two more hospitalizations, in 1954 and 1955: his need for alcohol and a work environment infested with drugs and enablers made sobriety a Herculean test. Complications always seemed to dog him. While he managed a string of important recordings of standards for Norman Granz's label, for example, the two became embroiled in a lawsuit about the company's releases of music against the pianist's wishes. His erratic behavior prompted his handlers to offer Mary Lou Williams, his friend and mentor, seventy-five dollars a week to look after him for his

Birdland gigs. She found the offer incredible, apparently because it put her, a world-class artist, on the level of a paid caretaker.[104]

Significantly, the drummer Art Taylor became a regular in Powell's trio at this time. As a musician who knew both the business and the aesthetics of bebop, Taylor would, for all intents and purposes, become an ethnographer of modern jazz when he published his book *Notes and Tones* in 1977. Taylor wanted to document the musicians' views as a testament to various moments in jazz history. He made a special point to ask them about their thoughts about Charlie Parker and Bud Powell to add to the historical record, which at that time was limited to journalistic accounts.[105]

Taylor became part of the Bud Powell Trio at Birdland with bassist George Duvivier, who worked with the pianist intermittently between 1953 and 1957. Duvivier—the man who wrote out "Glass Enclosure" for the publishing company—said that by this time "Bud had become almost a complete introvert. We had no personal communication— only music." Powell was a complete mystery to Duvivier. "I can't tell you what the man was like. And I don't think anyone who worked with him before or after I did can do much better!" Duvivier believed that Oscar Goodstein had wanted him to be a "babysitter," a job that he didn't even consider. While he called Powell "obviously a genius," he felt that Powell was deteriorating gradually, and it impressed him how much effort and concentration it took for him to play well. Some nights his playing was "pure genius"; at other times, he'd mix up the forms of songs. He and Taylor had to hang in there and try to keep up because rarely were there written parts, notwithstanding the occasions when someone would offer him a piece of their own music to sight read.[106]

In France, jazz fans such as Paudras gobbled up information on Powell's exploits as bebop became more popular all across Europe. He was thrilled when he read in the February 1955 issue of *Jazz Hot* that Powell had been voted the magazine's favorite pianist in a country that Powell had never visited.[107] Paudras was beside himself to learn that a recent gig in Cleveland had gotten Powell favorable reviews, and he then read the words that he'd been waiting for: "A European tour may also be coming up."[108] But would Powell be ready to travel internationally, given the ups and downs of his professional and personal life?

Bud Powell's journey from child prodigy to sought-out young professional to a beloved yet beleaguered legend has been created in and interpreted through several social orders, all of which mark him as a genius and jazz as a complicated, culturally heterogeneous art form. As the historical record shows, Powell's work existed on a continuum between the inner world of a romanticized artistic collective of musical experimentalists and a network of independent entrepreneurs who commodified the music with sometimes crass and mercenary tactics. Brimming below the surface of this simplified framework, however, are numerous interlocking discourses grounded in historical and material conditions that work to give Powell's genius its logic.

Powell's craft in improvisation and composition was often described as something magical, a gift able to enchant his international fans, nightclub and record company owners, and other musicians. The on-the-ground circumstances of his immediate social world—the mental health care system, the jazz labor industry, the spatial aspects of drug use and abuse in New York jazz clubs, his artistic and professional relationships with colleagues, his domestic connections with women— were all sites from which the sources and frustrations of his powerful legend were thought to emanate during his lifetime and beyond.

Over the course of Powell's life, developments in jazz criticism, a dynamic and international community theater of literary musing, shaped how the music—and, by extension, Powell's artistry—would be understood, even if Powell's music wasn't specifically indicated by name. This is true particularly for the generations of readers and listeners who came after him. As a body of work, this ordering of the aesthetics and cultural politics of jazz's social world took shape not in a vacuum, but within a legacy of "race writing" in the West. Indeed, the "blackness" of jazz (and Powell's music) belonged to a larger philosophy of socially grounded "culture and meaning making," as we have seen. We experience this kind of historical trajectory in issues of race and black health care as well. And they exist even in the ideas informing Powell's virtuoso status in an Afrological improvising tradition, one that, in Powell's hands, wore its Eurological connections on its sleeve as well.

Powell's genius, then, was staged in multifaceted and deeply historical social orders, structures, and systems of thought and creativity that gave his aesthetic agency a powerful and singular voice in jazz history.

4

Making the Changes

Jazz Manhood, Bebop Virtuosity, and a New Social Contract

In the wake of bebop, we no longer think of jazz
improvisation as a *way* of playing tunes but as an exacting
art form in itself that happens, as a rule, to use popular
music as a point of departure. In the hands of a jazz
improviser, a copyrighted popular song is less text than
pretext. Its crucial identifying feature—melody—is erased in
the heat of improvisation, leaving behind the more abstract
and malleable level of harmonic pattern. Out of the ashes of
popular song comes a new structure, a new aesthetic order,
shaped by the intelligence and virtuosity of the improviser;
and it is to that structure, and that structure alone, that our
attention should be drawn.

Scott DeVeaux, "'Nice Work If You Can Get It':
Thelonious Monk and Popular Song"

The epigraph above affirms that intense, aggressive virtuosity within
and on top of the structures of American popular song constituted the
heart of the bebop aesthetic. Combining these two seemingly opposite aesthetics in a "strategic multiplicity"—one that also included elements of blues—mirrored musically the social realm of many African
Americans at midcentury who were strategically and creatively pursuing equality on many other fronts. Scholar Eric Lott has called this a
"politics of style," a concept describing the specific mode of cultural
work the music achieved in its time.[1] The young black men in the bebop
movement found in its aesthetic and assorted politics a patriarchal,
heroic performance space, one that became the new musical language
of "jazz manhood."

By most accounts, Bud Powell was "the man" of bebop piano, and the early chapters of Peter Pullman's book *Wail: The Life of Bud Powell* describe a talented but introverted boy whose musical skills and seriousness about his craft paved the way for his meteoric rise in the New York jazz world.[2] According to various sources who knew Powell in his younger years, he had become enamored of the modernist sound elements in bebop before he was twenty years old. Former acquaintances shared stories of an increasingly impatient young man who sought out competitive situations in which he could show off his technical command in the new style in the tradition of the stride piano contests of previous generations. Otherwise soft-spoken and withdrawn, in purely musical settings Powell was known to want his own way—never with violence, but often with the seething insistence of someone with little regard for the feelings of others. Whether he was refusing to play a bandleader's desired number or brusquely removing another pianist (or competitor) from the instrument to brandish his own "weapons," Powell's single-minded, almost myopic focus on showcasing his own gifts was often excused by others as harmless, youthful unruliness. But his exposure to alcohol, drugs, a nocturnal lifestyle that had interrupted his education, and the overall phallocentric vibe of the scene no doubt caused the sheltered prodigy to grow up and man up fast—both artistically and otherwise—although one can surmise from various accounts that Powell was still very much an adolescent emotionally.

What were the technical specifics of this language of jazz manhood in which Powell would immerse himself? And in which historical and material notions of the gender/music relationship were this language and its social environment grounded? What were the terms of Powell's social contract as a black virtuoso in the bebop scene?

Although historians may still debate whether bebop was a revolutionary or an evolutionary style development, agreement exists on its core qualities. Most prominently, bebop consists of an enriched melodic, harmonic, and rhythmic vocabulary that required astute musicianship and a "virtuosic bravado."[3] Bebop's most significant contribution to the jazz tradition was in the area of improvisation, both in soloing and accompanying. Improvised bebop solos shared the melodic and rhythmic character of many bebop themes, including a frequent use of asymmetrical phrase structures; a harmonic vocabulary that employed ninths, elevenths, and thirteenths; and chromatic melodic lines that often stressed the weak beats of the measure. Swing, bebop's immediate stylistic predecessor, used more uniform phrases, structures, and accents and had less varied rhythmic patterns and less emphasis on harmonic dissonance.[4]

Frontline virtuosos such as Charlie Parker and Dizzy Gillespie attracted the lion's share of public attention as they wove intricate solos before awestruck listeners. Yet much of the musical enchantment of bebop emanated from its new conception of accompaniment in the rhythm sections, which created brilliant sonic tapestries supporting the dramatic solos. Pianists, drummers, guitarists, and bassists supported bebop's themes and solos with a rich and sometimes cacophonous mix of timbres, harmonic substitutions, and polyrhythmic accents that complemented and at the same time challenged the soloists. All the while, they maintained the fixed rhythmic pulse that linked the music to traditional black dance music forms. Bebop innovations brought about a heightened tension in melody, harmony, and rhythm that was, on some levels, a break with earlier styles of jazz. Thus bebop musicians struck a balance that both satisfied modernist ideals of musical "complexity" and situated their music conceptually under the umbrella of black Atlantic musical traditions.

The cultural work performed by the rhythm section is a crucial aspect of what a jazz performance might say or mean to audiences. Not only does an imaginative rhythm section inspire the frontline soloists, as scholar Ingrid Monson has argued, it also presents a profound model and metaphor of community "through the simultaneous interaction of musical sounds, people, and their musical and cultural histories."[5] Indeed, the dynamic grooves struck by modern jazz musicians such as Powell were as central to the music's influence as the work of frontline soloists. It was there—in the midst of the give and go of rhythms, subtle timbral shifts, and cagey harmonic embellishments— that audiences were able to discern that a new day had dawned in popular music, and that new communities and identities were being formed as well.

These new musical conceptions, together with a new social contract with the listening public, signaled that jazz had experienced a generic shift; that it had, in other words, become something new. Because social identities are "made" and often communicated to others within the context of expressive culture, one can look to concepts such as gender and genius to interpret modern jazz's generic development. How did bebop music precipitate jazz's change in pedigree? How did this transformation reflect and inform the way that musicians such as

Powell performed their social identities in the world? In what ways did the concept of genius gain currency in bebop, especially in the context of Powell's specific development and musical contributions?

In his discussion of gender and jazz in the 1930s, Patrick Burke argues that white masculinity in this context was constituted at "the tangled intersection of ideas about race, gender, labor, and musical practice."[6] In the after-hours cultural space of 52nd Street's Onyx Club, a popular speakeasy, white male musicians negotiated their own sense of identity through several means, including their emulation of stereotypes about black musical spontaneity and "hotness," the marginalization of women, and their antagonistic views about a supposed antithetical relationship between their lucrative gigs and "authentic expression." These musicians were not exceptions in this regard: many throughout the history of the music have negotiated their identities in the jazz world.[7] In this particular social setting, racial ventriloquism and anticommercial sentiments were rehearsed within a culture of urban bachelorhood. This was a powerful cocktail indeed.[8]

How might the setting of the Onyx Club help us understand the world of black male musicians who, like Powell, played bebop at a later historical moment? Was there another intersection of race, gender, labor, and musical practice uptown? "I am the Earl of Harlem," Powell was known to boast, and for good reason.[9] Uptown Manhattan in the 1940s was a thriving cultural space and home to nightspots that nurtured early bebop. Its after-hours nightclubs were extensions of the jooks and honkytonks black citizens had patronized as they sought respite in secular entertainment both in the South and later in the North. Historian Katrina Hazzard-Gordon calls the development of these establishments "the jook continuum." She traces the appearance of these venues to the post-Reconstruction period, which saw horrendous acts of violence by whites who disapproved of African Americans' unprecedented liberties.[10] The clubs were considered safe spaces for the celebration of culture.

As they operated with somewhat different social standings, white and black masculinities in the musical world of the 1940s shared little save the marginalization of female musicians, especially instrumentalists. Black musicians negotiated their immediate social worlds to procure for themselves some of the traditional advantages of male power—earning wages, spectacle, and hegemony over women—in the context of a growing black, urban, and artistic proletariat. Significant work in gender and music has, of course, been developed in studies of western art music and popular music studies. When we work with those insights into jazz and black music specifically, we must account for their similarities to and differences from both those realms.

By the early 1900s, a "classical sphere" network based on European traditions of compositions was clearly in place in America, and it included "performing groups, concert halls, conservatories, and enough public interest in these institutions to support them financially."[11] Involvement with classical music became at this time a set of activities—performance, promotion, and audience participation—in which "men and women articulated their anxieties about changing gender roles."[12] As women pushed for fulfilling lives outside the home and the domestic realm, careers in music provided new alternatives: professional women musicians became emblematic of women's desires for more satisfying public lives. Many formed civic clubs in which they exercised control over the community's musical life and other realms of the public sphere. For their part, men tempered their muses by emphasizing their enthusiasm for "boxing, wrestling, or other similar activities, or by expressing their interests [in music] solely as a civic and husbandly duty." Gender distinctions were a pressing concern, and America's classical music world was a potent place in which to struggle with them, indeed, to "arbitrate anew the meanings of masculinity and femininity" in modern industrialized society.[13]

During these same years, jazz emerged as a musical form distinct from classical-sphere music and its concerns, replete with varying ideas about gender, class, and, of course, race. Jazz became part of the popular sphere, and, as Richard Crawford has noted, "popular entertainment was well on its way to becoming modern 'show business.' And the workings of this new entertainment industry depended on a new approach to creating and marketing popular song."[14] The elements of this emerging structure created a space for a wide range of social formations. For example, it provided opportunities to work out gender roles in the public sphere, and African Americans were crucial in these new formations because the industry offered one of the precious few opportunities for them to be considered something more than servants and menial workers with the lowest pay.

THE POPULAR SPHERE AND MUSICAL MANHOOD

The great jazz composer and pianist Jelly Roll Morton's discussion of his childhood musical attitudes and aspirations in early-twentieth-century New Orleans gives us a snapshot of how race, gender, and class shaped his thinking. As Creoles, his class-conscious parents wanted him to play the "proper music heard at the French Opera House" and not popular music. As a child, he heard a man play a classical recital, and he was attracted to the music. But there was a problem. The gentleman had "long bushy hair, and, because the piano was known in our circle as an instrument for a lady, this confirmed for me my idea that if I played the piano I would be misunderstood." In his own words, Morton "didn't want to be called a sissy." Because of this aversion to one of the prevalent social meanings of the piano in his world, he decided to study other instruments, "such as violin, drums, and guitar, until one day at a party I saw a gentleman sit down at the piano and play a very good piece of ragtime. This particular gentleman had short hair and I decided then that the instrument was good for a gentleman same as it was for a lady."[15]

Fletcher Henderson's educated parents stressed piano lessons in the home as a crucial part of a thorough, well-rounded education in the Deep South at a time (the early twentieth century) when the instrument was a symbol of uplift and middle-class respectability. Everyone in the Henderson household read music and played the piano, although the repertoire was circumscribed to "classical and church music."[16] Because of this background, the pull of financial gain and masculinist success was strong and inevitable. Henderson would eventually forego his plans to earn a master's degree in chemistry at Columbia University to pursue a successful career in dance music. The music industry at this time, together with a heightened African American cultural presence in American consciousness, provided what Jeffrey Magee has called "unprecedented opportunities for African Americans with ambition and talent."[17] Henderson clearly possessed both, and by 1923, three years after he arrived in New York, he was thoroughly ensconced in the city's popular musical world.

One of his activities involved the new blues craze of the 1920s. Although he was not a blues or jazz musician per se when he came to New York, Henderson accepted the professional challenges of this environment, one far removed from his sheltered upbringing in the upper crust of the new black South. He enjoyed money, notoriety, and popularity with the ladies. Indeed, the music industry became a promising alternative realm for black men to make new meanings in masculinity, even well-educated, prepared men such as Henderson.

Here it is important to remember that the popular sphere also gave women a platform to attain the empowering visibility and wage-earning potential that defined traditional masculinities. The blues industry in particular provided women with their own stage on which to publicly negotiate gender roles. The rise of black popular culture was part of a larger shift in the 1920s that wrested the sole responsibility for black progress and representation away from the educated, literate men of the "Talented Tenth." In her study of 1920s blueswomen, Hazel Carby argues that black power and representation were up for grabs across the board—not just in the realm of music—as various constituencies jockeyed to publicly claim that their own group best represented "the experience of the race."[18] Thus black musical masculinity was performed in a larger cultural frame of diverse intra–African American struggles for social power, including but not limited to both men and women actively stepping out of traditional subservient roles.

We see multiple shifts occurring here. Popular music became an important province for African Americans, and classical music solidified their own idea of authenticity. Each realm was an important cultural territory for negotiating power through gendered meanings, and they would collide in the bebop movement. For black men, popular culture provided an arena of accomplishment that was thoroughly rooted in wage earning, visibility, and creative expression. Since the public aspect of popular culture remained, for the most part, segregated, it provided little threat to the "separate but equal" doctrine that policed race relations. In other words, there existed—on the surface, at least—few risks of direct sexual, financial, or social competition with white men.

The ascendancy of popular culture tended to flatten out class distinctions within the black community as well, as black middle-class musicians flocked to the unprecedented opportunities and prestige that it offered. Apparently, what the cultural arbiters of good taste considered "low-brow" was a shot at upward mobility for these "Others." What was perceived as a threat to virile masculinity and good class standing by Jelly Roll Morton's generation—particularly seen in his apparent view that "classical" music posed a threat to perceptions of his masculinity—was a springboard to becoming a sex symbol and iconic success for Duke Ellington, Willie "the Lion" Smith, and other, later musicians.[19] It is within this historical, social, and material grounding that bebop and the new idea of "jazz manhood" emerged.

SOUND, BODIES, AND SOCIAL CONTRACTS

As one considers the specific musical practices of bebop—what people heard and how they responded to it—it emerges as a gendered sonic field doing extraordinary cultural work. For many contemporary observers, bebop rhythm was the music's most radical and controversial feature when it first appeared. "Bebop rhythmics," Ross Russell wrote in the late 1940s, were "revolutionary," and these complex polyrhythms reflected "the spirit and temper of contemporary emotions." For Leonard Feather, a musician and critic, acquisition of the "bop beat" was the most difficult obstacle for "old-time jazzmen" who wanted to renew their playing style. He identifies three tendencies in the bop beat: (1) a lag-along approach where notes fall slightly behind the beat; (2) upbeat accents in which upbeats receive more emphasis than downbeats, especially at medium and medium-fast tempos; and (3) a double-time feel wherein soloists play "as if the chorus contained twice as many bars."[20] Thus, mastery of this rhythmic approach identified a musician as being part of the new jazz order. It united musicians under the bebop flag and became how they "represented"—to borrow a term from modern hip-hop culture parlance—their social affiliation with an avant-garde cultural movement.

Bebop rhythm implied an eighth-note subdivision of the basic jazz beat that was usually in 4/4 meter. That foundation encouraged musicians to create irregularly shaped melodic and rhythmic phrases that often shifted accents away from where they typically fell in earlier styles of jazz. These shifts occurred and were reinforced within solo improvisations, compositional procedures, and all aspects of the accompaniment. Bebop musicians deployed rhythm in flexible and dynamic ways, and when it was executed within the typically fast tempos of bebop performances, this specific brand of rhythmic virtuosity made the music a dazzling sonic display, one that some listeners found disorienting.[21] Though bebop's continuing influence has trained our contemporary ears to hear this rhythmic conception as logical, Russell claims that as late as 1948, some listeners still believed that bebop had "no beat" and that it was "rhythmically incoherent."[22] In tempo, accentuation, subdivision of the beat, and articulation, bebop's rhythmic innovations were the style's most fundamental and dramatic quality and rupture with the past.

It is, perhaps, no surprise that rhythm was considered the eye of this storm. More so than harmony and melody, rhythm is the element that unifies an ensemble and the bodies of audiences. As the component of music that moves the soundscape through time, and the element that is thus perceived as "bodily," it has the ability to cohere. Thus, when communities of musicians were perceived to be rhythmically incoherent—which beboppers were to some degree at first—we might think about such cases as sites where musicians could dramatically express new subjectivities that challenged the body politic. And bebop musicians did just that. By tweaking black musicians' historic and traditional role as primarily dance musicians who moved bodies, they participated in a social rupture of sorts, a subversion of the racial order of things. Black musicians, the logic went, should play dance music.

There are other fascinating developments in the American musical landscape that show the difficulties that occur when musicians refuse to "stay in their musical place." In her study of the genre-busting, market-challenging Black Rock Coalition (BRC), anthropologist Maureen Mahon shows how the group, formed in 1985, sought to wrest the signifier "rock 'n' roll" away from its signified "whiteness." Like bebop, "black rock was a direct challenge to the narrow understandings of black cultural production that dominated decision making in the music industry and in people's everyday thinking." The specific concerns of the BRC, particularly its "right to rock" mantra, were suggestive of issues beyond the music specifically: they spoke back to society's "inability to deal with the breadth and complexity of contemporary African American people and culture."[23] In other words, they broke the social contract: "black bodies" should not play rock.

We also see African Americans composers in the western art music tradition facing similar challenges as they continued to break through the barriers of racial stereotyping in musical practice. At a 1969 seminar, "Black Music in College and University Curricula"—a radical notion at that time—three black composers, T.J. Anderson, Hale Smith, and Olly Wilson, spoke about their philosophies as creators. It was, as many know, "nation time," an era of heightened black cultural nationalism during which black artists were justifying both their calls for inclusion in the canon and the validity of their work in the cause of black social activism.[24] Hale Smith noted that critics were unwilling to grant that blacks were intellectually capable of writing in the western art music tradition and believed that they were better suited for songwriting and jazz. And Olly Wilson, as an early experimenter in electronic media, argued for the expansion of black compositional possibilities beyond the status quo. Although for many years there had been an established presence of black composers such as Florence Price, William Dawson, William Grant Still, and Nathaniel Dett, among others, Anderson, Smith, and Wilson believed that in the late 1960s the black composer was still not fully accepted by America's concert culture.[25]

Historically, and in much the same way as bebop musicians, black rockers, and black art music composers, women composers had to fight calcified stereotypes in their quest for artistic equity and the recognition of their abilities, because, as scholar Judith Tick puts it, "the language of creative musical achievement" in the art world was patriarchal and, I would add, white. As a case in point, Mary Carr Moore (1873–1957), a contemporary composer of Charles Ives, noted that "so long as a woman contents herself with writing graceful little songs about springtime and the birdies, no one resents it or thinks her presumptuous; but woe be unto her if she dares attempt the larger forms!"[26] In somewhat of a departure from the norm, and unlike in the world of bebop, black women's works and performances were celebrated in the subcultural classical realm of African American music making. Black female classical-music critics such as Nora Douglas Holt, who wrote for the *Chicago Defender*, were respected figures, and the little-known composer Howard Swanson burst onto the national scene only after the famous contralto Marian Anderson had performed his "The Negro Speaks of Rivers" in 1949.[27]

The associations that we are socialized to make about organized sound and the bodies that make it are powerful, historically and culturally mediated, and govern what people think music means. And, as my quick review above proves, old ideas about music and social identities show how restrictive these associations can be in the lives and careers of musicians. Bebop, as an experimental musical language, was upon its appearance in the 1940s a style that challenged many assumptions about black male creativity and the power of pop and mass culture in the making of "art." As such, it can also be viewed as a model of how new social contracts for musical bodies can be established and how they can challenge older paradigms.

COMPOSITION/IMPROVISATION/INTERPRETATION

Bud Powell's recordings show that following his early years with Cootie Williams's band, the bebop style—this new sonic-socio experiment—constituted his compositional voice and performance rhetoric. But to speak here of composition and performance practice as if they were two different things is a little misleading. In modern jazz improvisation, composing and performing often occur simultaneously and represent theoretical points on a continuum. Music, broadly considered, is rarely "purely improvisational" or "permanently fixed."[28] In bebop, for example, compositional structures and performance events shifted between fixed and unfixed components: this dichotomy is simply more theoretical than practical.

Another point needs to be made here about the porous and malleable quality of bebop practice. Although they also wrote wholly original pieces, beboppers based many of their compositions on the harmonic structures of preexisting songs. Jazz musicians had long worked in this way, but modern jazz was so invested in the idea that one might call the technique one of the music's most distinguishing qualities. Leonard Feather, who was among the first to write technically about bebop's formal organization, noted in 1949 three types of sources favored among bebop musicians: the twelve-bar blues, Gershwin's song "I Got Rhythm" (known as "rhythm changes"), and the chord progressions of other popular songs.[29] Musicologist James Patrick labels this technique "melodic contrafact" after the term *contrafactum,* which describes text substitution in medieval music, linking the practice conceptually to western art music.[30]

On one level, the practice of melodic contrafact highlights excellently the interaction of the fixed and nonfixed aspects of jazz composition. It also situates this music in a specific creative legacy, because one can find resemblances to this procedure in other realms of African American music making. Patrick observes, and I concur, that it "connects bebop to earlier African American musical forms and compositional approaches in which old and new materials were combined to create new pieces." Think, for example, of the antebellum African American practice of embellishing, conflating, and in some instances newly composing songs based on standard church hymns. Patrick also notes the practice in early jazz styles such as Dixieland and Kansas City swing.[31] One can also mention the practice of digital sampling in hip-hop music as yet another important compositional method linked to this conceptual approach to music creation.

Clearly this creative formula positions bebop within the legacy of African American music's primarily oral past. But it also, quite ironically, became symbolic of African Americans' progress, education, and commercial viability. As early as 1949, Leonard Feather said that bebop represented growth and refinement among jazz musicians, calling bebop musicians' unique treatment of harmony and melody "advances" over previous jazz styles. He believed these changes occurred because jazz musicians had acquired "a little more knowledge of music" than their predecessors.[32] And these artistic advances could claim some practical, on-the-ground advantages. Max Roach noted the importance of melodic contrafact when bebop moved from Harlem to 52nd Street because, in his words, "people wanted to hear something they were familiar with, like 'How High the Moon,' 'What Is This Thing Called Love?' Can you play that? So in playing these things, the black musicians recognized that the royalties were going back to these people, like ASCAP, the Jerome Kerns, the Gershwins." Musicians lost potential royalties performing these standards, especially in recording situations. Thus, "bebopping" a popular song worked to their advantage in the studio: "If you made a record," Roach noted, "you could say, 'This is an original.'"[33] Melodic contrafact also benefited the small record companies that recorded bebop. For one thing, it provided them a way to avoid paying royalties to composers in accordance to the prevailing copyright laws. Second, it gave the musicians an efficiently speedy way to record four sides of "original" music within the three-hour limit enforced by union contracts.[34]

The practice became a mark of professionalism and an object of admiration among musicians. Tommy Potter, the bassist who played steadily with Charlie Parker in the late 1940s, recalls that the latter created stunning melodies with remarkable speed: "On the record dates he could create on the spot. . . . he'd write out eight bars, usually for the trumpet. He could transpose it for his alto without a score. The channel [the bridge] of the tune could be ad libbed."[35] Speaking retrospectively about the 1940s, Gillespie believed that bebop compositions improved popular music by adding new sounds to it: "I can hear a lotta the music that we created during those years now, in motion pictures and on television."[36] Roach added a racial (and gendered) perspective to Gillespie's views by highlighting the influence of black musicians on the American music scene: "The only reason that the music of the Gershwins and all these people lived during that period was because all the black people, the Billie Holidays, Ella Fitzgeralds, Dizzy Gillespies, Charlie Parkers, the Monks, the Coleman Hawkinses projected this music, used this music and kept it alive."[37] Roach's bird's-eye observations can be contextualized within the broader landscape and history of American music, which has traditionally been a performer's world rather than primarily one of composers and their works.[38]

Performers may have ruled the landscape in some ways, but in others they did not. Gillespie's attitude toward the financial end of bebop composition counters the prevailing view that bebop musicians cared little about commercial rewards: "All the big money," he writes, "went to the guys who owned the music, not to the guys who played it. . . . Our protests against being cheated and ripped off never meant we stood against making money." On the contrary, Gillespie claims that "being politically inclined against commercialism or trying to take over anything never figured too prominently with me."[39] It's worth mentioning here that owning the rights to bebop compositions was a priority to record company owners such as Henry Lubinsky of the Savoy label.[40]

Both Roach's and Gillespie's beliefs about bebop, commercialism, and race naturally invite comparison to those of the Onyx Club gang, whose ideas about race, gender, labor, authenticity, and musical practice became the way their masculinity was expressed. We can start with an indisputable fact: The jazz world of critics, audiences, and musicians mirrored that of the larger society. It was male-dominated and it marginalized women, except perhaps in the case of singing. It is also true that the idea of "the popular" was generally coded as feminine when compared to more "artistic" and "serious" endeavors, such as the act of composition in the western art music tradition. Nonetheless, multiple variations and shadings abound on this reliable theme of inequality.

If we seriously consider the statements of Max Roach and others, for example, it appears that the act of interpreting a popular song—as a straight rendition or as a melodic contrafact—was viewed as artistically important and fulfilling. In this segregated segment of the music business, engagement with popular culture was not considered artistically inferior, as it might have been in other artistic communities. Commercial viability was pursued, although with an insistence that artistic value not be traded off. In other words, mastery of the business aspects of the industry and the experimental language of bebop were not seen as mutually exclusive enterprises. As an extension of a long history of African American musical interpretation or versioning, one in which Billie Holiday, Ella Fitzgerald, Mary Lou Williams, and Sarah Vaughan were certainly pioneers and masters, artistic authenticity in jazz was not the sole province of the male instrumentalist. In this sound world, interpretation, performance, and composition seemed to enjoy parity. Moreover, the bundle of social codes with which Onyx Club musicians negotiated their expressed masculinity—authenticity, anti-commercialism, and so on—was in many cases inverted by black musicians because they had to work out masculinity on their own terms and in their own specific social circumstances.

This revision of masculinist musical expression, one that seemed to equate (if not privilege) interpretation and commercial viability with individualized composition and cloistered elitism, shows how complex, diffuse, and contradictory gendered ideologies can be. They cannot be interpreted in the same way across time, genre, and geography. As Judith Tick has shown in a brilliant study of Charles Ives, notions about gender and musicianship gradually shifted over the twentieth century from a "Victorian faith in sexual polarity" to more contradictory ideals that mirrored society's changing historical contingencies. In an important caution to scholars, Tick warns that stubborn notions from the past still resonate in the present era because gender ideologies are constantly reconfiguring themselves:

> In our gender ideology of music the "masculinization" of high art has been no less powerful and pervasive than the "feminization" of musical "accomplishment," these associations retaining some resonance even today. Unless we distance ourselves from this legacy, we run the risk of cementing the orthodoxies of "separate spheres" into our own interpretations, rather than recognizing the continuum of possible adaptations and resistances between individuals and society and between men and women who, as composers and musicians, are bound together as much as torn apart by the ideology surrounding music and gender.[41]

MANNING UP BEBOP

With these ideas in mind, we can see how musicologists "butched up" bebop discourse by making associations between it and western art music, and thus facilitated its move from pop to art. Frank Tirro, for example, writing in 1967, called bebop composition practice a "silent theme" tradition, or *musica reservata,* referencing a Renaissance music practice. "It is a practice that operates on two levels, one sounded, and therefore open to the public, and one silent but implied, and therefore hidden and reserved for initiates who have been introduced to, and are capable of understanding, the secret."[42] Tirro's analogy supports his theory that bebop was a self-conscious attempt to raise "the quality of jazz from the level of utilitarian dance music to that of a chamber art form."[43]

Richard Crawford has compared the persistent use of harmonic structures such as rhythm changes to a similar one in the western art music tradition: "The harmonic structure of 'I Got Rhythm' won a place in Parker's imagination, much as the theme of the *Eroica* Variations or perhaps Diabelli's Waltz had in Beethoven's—though Beethoven concentrated his efforts on lengthy, integrated compositions, while Parker's 'I Got Rhythm' variations are scattered widely among many performances."[44] Both Tirro and Crawford were presenting jazz scholarship in an academic world with a growing knowledge of jazz and black vernacular music. Their work participated in an important kind of cultural politics that cleared space within influential institutions such as university music departments, which now support jazz as an American art.

When thinking about these moves, it is instructive to consider how, on the one hand, writers have interpreted bebop's compositional practice within a western art music conceptual framework and, on the other hand, how they have considered it as a war on popular music, especially Tin Pan Alley song. If this was indeed a war, jazz—with bebop's help—ultimately won the spoils of aesthetic and academic prestige. As Scott DeVeaux argues, jazz criticism has been especially focused on pointing to bebop improvisation's superiority over "mere commercial music."[45] The purpose of bebop improvisation, he writes, "was not so much to displace or erase the original but to offer a personal interpretation of it. These interpretations, of course, were designed to display the artistry of the improviser through dizzying displays of virtuosic passagework, ingenious harmonic substitutions, and the like. All of this, admittedly, led in the direction of obscuring the original tune."[46] But compositional practices that emphasized constant repetition of harmonic patterns were an obstacle in bebop's road to its status as a bona fide high art and a masculinist endeavor.

In his infamous repudiation of popular music, Theodor Adorno wrote in 1941 that the rigid use of set harmonic patterns rendered jazz improvisation a "pseudo-individualization" that endowed "cultural mass production with the halo of free choice or open market on the basis of standardization itself."[47] This sentiment reflects his broader ideas about popular music as primitive, childish, and hysterical, and they rub against some accepted ideals of elite art that many argue exist in jazz. Such a disparaging depiction of pseudo-individualization, for example, disallows a reading of jazz solos as profound expressions of individual subjectivity. But here we have another instance of musicians adapting, resisting, and playing with inherited cultural signs.

Bebop's repeating choruses provided a kind of ceremonial space for performers to display technical virtuosity and to exploit the harmonic, melodic, and rhythmic potential of the songs. Although the three-minute time limit of mid-1940s recordings precluded the immediate experience of extended repetition, they stand as miniature abstractions of longer live jazz performances. As many others have noted, the desire to revise and improve on the familiar concurs with Henry Louis Gates's now ubiquitous formulation "signifyin(g)," an imperative he traces across black expressive culture: "Signifyin(g) in jazz performances and in the play of black language games is a mode of formal revision, it depends for its effects on troping, it is often characterized by pastiche, and most crucially, it turns on repetition of formal structures and their differences."[48] In other words, individual expressions of virtuosity are embedded in a cultural framework and a collective community of listeners bound by their investment in a specific musical legacy. The source of the structure in which improvisation took place was less important than the cultural work performed during it.

In this system of "musicking," the theme or structure not only becomes silent or secret; its "meaning is devalued, while the signifier [the performer or the improvisation] is valorized."[49] In a socially determined manner, this artistic configuration highlights the musical personality being forwarded in the performance. Thus the cliché is not coded as childish but as profound, as Anne Danielsen argues: it asserts its "proper role as that which gives form, becoming a presupposition for the individual to appear. The formal becomes the springboard for the personal: familiarity with a figure makes it easier to distinguish a special touch."[50] This self-fashioning can been witnessed clearly in the example of Miles Davis, notorious for his continual pursuit of new expressive modes, including bebop, cool, hard bop, fusion, and hip-hop. Jeffrey Magee writes that Davis's continual return to the twelve-bar blues throughout his numerous stylistic explorations over some four decades reveals the trumpeter's negotiations of the complexities of modern social identity. The blues template—ubiquitous to the point of invisibility, and familiar to the point of transparency—allowed Davis to play with relationships among genre, style, and aesthetic agency without the burden of recreating a frame for his "self-construction."[51]

THE SELF-FASHIONING BLACK VIRTUOSO

Among all the great bebop pianists active in the mid-1940s—Al Haig, Clyde Hart, George Wallingford, Thelonious Monk, Dodo

Marmarosa—Bud Powell was the first to lead a piano trio date, a benchmark accomplishment for any jazz pianist. Apparently it had become clear to those around him that Powell had outgrown the quintet format. As Gillespie put it: "We needed a piano player to stay outta the way. The one that stayed outta the way best was the one best for us. . . . Bud's importance was as a great soloist, not necessarily an accompanist. He was too much of a rebel for that."[52] Powell's refusal to stay "outta the way" put his playing on an artistic footing equal to that of other front-line musicians in the bebop ensemble sensibility. (Certainly, Kenny Clarke and Max Roach accomplished the same for drumming.) What remains remarkable is that he was both a recognized master of bebop's aesthetic codes and a rebel well before his twenty-third birthday. As we have learned above, bebop could be interpreted through multiple lenses in both western art music history and in practices specific to African American culture. This pedigree of multiplicity made the music of "cullud boys" and "flatted fifths" a powerful space for Powell to explore his own muse, to self-fashion an artistic identity, and change the course of jazz pianism by exploiting and moving against tradition.

Although Powell developed a singular voice, he drew stylistically from other piano giants, including Earl "Fatha" Hines, Teddy Wilson, Billy Kyle, Monk, and Art Tatum. Yet his contributions were singular, an amalgam of approaches. One standard reference book characterizes Powell's work as transforming "the jazz pianism of his time" with the "spare manner that he devised in the early 1940s; rapid melodic lines in the right hand punctuated by irregularly spaced, dissonant chords in the left."[53] His dominant right-hand emphasis—a stylistic extension of Hines's and Wilson's innovations—allowed Powell to construct linear solos with all the speed, agility, and thrust of bebop wind players. During the solos, Powell's left hand played sparse chord voicings—usually thirds, fifths, sevenths, and tenths—allowing him to reinforce the harmonic structure of a piece during his own soloing.

Powell dramatized his melodic inventions with an approach that can be described by the term "againstness."[54] He embellished the function of the piano in the bebop ensemble by working *against* certain aspects of typical jazz performance style, most notably in the area of rhythm and, to a lesser degree, in the way he used the piano. Powell's accompanying style added another layer of rhythmic complexity to the bebop ensemble while intensifying the momentum of the overall performance. Furthermore, the dramatic, exuberant nature of his solos—their asymmetrical phrasing, sinewy melodic lines that often overrode standard cadential rest-

ing points, and, in his heyday, an almost flawlessly even articulation—
marked the piano as an important voice within the modern jazz ensemble.
By extending the melodic, harmonic, and percussive possibilities of the
piano, Powell managed to become a front-line soloist in the bebop ensemble while helping to define the pianist's duties in modern jazz.

The unflinching antipianism he projected in bebop ensemble playing, for example, could be linked to some historical conventions of
black vernacular music making. Black musicians in America have historically adapted European-originated instruments for their own aesthetic purposes "with little regard for whether that technique con-
formed to the instrument's 'proper' use by European standards."[55]
Powell's multifaceted approach—he synthesized a number of influences
to create it—debunks the widely accepted axiom that he merely applied
Parker's innovations to the piano. Powell's style of accompanying and
soloing became *the* standard for early bebop piano technique. And his
early recordings suggest that he began to develop his singular voice as
a young apprentice in the band of Cootie Williams.

MAKING JAZZ GENIUS

The idea of musical genius is much more than a description of an
extraordinary endowment; it is also the product of a complex social
process. Hypersexuality, physical malady, drug addiction, western
and African musical priorities, the debates surrounding black athletic
and intellectual prowess, and bebop as a social and musical paradigm,
among other factors, all figure in the present story. And, as others
before me have noted, gender and race form important, though somewhat underanalyzed, factors in the process of genius designation.[56]

It should not surprise us that contemporary female scholars in jazz
studies have been in the forefront of considerations of gender and
genius in jazz. Cultural critic Farah Griffin has taken the issue head-on
in her portrayal of Billie Holiday. She writes:

> Billie Holiday was a musical genius. Until the recent celebrations of Nobel
> Prize Laureate Toni Morrison, few were willing to grant black women the
> title genius. Since the earliest days of our nation, black women were thought
> to be incapable of possessing genius; their achievements were considered
> the very opposite of intellectual accomplishment. All persons of African
> descent were thought to be unfit for advanced intellectual endeavor. Black
> women in particular were body, feeling, emotion and sexuality. This holds
> true even in comparison to white women; if white women's abilities were
> questioned and debated, their humanity was not.[57]

Mary Lou Williams, another compelling example of black female genius, shows us that the issue of gender in black musical genius is a complex site of negotiation, especially in jazz. Nichole Rustin clears space to rightly include the brilliance of musicians such as Holiday and Williams by stretching the bounds of what has been traditionally been thought of as masculine and feminine. She shows that gender is one of the oddly invisible structures in which jazz genius has been traditionally understood. If we think deeply about genius in jazz this way—as something steeped in gendered discourse—it broadens our understanding of what counts as "the masculine" in realms outside the music world.[58]

Writing in 2001, in the context of a wave of scholarship named the New Jazz Studies, Sherrie Tucker argued persuasively for the inclusion of gender in jazz studies in many publications.[59] Rather than seeing her project as solely aimed at recovering the history of women participating in jazz, Tucker suggested a more radical strategy. She pushed for the placement of jazz studies over the field of gender as a way to understand how the latter structures all aspects of the jazz field. While the compensatory histories of women in jazz are useful and long overdue, the critical study of gender in jazz studies should involve more than the "women were there, too" framework. All this work demands that we see jazz*men* as possessing gendered identities, too: the music was an activity in which they negotiated their sense of manhood in American society.

Although we've come a long way since the days when women's bodies were used as a sign of music being "not real jazz" in publications such as *Down Beat,* the time is ripe for critical expansion. As Tucker argued, we "need to conceive of gender not as a synonym for women, and not just as a critical description of sex and gender roles, but as one of the primary fields 'within which or by means of which power is articulated.'"[60] Her approach shows how the analytical category of gender can explain the power of jazz performances at different historical moments. Such a critique enhances other analytical categories already well established in jazz studies: race, ethnicity, class, sexuality, national identity, empire, and capitalism.[61] Consideration of gender studies helps us understand that performed aspects of identity—both masculinities and femininities—are expressed in complex, interdependent ways and should not be considered as simplistic binaries. Jazz's historically masculinist profile can certainly benefit from such distinctions and will make our theories of identity in the music less monolithic. Powell's work is a wellspring for such considerations.

Anthropologist Sherrie Ortner, like Tucker and others, believes that we cannot stress power enough in narratives of expression culture. Indeed, "systemic practices of power and domination and small and large acts of resistance" are embedded in cultural practices such as music.[62] Yet this work should "not presume that agents are free individuals . . . [and] not construct the agent as a bourgeois subject."[63] This caution rings loud and clear in the study of musical genius, a concept that in my view is the ultimate construction of the bourgeois subject, with its powerful images of free-willed artists creating timeless works that transcend their historical and social settings. Rethinking genius with gender in mind encourages us to reconsider agency, identity, and subjectivity across the board, particularly with regard to musicians such as Powell and the ways that audiences members have made meaning from his music.

Bringing it all together are the ideas on power, identity, social structure, agency, and musical practice set forth by Susan McClary in her landmark study *Feminine Endings* (1991). McClary makes the case for the development of a feminist critique in the field of musicology, and it is useful to revisit this influential work as the study of gender gains its footing in jazz studies.[64] Working against the privileging of "chronology" in music history, McClary proposes an alternative approach. Historical chronology tends to flatten out issues of power and struggle (e.g., gender, sexuality, race, and class) in music history to the service of organic style development. But even the supposedly nonrepresentational instrumental music of the canon can be analyzed with respect to its registration of historically contingent social energies. Such analysis uncovers, among other things, how institutions and power structures have sought to police knowledge, expressive culture, sexuality, the body, and so on, and how historical agents have fought back against these efforts. As a viable factor in these struggles, music circulates social energies throughout society in potent and, of course, pleasurable ways.

Much of this energy occurs at the borders of a perceived musical style or genre. And here is where the case for gender study gets compelling with regard to jazz, bebop, and Powell. McClary argues that "genres and conventions crystallize because they are embraced as natural by a certain community: they define the limits of what counts as proper musical behavior."[65] Thus, the occasions of stylistic disruption—those times when jazz musicians seemed to push the limit of acceptable generic expectations—are important sites in which to tease out gendered meanings: in the space between convention and innovation exists the stories of power struggle through experimentation. In other words, as musicians push against a listening community's acceptable codes of musical behavior, they are usually articulating who they believe they are in the world through displays of musical prowess, stylistic challenge, and experimentation.

The disruptive appearance of bebop, then, provides an excellent opportunity to examine jazz and gender. This work must develop from understanding how the western system of tonality has governed music history, creativity, and interpretation. These supposedly abstract conventions have, in fact, socialized audiences to experience struggle, fulfillment, repose, and climax, among other states of being, as part and parcel of the listening experience. Backed by a codified body of theoretical treatises steeped in conventions that assigned masculine and feminine identities to various musical procedures, analysts have shown how western music helped to shape the social realities of its subjects. These ideals were further fortified as they were employed in the narrative conventions of opera, an art world in which gender roles were central to its dramaturgy and made larger than life through its glorification of the spectacular. All of this has circulated, by the way, within a network of ideologies in which popular and "Other" cultures were historically rendered as feminine, providing another example of how musicality and gender were diligently policed.

To what degree, we must ask, are these patterns present in jazz history? How have they differed? And how have musical theories revealed the practice and politics of "jazzmanhood" in instrumental jazz? Jazz, like many American musical forms, is grounded in multiple cultural heritages. How do we account for this multiplicity in the analytical framework? A theory of gender in jazz has to situate specific ideologies of musicality, masculinity, femininity, tonality, and "the popular" in terms that are historically and socially specific to jazz in general and have some resonance with cultural values in American musical communities particularly. Does phallic power—in the guise of musical transcendence—operate the same way in jazz that it does in the western traditions in which feminist musical criticism first emerged?

David Ake has provided an excellent example. His study of Ornette Coleman examines another stylistic rupture in jazz: the appearance of free jazz, or the New Thing. Coleman and his musical contributions represent, for Ake, an alternative masculinity to the one forwarded by the beboppers who preceded him. He redefined the terms of musical prowess in jazz that had long connected a particular brand of "instrumental proficiency with standards of excellence, power, and manhood."[66] Coleman achieved this through his well-formed, unconventional opinions, his general comportment, and, most importantly, his musical innovations in his late-1950s compositions. His pushing out at the edges of bebop virtuosity and other orthodoxies of jazz practice, Ake says, allowed him to "make" another kind of masculinity. What about Powell's expression of bebop, a style dependent on a hyperintensification of functional harmony and steeped in a virtuosic display that would become jazz's raison d'être? What were the technical formations through which Powell expressed his identity?

5

Exploding Narratives and Structures in the Art of Bud Powell

When one listens to a string of Bud Powell recordings, particularly the trio and solo numbers, they convey the feeling of short studies for the piano. The experience also reveals a style constituted of gushes of spectacular melodic flourishes—tight scalar runs that are set off by grand gestures of fanfare and a flair for the dramatic. Powell embeds in this idiosyncratic rhetoric a tour of the history of jazz piano: one can hear stride, Earl "Fatha" Hines's "trumpet style," and Art Tatum's virtuosic bravado, among other references. And miraculously, all these approaches are subsumed in the language of bebop. Powell's work is a study in contrast as he moves from moods of introspection to ostentatious verbosity, sometimes in a single performance. His musical imagination seems to be a boundless force, undaunted by tricky harmonic terrains or flying tempos. Because of the repeatability that's allowed through recording technology, these performances take on the character of compositions—logical, shapely, and ordered.

Powell's music, and the bebop movement in general, has been interpreted as art—serious black art—and as a symbol of Afro-modernity and a musical avant-garde. Blues culture, jam-session aesthetics, virtuoso sensibilities with legacies from two "old worlds" (Europe and Africa), and the formal structures and market-driven tendencies of pop culture all came together in bebop. Indeed, Powell and his comrades participated in what musician and scholar Salim Washington has characterized as "a continuous search for expansion of the formal parameters" of their art form.[1] The following discussion sinks into the details of Powell's music and that of his colleagues. It describes the rhetorical strategies he developed in his quest to achieve an individualized voice as an improviser and composer in the idiom. The anatomy of Powell's work reveals how he manipulated the musical schemata that were being codified around him and how he shaped them to meet his own aesthetic purposes and technical coordinates. By moving through various recordings, we can see the emergence of his idiosyncratic approach. First, let's think about Powell in his role as the improvising virtuoso soloist. How do we begin to account for his power and prestige in this specific domain?

Pianist, composer, and scholar Vijay Iyer has outlined a way for us to contemplate how improvising solos in the jazz tradition "tells a story." Citing the lack of analytical tools to adequately unpack this cliché of jazz discourse (what exactly, for example, is a solo saying in narrative terms?), Iyer builds on previous paradigms that emphasized things such as the improvised solo's "musical coherence" in relationship to western music; the notion of the "exchange of personal narratives" in soloing; and the notions of the "telegraphic model of communication" and group interplay or "sustained antiphony."[2] Although it is widely understood that telling a story typically means making a profound instrumental statement in the solo, Iyer teases out a more thorough understanding. The achievement of a logical motivic coherence, he argues, is but one of many possible qualities of a successful jazz solo.

Iyer's views circle around the notion of musical practice as a kind of labor. The story or narrative in a solo emerges from "the minute laborious acts that make up musical activity . . . [a]nd can be read as a celebration of the athletics of black musical performance (or perhaps the performativity of black musical athletics)."[3] Iyer calls this idea "traces of embodiment," as it explores how bodily metaphors might help us unpack the solo's story; indeed, it explores how solos "signify" through an abundance of "microscopic details" rather than solely through their overall structural coherence. "The story dwells not just in one solo at a time, but also in a single note, and equally in an entire lifetime of improvisations. In short, the story is revealed not as a simple linear narrative, but as a fractured, exploded one. It is what we take to be the shifting, multiple, continually reconstructed subjectivities of the improvisors [sic] encoded in a diverse variety of sonic symbols, occurring at different levels and subject to different stylistic controls."[4] Narratives such as a jazz solo, then, might be thought of as mosaics, "puzzling shards" that explode in performance.

Iyer recognizes that music possesses a bundle of attributes that make possible its communicative power. Its kinetic basis, together with the fact that, like speech, it is a process, is interactive, and its semiotic dimensions allow a musician to forward, through sound, highly personalized expressions that over time collate and become his or her personalized "voice." Furthermore, a special quality that listeners experience in improvised music differentiates it from composed music: the "visceral fact of the shared sense of time: the sense that the improvisor is working, creating, generating musical material at the same time in which we are coperforming as listeners."[5] Listeners, in other words, are sharing and doing their own empathetic "work" with performers in real time. We perceive, then, an "exploding narrative" in jazz improvisation. The narrative, Iyer argues, "is conveyed both musically through the skillful, individualistic, improvisatory manipulation of expressive parameters in combination, as well as *extramusically,* in the sense that these sonic symbols 'point' to a certain physical, social, and cultural comportment, a certain way of being embodied. Kinesthetics, performativity, personal sound, temporality—all these traces of embodiment generate, reflect, and refract stories into innumerable splinters and shards."[6]

Powell's professional recording career began when he was a nineteen-year-old prodigy with the Cootie Williams band, full of fire, hope, and a future. A decidedly formalist look at his contributions in the band shows him slowly developing into a masterful storyteller, one whose sonic narratives would eventually mesmerize his audiences with their intense rhetoric.

THE COOTIE WILLIAMS RECORDINGS

In the early 1940s, the Cootie Williams band was considered an eclectic ensemble whose composite style combined jump blues, swing, and the fledgling bebop experiment. On January 4, 1944, the Cootie Williams Sextet recorded four sides for the Hit label that display the group's particular brand of variety. The session produced the original tunes "You Talk a Little Trash," "Floogie Boo," "I Don't Know," and "Gotta Do Some War Work Baby."

The featured personnel are a scaled-down combo from Williams's large orchestra: Williams (trumpet, vocals); Eddie Vinson (alto saxophone, vocals); Eddie "Lockjaw" Davis (tenor saxophone); Powell (piano); Norman Keenan (bass); and Sylvester "Vess" Payne (drums). The band plays swing-oriented arrangements, and the pieces churn along at moderate tempos (except for "Floogie Boo"), and Payne's drumming provides a straightforward beat in 4/4, peppered sparingly with accents. Keenan restricts his part to outlining the chord changes four notes to the bar. Each of the four tunes is in a thirty-two-bar A-A-B-A form, and three are contrafacts: "You Talk a Little Trash" is rhythm changes in E-flat. "Floogie Boo" is composed of rhythm changes with a bridge section from "Honeysuckle Rose"; and the standard "Exactly Like You" provides the harmonic framework for the A sections of "I Don't Know." "Gotta Do Some War Work Baby" features vocals by Williams and appears to be an original progression.

Although Powell is not prominently featured as a soloist on the session, he asserts his presence with playing that brims with energy and imagination. He provides some of the spontaneous-sounding two- and four-bar introductions that would become his trademark; his comping is solid, spurring on the soloists as well as propelling the ensemble as a whole with a purposeful, rhythmic vitality and pristine Count Basie–like fills. An example of Powell's seasoned soloing ability at this early time is the fully developed statement on "Floogie Boo," the fastest piece on the session (example 1).

Powell's solo in the third chorus of "Floogie Boo" differs notably from other solos on the session. The way he plays the familiar chord changes here shows him developing an idiom in which chromatic pitches, dissonances, and irregular accents play a larger role than in the swing style. Lacking pauses, the solo generates a powerful forward momentum through a consistent flow of eighth notes, intermittently dashed with triplet design elements. Although Powell employs chromaticism sparingly in this solo, when he does use it, the effect makes his work sound more "complex" than that of the other soloists. In m. 4, the B-natural (accented on the downbeat), A-flat, and F-sharp all form dissonances with the C minor 7 chord over which they are heard. (Similar types of chromaticism appear in mm. 5 and 6.) On the last two beats of m. 4, Powell outlines an E-flat major 7—E-flat, G, B-flat, D— on top of the F7 chord. Although these pitches are not chromatic, they add harmonic tension to the passage. Likewise, in the first two beats of m. 8, Powell superimposes a B-flat chord on top of the C minor 7, creating a similar effect.

Another distinctive feature of the solo is how Powell exploits the

EXAMPLE 1. Powell solo, "Floogie Boo," third chorus, mm. 1–16.

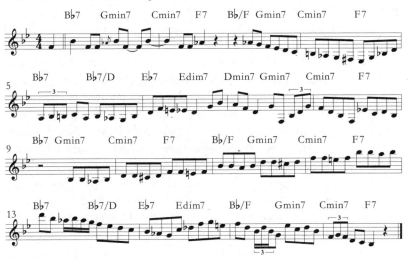

space between the formulaic or cliché and what would be heard as more innovative gestures. The term *formulaic* is not meant in a negative sense here: Powell had a firm command of established riffs and stylistic approaches appropriate to the musical context in which these recordings were made, and he used them. He begins the solo with a slightly syncopated blues lick (mm. 1–2) consisting of a B-flat, F, and a lowered seventh-scale degree, A-flat. In mm. 3–8, however, he plays a more inventive and multidirectional melody with the chromatic shadings noted above. After a two-beat pause in m. 9, Powell creates a tonal sequence that spans two octaves. The gesture outlines the tonic B-flat chord in a regular, and somewhat predictable, rhythmic pattern—although the tune's harmonic structure does not fit the sequence exactly. In mm. 13–16, Powell shifts back to the more rhythmically varied, weaving line associated with bebop style. The run begins with the highest pitch of the solo and pours out into a combination of motives that contains a scale passage, disjunctive leaps, arpeggios, and brief melodic figures. Essentially, Powell's collage of approaches here is a rhetorical strategy important to his early solos. In his continual stylistic shifting (in the "Floogie Boo" solo, he plays a little blues, a little swing, and a little of what was soon to be called bebop), Powell shows that traversing stylistic idioms was an essential part of his early professional life. On "I Don't Know," Powell's brief, flourishing solo passage contains a double-time gesture that momentarily shifts the feeling of regularly placed accents in the chorus. That feature became, as we shall see, a standard feature of bebop solos.

Powell's zigzags between the conventions of swing/blues and a newer style are what make his work at this point in his career so rhetorically rich. In our search for innovations, we often dismiss the formulaic as cliché, as unimportant to the larger scheme of things. This is especially true when the point of a research project is to highlight what is novel or "new" about a musical gesture. But, as Susan McClary argues persuasively, "conventions always operate as part of the signifying apparatus, even when they occupy the ground over which explicit references and encodings occur: in other words, it is not deviations alone that signify but the norms as well. Indeed, the deviations of particular pieces could not signify if we did not invest a great deal in the conventions up against which they become meaningful."[7] Thus Powell's playing, with its signs of swing convention and bebop innovation, can be read as significant at its historical moment: the man was articulating his sense of an emerging new identity in a musical setting where he could have just as easily played what his predecessors played. He needed the referential framework of swing to work against so that his stylistic push could be clearly discerned.

Two days later, the sextet returned to the studio to record four more sides, none of them composed by band members. These sides—"My Old Flame," "Sweet Lorraine," "Honeysuckle Rose," and Ellington's "Echoes of Harlem"—further demonstrate the eclectic sweep of Williams's repertory. The ballad "My Old Flame," by Arthur Johnson and Sam Coslow (1934), first appeared in the film *Belle of the Nineties*.[8] The other popular song on the session, "Sweet Lorraine" (by Mitchell Parrish and Clifford Burwell), dates back to 1928. Many artists had recorded the tune before Williams, including Art Tatum, Joe Venuti, Artie Shaw, Teddy Wilson, Nat Cole, and Hoagy Carmichael, among others, and for Tatum it had become something of a signature tune.[9] On both these numbers, the soloists restrict themselves to paraphrasing the melody; they employ improvisation only to fill in or to intensify the aura of the song. "Echoes of Harlem" dates back to Williams's time as a featured soloist with Duke Ellington, who recorded the piece in 1936. This version of "Echoes" is taken at a slower tempo than the original, among other changes.[10] Williams's masterful interpretation seems the main point of this performance because he is the only soloist. Powell's chord voicings add a flavor that the recording would otherwise lack, especially given the absence of Ellington's original orchestration. (Williams recorded the piece again

EXAMPLE 2. Substitution chords and melody, "Honeysuckle Rose," mm. 25–28.

in 1946 with his large orchestra. Since the three recordings differ, they make an interesting study in the interaction between the "composed" and "improvised" aspects of a jazz performance.)

The last tune on this date, "Honeysuckle Rose" (1929), a standard by Thomas "Fats" Waller and Andy Razaf, seems closest in spirit to the January 4 session.[11] The melody—performed in unison by Williams, Vinson, and Davis—strays far from Waller's original tune. Each A section possesses a different melody, adding variety to the song's A-A-B-A structure. The first four measures of the last A section are revamped to introduce a melodic sequence (example 2), a familiar compositional device of bebop. As they do in "Floogie Boo," the harmonic conceptualization and rhythmic inflection of Powell's sixteen-bar solo reflect a confidence and maturity that belie his young age. In general, Powell's contribution to the session is solid, if restrained. Unlike his innovative work on "Floogie Boo," his brief solos basically paraphrase the melodies of the respective songs, an approach well suited to this performance context. He supports the other soloists by laying down the changes simply, occasionally tossing in a clean, well-placed Tatumesque scale or arpeggio for emotional intensity.

In addition to the small-group work, Williams's big band also recorded four tunes on the January 6 session.[12] Its repertory was composed of dance-oriented numbers, each featuring vocalists. Pearl Bailey's vocals on "Now I Know" and "Tess's Torch Song" are undistinguished, tentative, and a little flat in pitch. Powell's accompaniment is barely audible on the large group pieces. Eddie Vinson's vocal work on the bluesy "Red Blues" and "Things Ain't What They Used to Be" provides an early template for what would become a very popular rhythm-and-blues singing style. The key centers always seem to place each song in the upper register of Vinson's tenor voice. Furthermore, in order to achieve greater expressiveness, Vinson frequently flips up into a sudden falsetto and then drops back down into his chest voice at key points in a phrase. The effect conveys the soulful immediacy of a stylized blues shout, a device that many later rhythm-and-blues singers would employ to their audience's sheer delight.

EXAMPLE 3. Powell solo, "Perdido," mm. 1–16.

Powell also played live broadcasts while in Williams's orchestra, and some airchecks from these performances still exist. These broadcasts differ from the standard commercial recordings in that they allowed the performers to play longer solos. Thus they provide evidence of Powell's growing prowess as a modern jazz soloist. The band's arrangement of Juan Tizol's "Perdido," another Ellington band chestnut, taken from a broadcast in early January 1944, provides another clear example of Powell's emerging solo style (example 3). He opens with a cascade of descending triplet figures that demonstrate his infectious technical command. The idea of "againstness" exists in this solo—and, as noted earlier, in bebop in general—on at least two levels: in his experimentation with phrase structure and in the articulation of the accents. Bebop soloing, for the most part, derives much of its musical interest from avoiding the expected resting points of a phrase. Powell uses this technique in "Perdido" in two ways: by creating a rhythmically discontinuous melodic line consisting of rests, triplets, sixteenth notes, and ties that give the eighth-note propulsion a feeling of flexibility and fluidity; and by cutting across the phrase structures of pieces, a technique that is particularly effective when listeners know the original tune. Powell exploits both techniques here to great effect.

After the cascade of triplets in the first measure, Powell avoids the landing point at the end of the phrase with an eighth rest on the downbeat of bar 2. An upbeat accent anticipating the C in m. 4 and the gesture-within-a-phrase that composes the last three notes of m. 5 and the first three of m. 6 combine (along with the opening measure) to make a supple melodic line that works against "Perdido"'s phrase structure. In contrast, the downbeat of bar 7 affirms the original tune: it cadences in the same place. Almost immediately, however, Powell again works against the phrase structure with a new figure in m. 8, a full bar ahead of where the melody resumes in the original. Powell follows the rifflike figure with six flowing measures of rhythmically varied solo line that also breaks where the original tune does—after the downbeat of m. 15. After the brief pause (one beat), the final notes of the solo descend smoothly into the tune's bridge section. Judging from the musical evidence, Powell was less interested in mixing idioms in the rhetoric of this solo than in "Floogie Boo."

As Powell moved away from swing style's conventions, he sometimes entered territory where virtuosic display seemed to get away from him a bit. Throughout the medium-tempo blues number "When My Baby Left Me," for example, Powell's constant fills under Vinson's vocals seem too busy—especially when played against the band's unison ostinato lines and Cootie's trumpet fills. At the same time, his command of a number of jazz/blues piano styles is admirable. On "Royal Garden Blues," his two-chorus solo includes block chord passages, a technique that would become a favored device of such pianists as George Shearing and Erroll Garner. And on a live version of "Roll 'Em," a fast jump blues composed by friend and fellow pianist Mary Lou Williams, Powell plays a solo that alternates among a riff-based approach, heavy stridelike left-hand work, and bebop passages accompanied by sparse chords. In the second chorus, Powell's blues licks in mm. 1–2 contrast with the more inventive run in bars 3–4. In mm. 6–8, the same riff is played in "Floogie Boo" (example 4). Powell uses these different idioms for maximum communication during his brief opportunities to solo, an indication that we should not simply think of his emerging style as a mere imitation of Charlie Parker.

Powell traveled extensively with Williams's orchestra and gained valuable professional experience, but many times his musical contributions were buried in the sound of the large ensemble. Through his work with Williams, he was also exposed to a black professional world that promoted variety, one in which singers, instrumentalists, dancers, and comedians shared the stage. He made his last commercial recordings

EXAMPLE 4. Powell solo, "Roll 'Em," mm. 1–8.

with the band on August 22, 1944, and he would thereafter be publicly identified with bebop's inner circle of musicians. The group's song list that day remained committed to its aesthetic of eclecticism—from Louis Jordan's "Is You Is or Is You Ain't My Baby?" to Thelonious Monk's "'Round Midnight"—and spanned the spectrum. Powell's next recording dates, however, would up the artistic ante as he moved gradually into choppier creative waters.

THE 1946 SIDEMAN RECORDINGS

In his first year of recording, Powell proved that he was a good swing musician, comfortable in several styles of popular music. But his fame would come in the specialized context of bebop. Over the next couple of years, as he and the other beboppers crystallized their ideas, a new jazz idiom gradually emerged. As I noted earlier, throughout 1945 Powell's health difficulties probably limited his musical output. But by 1946, he had rebounded and was a central force in extending the influence of the new bebop style in a year of active recording. Leonard Feather notes that "by 1946, bebop recording had reached a phenomenal level both in quantity and quality," although the lines dividing bebop from the previous jazz were still somewhat unclear.[13] Powell's 1946 sideman recordings provide a look at the next stage of his artistic and professional development, and they document bebop's formal qualities on the brink of the style's crystallization. He created this work

EXAMPLE 5. Powell solo, "Long, Tall Dexter," ninth chorus, mm. 1–12.

in a "center collectivity," a group of young musicians who formed the creative leadership of the movement.[14]

Tenor saxophonist Dexter Gordon was one of the first on his instrument to adopt the bebop style. He led a session for the Savoy label on January 29, 1946, that featured Powell, Roach, bassist Curley Russell, and the lesser-known Leonard Hawkins on trumpet. The date is made up of three original compositions, "Long, Tall Dexter," "Dexter Rides Again," and "Dexter Digs In," and one precomposed ballad, "I Can't Escape from You." Taken together, the four tunes are prototypes for many other recordings of the bebop era. Both in their formal construction and performance practice, they typify bebop convention.[15]

The tempo of "Long, Tall Dexter," like the other two originals on this session, moves at a medium-fast pace. Roach introduces the tune, a blues in B-flat, with a two-measure drum solo; Gordon and Hawkins play the theme with precision an octave apart for two choruses. As the leader, Gordon takes four inspired solo choruses—more than Hawkins and Powell, who get two each. Powell plays a fine solo exhibiting the fluidity of the bebop idiom. The first chorus of the solo (example 5) reveals how Powell retained at least one aspect of vocal blues rhetoric in the context of the bebop instrumental style. Like a typical vocal blues, the chorus contains three four-bar phrases, but Powell plays with

EXAMPLE 6. Melody, "Long, Tall Dexter."

the well-known form. Each phrase shares a descending contour and a similar rhythmic vocabulary (i.e., eighth notes, triplets). The first phrase begins with a syncopated figure and continues until the last beat of m. 3. In bar 4, Powell anticipates the second phrase with a figure that propels the melodic line toward the subdominant harmony, a crucial point of arrival in the blues form. Measure 8 prepares the dominant harmony with the fastest harmonic rhythm in the piece: two chord changes rather than one per bar. Powell highlights the passage with a brief nod to Earl Hines's "trumpet style" piano (the use of octaves) that dramatically ascends. The chorus's final phrase begins in m. 9 with an upbeat to beat 3, providing another shift in the phrase structure. Powell concludes the chorus with a return to the single-note texture of the first two phrases.

"Long, Tall Dexter"'s harmonic framework, as noted, is a twelve-bar blues, a cyclic progression that formed the basis for many bebop themes. Blues bebop themes can be found in three basic formal types: A-A-A, A-A-B, and through-composed (or without repetition: A-B-C). The first type of theme is composed of three repeating four-bar phrases, sometimes with a slight variation on the last phrase (A-A-A'; example 6). The second type has a contrasting last phrase resembling the melodic scheme of classic vocal blues. Through-composed themes contain no pattern of repetition, variation, or contrast among their four-measure phrases. "Long, Tall Dexter" fits the A-A-B type scheme, with the melody in the fifth and sixth measures slightly adjusted to accommodate the subdominant harmony (example 7).

Bebop musicians routinely embellished this basic progression to add

EXAMPLE 7. Twelve-bar blues structural harmonies.

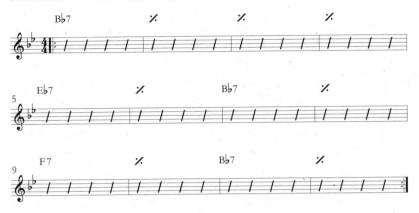

EXAMPLE 8. Substitution chords, "Long, Tall Dexter," third and seventh choruses.

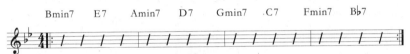

harmonic interest, complexity, and individuality to their compositions. This occurs in "Long, Tall Dexter": at the beginning of Gordon's and Hawkins's solos—the third and seventh choruses, respectively—the band plays chord substitutions based on a circle-of-fifths movement that arrives at the subdominant harmony in the fifth measure. In m. 10 of the theme, the C-flat 7 chord (designed to accommodate the melodic material Gordon has transposed up a half-step) substitutes for the dominant harmony (F7). I detail in example 7 (above) a typical twelve-bar blues progression; example 8 illustrates the harmonic embellishments.

Gordon and Powell cowrote "Dexter Rides Again," a piece in thirty-two-bar, A-A-B-A form. The theme is not a contrafact; it appears to be based on an original harmonic progression. Nonblues bebop themes such as "Dexter Rides Again" can be classified into A-A-B-A, A-B-A-C, and A-B-A-B′ formal schemes. The A-A-B-A category constitutes the largest class of nonblues bebop themes. Since many of these themes do not possess composed melodies in the B section (mm. 17–24), one soloist usually improvises during these measures. (Improvised B sections are often found in tunes based on the rhythm changes.) Many A-A-B-A themes repeat melodic material almost exactly in all three A sections of the piece, while others paraphrase. Bebop musicians also used other models when composing their themes: A-B-A-C themes feature a return of the A section in m. 17, and A-B-A-B′ and A-B-A-C themes are similar but may be distinguished by comparing the melodic content of mm. 9–16 and 25–32.[16]

All A sections of "Dexter Rides Again" are identical and fit perfectly the A-A-B-A scheme. The simple harmonic progression of the A section shifts between two chords—F major 7 and G-flat major 7—using one per measure. The B section provides contrast with a secondary dominant move that tonicizes the subdominant (B-flat) in mm. 11–12; then, with another secondary dominant chord (A-flat 7), the progression moves to a D-flat 7 chord that acts as an augmented sixth chord that resolves to a C7 chord, which is the dominant chord of the A-section's tonal center.

The melodic organization of this composition gives it a distinct bebop flavor. The melody begins with a two-measure phrase—two short motives separated by rests and consisting of descending intervals, a minor third and then a minor second (mm. 1–2). The second phrase (mm. 3–4) expands that pattern rhythmically with a descending eighth-note passage that outlines the F major 7 of the supporting harmony and comes to rest on the fifth of the G-flat major 7 chord. The last note of m. 3 and the first of m. 4 (E-flat and D-flat) reproduce the motive that begins the tune and the one that spans mm. 1–2. In addition, bar 5 begins with the same A-C over an F chord with which Gordon and Powell began the tune. The third and last phrase (mm. 5–8) contains hints of the first two but differs significantly. It begins with the motive of the first phrase and an interval inversion of the second phrase (m. 5). The next passage contains a major sixth leap (an inversion of the minor third interval of the opening motive), a scale passage based on the G-flat major 7 (m. 6) and a melodic cadential gesture with an E-flat that forms a cross-relation with the F major 7 below it (m. 7). Finally, a measure of rest completes the 2+2+4 phrase pattern of the A section.

The B section (bridge) has a regular phrase pattern: 2+2 and 2+2. But it also exhibits much melodic and rhythmic variety within that scheme. Measures 9–10 consist of an ascending sequence whose structural pitches outline an F chord. The half-step figure at the end of the melody in m. 7 predominates in the first line of the bridge. In mm. 11–12, the composers answer the phrase with a descending scale passage that reinforces the tonicized B-flat tonality. The next two phrases (mm. 13–16) present new melodic material: Both are scalelike passages that

EXAMPLE 9. A and B sections, "Dexter Rides Again."

continue the upbeat accents that unify the piece. In fact, within both the A and B sections, only one phrase begins on the downbeat. In mm. 9 and 13, the accent falls on the downbeat, but elsewhere the upbeat is accented. In sum, Gordon and Powell have taken a rather simple harmonic scheme and added interest primarily through melodic invention and rhythmic variety.

Gordon, Powell, and the others saturate the performance realm of "Dexter Rides Again" with bebop practice as well as with attributes of their individual styles. In the second chorus of his solo, Gordon quotes a bit of "Jingle Bells," demonstrating his custom of injecting familiar strains of melodies into a solo. (He made the habit a constant feature of his style throughout his long career.)[17] Furthermore, Powell's comping on "Dexter Rides Again" reminds the listener that soloing shows only part of his skill and inspiration as a performer. He was also an excellent accompanist, and this piece shows that side of him in action. Especially telling is the rhythmic aspect of his accompanying, which is best heard as a collaborative event with Roach. Powell plays a stream of diversely voiced chords, sometimes on downbeats and sometimes simultaneously with Roach's accents. At other points, Powell stresses unaccented beats and creates rhythmic contrast with the soloist and the other rhythm section players. In fact, Roach and Powell seem to be in a "conversation of rhythms" throughout Gordon's and Hawkins's solos. During Powell's solo, Roach switches from louder playing on the ride cymbal to softer work on the hi-hat. This strategy not only allows Powell's solo (and his well-known audible grunts) to be clearly heard, but also dramatically reduces the group's volume level. Finally, within all this activity, Russell consistently outlines the theme's chord progression by playing four notes to the bar.

Both Feather and Russell agree that the changing role and style of the drummer were of singular importance to the bebop idiom and, one realizes in retrospect, to American music in general. Drummers Kenneth "Klook" Clarke (1914–85) and, later, Max Roach (born 1924) are credited with creating a new style of drumming that many believe elevated jazz drummers from the role of "*accompanying timekeeper* to active participant in the creative music-making process."[18] Anthony Brown writes that the "development of modern jazz drumset artistry can be traced from Kenny Clarke's earliest experiments while performing with big bands of the late 1930s, through several less prominent drummers, to its full fruition as documented in the drumming style of Max Roach's performances with the Charlie Parker Quintet during the late 1940s."[19] Brown summarizes Clarke's mature playing style, and modern jazz drumming in general, as "fixed rhythmic patterns maintained on the ride cymbal, hi-hat cymbals marking beats 2 and 4, and the snare and bass drums used to accentuate and punctuate the rhythmic flow."[20] Taken together, these techniques became known as "coordinated independence," the technique of drummers maintaining "a continuous four-voice, polyrhythmical structure" with their four limbs.[21]

Essentially, Clarke reintroduced to jazz what could be considered a "traditional West African musical conception, wherein a metallophone (bell) and idiophone (rattle) maintain the fixed rhythmic patterns and drums provide the variable rhythmic embellishments."[22] Clarke's innovations had extensive influence beyond jazz:

> Inevitably, Clarke's percussion innovations had a profound impact on the direction of American music. By employing a metallophone (a cymbal [functioning as the bell]) to maintain the fixed rhythmic pattern, and the drums to provide a polyrhythmic foundation, Clarke paved the way for the

drumset's ultimate return to its West African conceptual origins. The ubiquitous sound of the snare drum accent in beats 2 and 4, heard in the music
played incessantly on AM and FM radio, is a transference of the hi-hat pattern that characterizes modern jazz drumming. Today, due primarily to the
global influence of American music, this originally African rhythmic framework is found in the popular music of virtually every nation on the planet.[23]

Brown attributes Roach's originality and singular influence to "his
increased incorporation of textural rather than strictly rhythmical elements into his percussion vocabulary, including his integration of the
various 'instruments' of the drumset to create a more balanced, heterogeneous sound."[24] As an "equal partner" in the band's overall sound, a
bebop drummer freely explored the textural and tonal possibilities of
the drum set. In early bebop recordings, some of these effects were lost
due to the limitations of recording technology. But in live performance,
bebop drummers, as Russell observes, "seem to set the air around them
in motion and have an exhilarating effect on both listener and fellow
musician."[25]

Russell describes the string bass player in the bebop ensemble as
the "work-horse," whose requirements for masterful modern work
included "a crisp plunging sound" like that of Oscar Pettiford.[26] The
bassist's primary responsibility was to provide harmonic support and
to maintain a steady pulse against the other improvisatory rhythmic
inventions that occurred during the performance. Russell fills that role
on every side of the Gordon session. Essentially, the bassist helped to
supply a metronomic sense to the performance.

By 1946, as the remainder of Powell's sessions show, bebop musicians had developed composing techniques that emphasized variety
within an established set of procedures. Therefore, it is helpful here to
outline a few of James Williams's observations that apply to many of
these compositions. One way to discuss thirty-two-bar bebop compositions such as "Dexter Rides Again" and "Dexter Digs In" (another
tune on the Gordon session) is to think of their framework in eight-
measure modules. Williams uses the term *model* to designate "the harmonic progression which serves as a common element among various
jazz themes."[27] Thus, just as blues themes share a common harmonic
structure, many nonblues bebop themes do, too. Since the harmonic
frameworks of many bebop themes are often based on more than one
source (e.g., the A section of "I Got Rhythm" and the B section of
"Honeysuckle Rose"), Williams argues that it is helpful "to think of
a model as an eight-measure harmonic scheme rather than a thirty-

EXAMPLE 10. B section, "Dexter Digs In," mm. 17–24.

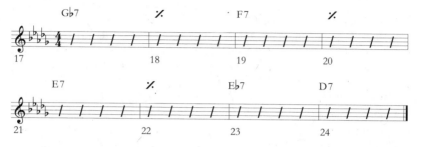

two-measure formula" for at least two reasons: (1) within eight-measure modules, the borrowed harmonic framework "remains relatively intact"; and (2) in eight-measure models, "the variation can be more precisely described when the unit is shorter."[28]

Most A-section models such as the one in "Dexter Digs In" are based on rhythm changes. Like the blues harmonic model, many variations on this basic model exist among bebop themes. Many B-section models are based on the bridge section of "I Got Rhythm." Generally, B sections serve to provide a conspicuous tonal contrast to the A section. Furthermore, the B section of rhythm changes has a simple harmonic plan: "A cycle of dominant sevenths, the last of which is the primary dominant seventh of the tonic key of the theme. . . . Since dominant sevenths chords with roots a tritone apart are virtually interchangeable in bebop . . . the progression may utilize root motion of descending fifths, descending minor seconds, or a combination of the two. . . . Another significant aspect of the model is its regular harmonic rhythm; each chord customarily spans two measures."[29]

B-section models include those based on Fats Waller's song "Honeysuckle Rose," which, according to Williams, has had more variations based on it than the B section of rhythm changes. Other popular ones are Edgar Sampson's "Stompin' at the Savoy" and Gershwin's "Oh, Lady Be Good."[30] A common feature of all these B-section progressions is the use of stepwise descents in the bass. Gordon's "Dexter Digs In" provides a clear example of several of these formulas.

The harmonic structure of "Dexter Digs In" carries an A-section model based on rhythm changes in D-flat. Although Gordon's variation is essentially a repeating 4+4 scheme, the progression makes the required arrival at the subdominant (G-flat) in m. 6. The B section is a series of dominant-seventh chords that descend chromatically based

EXAMPLE 11. B section, "Stomping at the Savoy," mm. 17–24.

on a B-section model of "Stompin' at the Savoy." After moving to the subdominant chord in m. 17, Gordon employs the "tritone substitution" technique described above. In this example, F7 (m. 19) substitutes for "Stompin'"'s B7, E-flat 7 (m. 23) for the original A7, and D7 (m. 24) for Sampson's A-flat 7, which makes the bridge's transition to the D-flat tonic. Gordon wrote no melody for the bridge, so Powell solos, fulfilling another tendency in bebop compositions. The fact that Powell's solo serves as the bridge's melody may explain why he is listed as co-composer.

Although Powell and other beboppers discovered and elaborated a new style, they also celebrated their connection to "mainstream" American popular music. The ballad "I Can't Escape from You," by Leo Robin and Richard A. Whiting, is the only piece from the session not composed by the performers. Unlike the other compositions, "I Can't Escape" probably would have been immediately recognizable to audiences in 1946. It originated in a 1936 musical film called *Rhythm on the Range* with Bing Crosby and Martha Raye.[31] (Crosby recorded the song with Jimmy Dorsey and His Orchestra in 1936, and other groups did as well, including black swing bands such as Jimmy Lunceford and His Orchestra and Erskine Hawkins and His 'Bama State Collegians.)[32] Gordon's interpretation put him at center stage in this performance. Throughout the entire recording, his romantic "storytelling," along with his rich, controlled vibrato, guides the listener. Powell's playing complements Gordon's placid delivery with unobtrusive scale passages, arpeggios, and block chords that add interest but never detract from the soloist.

The month following Gordon's Savoy session, Powell was slated for more work with Gillespie, but his temperament kept him from making the engagement. In February 1946, Clark Monroe, owner of Harlem's

Uptown House and 52nd Street's Spotlite, provided Gillespie a venue to build an authentic bebop ensemble upon his return from California. Undaunted by bebop's lukewarm reception in the West, Gillespie organized a small group composed of Milt Jackson, Ray Brown, Stan Levey, Al Haig, and Sonny Stitt, who replaced Parker.[33] Encouraged by the success of the Spotlite engagement, Gillespie expanded his group to a big band, a well-established format for swing but a relatively unexplored one for bebop. He and his arranger Walter Gilbert Fuller chose the musicians and rehearsed for five days before the opening. Powell was Gillespie's first choice as pianist for the big band, but the plan did not work out: "When I formed the new band, I hired Bud Powell on piano and Max on drums. The money was a little erratic, and Bud was super-erratic, and I had to do something about that, so I got Monk."[34]

Despite signs of growing personal instability, Powell continued playing in New York nightclubs throughout 1946, apparently living in a domestic situation that provided him the financial freedom to experiment with his music. Jackie McLean recalls that as late as 1947, when he first met Powell, the twenty-three-year-old pianist was living at home with his parents. Working against stereotypes of jazz musicians, McLean describes Powell as a "homebody" who rarely ventured out except to perform.[35] As he continued to play, he must have attracted growing attention in the jazz world, for his professional associations began to expand. On May 7 came another recording opportunity for Powell, this time accompanying a female singer who began her professional career in close company with the young beboppers.

Born in the same year as Powell, Sarah Lois Vaughan was nurtured musically in a Newark, New Jersey, Baptist church. She joined Earl Hines's band in 1943 as his vocalist and second pianist. There she met Gillespie, Parker, and others who would soon make up bebop's inner circle. When vocalist Billy Eckstine formed his own band in 1944, Vaughan joined him, continuing her association with other modern jazz musicians also playing in the group.[36] The May 7 session for the Musicraft label (recorded during her important engagement at Café Society, an upscale New York nightclub) was Vaughan's first as a leader and a sure sign that her star was rising. Composer, pianist, and arranger Tadd Dameron served as the date's musical director and hired Powell along with the other instrumentalists.[37]

Apparently aimed at getting Vaughan's name before a wide audience, the four songs recorded that day are arranged for jazz combo and a string section.[38] Dameron's composition "If You Could See Me

Now" is the only material associated with the bebop repertory on the session.[39] Vaughan's rather sentimental treatment of the piece, Freddie Webster's soaring trumpet introduction, and Dameron's arrangement place the performance more in the realm of swing than of bebop. Vaughan sticks closely to the original melody. Nonetheless, all the musical building blocks from which she constructed her mature style are present here: the remarkable range, the emotional content extending from coy to dramatic, her excellent vocal control and delivery, and her signature vibrato.

As in his performance in "I Can't Escape from You," Powell's accompaniment ideally suits the setting. His melodic fills delicately ornament Dameron's arrangement, and he never upstages Vaughan's vocals. Powell's playing here shows a growing seasoning, and his presence on the session—a vocalist's debut—indicates that in 1946 bebop was certainly not yet considered a modernistic style that tested the limits of audience understanding. Furthermore, this pop/jazz session in repertory and in performance practice demonstrates the scope of musical demands placed on beboppers in 1946. Vaughan, of course, went on to forge a career that moved comfortably—and artistically—between jazz and more pop/easy-listening settings. Powell's future work and that of Dameron, however, ultimately would be perceived in narrower terms: strictly within the bebop idiom. As the Williams, Gordon, and Vaughan sessions indicate, by 1946 Powell and many of his colleagues had embraced and mastered a broad spectrum of jazz and popular styles, not just bebop. Furthermore, they drew on many sources for their repertory: pop ballads, bebop originals, and themes based on melodic contrafacts. Powell's success on these recordings shows that he had mastered the demands of the trade.

Nevertheless, by this time a definitive and recognizable bebop style did exist. All the factors that constituted the style—repertory, soloing, accompanying, and other aspects of performance practice—can be heard in the 1946 Powell recordings discussed above. Although Powell's work conforms to bebop's established procedures, it also pushes the envelope of what was expected, especially in the area of composition. And pieces written by Powell later in his career, such as "Un Poco Loco," "Glass Enclosure," "Parisian Thoroughfare," and others, demonstrate the breadth of his compositional gifts, arguably because they all seemed atypical of one or more aspects of standard bebop practice. Powell laid the foundation for those achievements in his early career.

In addition to the maturation of bebop composition practice, improvised solos in the style had also settled into a level of achievement that had become codified into a dynamic and abstract relationship to the harmonic environment of the composition. Powell's solo on George Gershwin's "Nice Work If You Can Get It" shows him as a mature bebop improviser in a way that previous examples have not. The musical details are not presented, however, as a way to show how "advanced" bebop solos were compared to previous styles. Rather, they show how the arrangement of "sonic symbols," in George Lewis's words, are "often constructed with a view toward social instrumentality" for many African American improvisers. "New improvisative and compositional styles," he writes, "are often identified with ideals of race advancement and, more importantly, as resistive ripostes to perceived opposition to black social expression and economic advancement by the dominant white American culture."[40]

Gershwin composed "Nice Work" in 1937. The song first appeared in the musical film *A Damsel in Distress*,[41] and shortly thereafter several performers recorded it, including the Andrews Sisters, Tommy Dorsey, Benny Goodman, Maxine Sullivan, and Teddy Wilson.[42] "Nice Work" was among the repertory bebop musicians favored in Minton's jam sessions. (Monk also recorded the tune on his first date as a leader, in September 1947 for Blue Note.) Besides its apparent popularity, the song's formal qualities were probably attractive to modern jazz musicians. As a harmonic structure, "Nice Work" conforms to the circle-of-fifths paradigm; it is also in A-A-B-A form with a two-bar stretch in the last phrase. The first two bars of the piece contain four secondary dominant seventh chords with root movement in fifths. The harmonic treatment obscures the A-flat tonic that is not really firmly established until bar 6. Theorist Henry Martin has observed how "many popular jazz songs project a key by arrival rather than by simple prolongation of a single tonality designated early on. This practice can be detected throughout jazz history, even in songs written as early as 1921."[43]

Powell recorded "Nice Work" on his leader session. He performs it in A-flat—a half-step higher than Gershwin's sheet music—the key in which Monk also recorded the tune. Since both pianists played the song in that key, it was probably the one informally established in jam sessions. After a percussive solo introduction, Powell presents the melody intact, adding melodic embellishments only during pauses in the melody. During the solo, he truncates Gershwin's two-bar extension into a one-measure tag that he maintains throughout the two-chorus solo. The solo itself is a marvel of melodic invention, a continuous flow of sound embodying many of the qualities of the best bebop improvisation, using harmonic progressions as a spur to melodic invention.

Powell takes a *prestissimo* tempo here, and the way he subdivides the beat produces a rapid, driving melodic flow. The eighth note is the predominant note value throughout the entire solo, though triplet and (even fewer) sixteenth-note figures add rhythmic contrast (example 12). Powell's secure technique is clearly evident: the certainty with which he executes the melodic line sounds at once relaxed and on the edge of his abilities. Although it is difficult to determine exactly at this fast tempo, Powell's articulation seems varied throughout the solo, a technique that prevents a hypnotic quality from entering his work. Sometimes Powell stresses the downbeat of a measure, and at other times he accents all the notes within a phrase. In fact, the extensive presence of eighth notes here makes the variety of Powell's articulation that much more important to the solo's overall effect. Powell's left-hand work consists of frequent use of third, fifth, and seventh intervals. The accompaniment reinforces the harmonic structure of the song and adds another layer of rhythmic complexity to the solo.

The rhetoric of Powell's treatment of "Nice Work"'s phrase structure constitutes another point of variety in the solo. The way Powell "plays through" some sections of the tune and pauses at others conforms to what seems to be a general principle of his musicianship: exploiting the tension between convention and againstness. For example, when Powell plays through the eight-bar phrase units between mm. 8 and 9, he elides the tune's phrase structure, makes the two sections feel seamless, and works against the listener's expectations. At the same time, however, he musically acknowledges the arrival of the new section: The melody spanning mm. 8–9 climaxes on the G—the highest note of the unit—and sounds on the downbeat of the section's first downbeat. Powell approaches elision differently between mm. 24 and 25. The juncture between the bridge and the last A is totally obscured because of the momentum of a melodic line that begins in m. 21 and does not stop until the last beat of m. 27, and then only briefly with a quarter rest. When Powell does pause at the end of sections (e.g., mm. 16 and 33), he allows the listener to hear the tune's original architecture, to absorb the preceding solo rhetoric, and to prepare for what is already on its way down the pipeline.

In general, when Powell plays descending melodic lines, they move by stepwise motion (mm. 1, 7, 9, 23, 24), a technique that also governs the four compositions discussed above. Ascending lines often arpeg-

EXAMPLE 12. Excerpt, Powell solo, "Nice Work If You Can Get It," mm. 1–36.
Transcription by John Mehegan.

giate (mm. 3, 8, 15, 22, 34, 35), although descending arpeggios are also present (mm. 12, 17, 18, 19, 25). Powell uses a high degree of chromaticism throughout, but nonharmonic tones usually resolve to a pitch consonant with the underlying harmony (mm. 2, 7, 9, 14, 15). Powell employs melodic tensions to a much lesser degree than in his compositions, although he does not totally abandon the technique.

Two events in the solo show how Powell achieved some of the emotional intensity for which his playing was noted. In each example, he uses flow against disjunction to generate some excitement. First, in mm. 10–11, Powell appears to stumble, giving the impression that he's made a false start. The mistake, however, seems to supply Powell with a burst of creative energy: the melodic line that follows (the last two beats of m. 11 through m. 16) constitutes one of the more beautifully crafted sections of the solo. In the second example (mm. 34–35), Powell begins the second chorus with an inventive sequence that contains tensions at the end of every triplet figure. Two features make the gesture stand out: it contains the highest notes of the entire solo, and it is the solo's most rhythmically disjunctive section. Powell follows the sequence—as he did in the first example—with an intense outpouring of melodic invention that works against the feeling of disruption he created with the gesture. Both examples show Powell achieving the urgent, spontaneous-sounding vitality so crucial to the bebop aesthetic.

Finally, Powell fashions each idea in this solo to "Nice Work"'s two-chords-per-measure harmonic rhythm. But the solo never simply runs the changes; it possesses the refreshing melodic coherence and expressiveness found in the best of Charlie Parker's solos. It *says* something. Powell seems to be announcing that he is inventing the solo on the spot and that he can take risks and land on his feet. At the same time, the lack of blues-inflected nuances make it unlike a lot of Parker's work and certainly different from the solos in Cootie Williams's band. Furthermore, the absence of any reference to "Nice Work"'s melody makes it doubtful that Powell built this solo from a single idea or motive. Thus the solo probably is more formulaic in conception, developed from a diverse set of fragmentary ideas. (A good example is found in mms. 1 and 8, where Powell repeats himself almost verbatim.) He used his repertoire of formulas and his rhetoric much as other great improvisers did: as the building blocks of his style and as a foundation for ceaseless variation. He had developed a voice in the exploding narrative riches of his solos.

VOICE, INFLUENCE, AND THE COLLECTIVE FORMATION IN BEBOP

The discussion of the microscopic details and structural framing of Powell's solo voice highlights the individual inner logic of his work, but another important point should be made here. Powell was part of a growing collective of musicians who together were charting new sonic and sociocultural territories in American music. Despite our tendency to valorize the genius of the major innovators of this revolution, the emerging corporate energies of bebop's growing cadre of disciples are also a big part of the story. Before considering more specifics of and broader ideas about Powell's compositional palette, let's consider bebop's growing and deepening squad of acolytes.

The summer of 1946 was especially productive for Powell, and it was significant for the bebop style, too, as its inner circle continued to widen with new talent. Between June 26 and September 6, Powell recorded twenty sides for the Savoy and Swing labels during the course of five dates. Of the sixteen recordings from these sessions available to this researcher, one is a contrafact based on "Just You, Just Me," two are based on twelve-bar blues, two are original progressions, and eleven use variations on rhythm changes (among other progressions) as a harmonic structure. Powell contributed three compositions to these sessions: "Bebop in Pastel," "Fool's Fancy," and "Webb City." In addition, on January 10, 1947, Powell made his first recording as a leader for the Deluxe label (later released on Roost). Powell's only composition on that session is "Bud's Bubble." Taken together, these four compositions provide a profile of Powell's early compositional style.

Powell recorded these pieces in the context of sessions that show James Louis "J.J." Johnson, Edward "Sonny" Stitt, and Theodore "Fats" Navarro, Jr.—three of early bebop's most prodigious players—embarking on important careers in jazz. (Clarke, another session leader, had already influenced jazz drumming, and he would continue to do so.) But Stitt's and Navarro's contributions in particular highlight a crucial issue in the diffusion of the bebop style: influence. Stitt's debt to Charlie Parker's style is well known; and Gillespie profoundly influenced many later trumpeters, including Navarro. Thus, beyond documenting Powell's growth and the crystallization of the bebop sound, these recordings show the bebop style spawning bona fide disciples. The bebop posse was growing.

Trombonist J.J. Johnson was born in 1924, the same year as Powell and Sarah Vaughan. In 1942, he left his native Indianapolis to join

Snookum Russell's band. There he met trumpeter Fats Navarro, who influenced him considerably. Johnson insists as well that his chief models were "Pres [Lester Young] and Roy [Eldridge], then Diz and Bird." Later that year, Johnson joined Benny Carter's band, which at various times included Max Roach and Curley Russell.[44] After a short stint with Count Basie in 1945, Johnson began to appear in 52nd Street clubs, desiring to focus on his small-group playing.[45] On the Street, Johnson's playing blossomed. Ira Gitler recalls first hearing him sitting in with Gillespie at the Spotlite; Gitler was "open-mouthed at his amazing dexterity."[46] In 1946, Johnson found kindred spirits when he fronted a band at the Spotlite that included Powell, Navarro, Russell, Roach, and tenor saxophonist Stan Getz.[47]

Sonny Stitt (1924–82) joined Billy Eckstine's band in 1945 and quickly embraced the new ideas being played there. As noted above, when Gillespie returned from California without Parker, Stitt replaced the saxophonist at the important Spotlite engagement. In fact, Stitt made his first recordings with Gillespie's combo and big band in May and July 1946. Gil Fuller, who collaborated with the arrangements on these sessions, recalled that Stitt "could play his can off during those days."[48] When Fuller produced Stitt's Savoy recordings—his first as a leader—in August that year, the two had already worked together closely. Despite a few incarcerations that had checkered his career, Stitt was among the first saxophonists to closely simulate Parker's style. Indeed, his emulation of Parker's melodic approach and timbre was so spot-on that bebop theorist Thomas Owens has observed that "only small details of phrasing and articulation—an occasional slight hesitation in connecting notes in a Parkeresque phrase, or a subtly different way of tonguing—betray the imitator."[49] That Parker, one of the earliest bebop musicians, was inspiring imitators and protégés as early as 1946 shows that bebop style was destined to be more than just a passing fad.

Fats Navarro (1923–50) first rose to prominence when he joined Eckstine's band as Gillespie's replacement in January 1945. He so capably filled the void in the group that, Eckstine noted, "You would hardly know that Diz had left the band. Fats played Dizzy's solos, *not* note for note, but his ideas on Dizzy's parts and the feeling was the same."[50] Navarro's talents quickly moved him into bebop's orbit, and although Gillespie obviously had influenced Navarro, he developed his own style. "The other guys were too busy trying to get to Dizzy," Teddy Reig once stated, "but Fats was *Fats*."[51]

An aspect of Henry Louis Gates's well-known notion of Signifyin(g) is a useful analytical frame here, perhaps obviously so. "Signifyin(g)," Gates writes, "epitomizes all of the rhetorical play in the black vernacular. Its self-consciously open rhetorical status, then, functions as a kind of writing, wherein rhetoric is writing of speech, of oral discourse."[52] Musical Signifyin(g)—an idea elaborated on by Samuel Floyd—in the black vernacular tradition embodies numerous levels of repetition with respect to repertory and specific musical techniques. That repetition or reinterpretation of materials usually is a gesture of "admiration and respect."[53] It's how genres and traditions come into being and how sonic collectivities form and become socially important. Furthermore, as John P. Murphy has argued, this self-referential tendency in the jazz tradition is one of the qualities that audiences and musicians find so compelling. "Rather than anxiously concealing their influences, some jazz improvisers . . . make them obvious, and celebrate their debt to their precursors. . . . By invoking and reworking music that is familiar to the audience, the jazz performer involves the audience in the process and makes it meaningful for those who recognize the sources."[54] (One could obviously draw parallels to the process of melodic contrafact here.)

In both Stitt's and Navarro's cases, their obvious debts to Parker and Gillespie, respectively, earned them prestige in the jazz community and fostered a growing sense of tradition among bebop musicians. Similarly, as Powell's recordings began to circulate among other pianists, the shadow and excitement of his influence enhanced the nascent sense of community and tradition in bebop.[55] This, together with the growing idiosyncratic nature of his compositional voice, helped to make him a standout in that creative circle.

SONG STRUCTURE IN POWELL'S COMPOSITIONS

Powell built a solo and compositional style on the works that proved important not only to early bebop, but also to later developments in jazz such as hard bop, the cool movement, and even free jazz. Avant-garde pianist Cecil Taylor has commented on Powell's influence on his own musical approach: "There was a lot of music going in my early years in Boston. Like I heard Bud [Powell] at this time, and even though I felt it was a spiritually different music, I couldn't identify with it. Later on I heard Bud's recording of *Un Poco Loco,* and it completely extinguished the Tristano influence which was strong in me in the early Fifties."[56] In another example, Miles Davis featured Powell's composition "Budo"

EXAMPLE 13. "Fool's Fancy."

(a.k.a. "Hallucinations") on his acclaimed *Birth of the Cool* session in 1949. Powell's younger brother and protégé, Richie, was the pianist in what many believe was the quintessential hard bop combo, the Clifford Brown / Max Roach Quintet. And Powell's early Blue Note sessions, featuring saxophonist Sonny Rollins and Roach, foreshadowed some of the stylistic qualities of hard bop.

"Fool's Fancy"

Powell first recorded "Fool's Fancy" on August 23, 1946, on a session led by Sonny Stitt. Along with Powell and Stitt (alto sax), the other musicians included Kenny Dorham (trumpet), Al Hall (bass), and Wallace Bishop (drums). The theme is a contrafact based on rhythm changes (example 13). The tune is also known by the name "Wail," a version of which can be heard on Powell's Blue Note recordings. Some of Powell's compositional approaches in "Fool's Fancy" are standard bebop practice, while other of his ideas push at its boundaries. Powell uses a "standard" variation of rhythm changes in E-flat to form the harmonic basis of this piece. The harmonic rhythm moves two chords per measure in the A section and one chord per two bars in the B section. .

In his unorthodox use of form here—he uses an A-B-C-B schematic design—Powell begins to deviate from established patterns, and what emerges shows a singular compositional voice. He varies the way that he groups melodic gestures within the song's phrases. The first sixteen bars contain two eight-measure models, each organized in 4+4 units, but Powell's technique works against that underlying regularity. In the first eight measures, for example, an antecedent/consequent relationship exists between bars 1 and 2 and 3 and 4, as well as with bars 5 and 6 and 7 and 8. Yet each of these units exhibits such melodic and rhythmic variety within itself that it sounds irregular and asymmetrical. Each four-bar unit ends similarly, however, with a falling interval (m. 4 and m. 8); the last note in m. 8 lands on a nondiatonic tension, a flatted fifth. .

At the beginning of the B section, m. 9 brings a hint of reference to A—the harmonic schemes supporting each phrase are almost identical, and the melody ascends similarly, though not in exactly the same way. Powell then takes the melody to another level of intensity with a cross-rhythm composed of a three-beat unit that starts on beat 4 of m. 9 and goes through m. 11. One of its results is to make mm. 9–12 a four-measure melodic unit—a longer and more complete melodic statement than anything played earlier. The phrase ends with a falling perfect fifth (E-flat to A-flat) in m. 12, the same type of gesture heard in section A. After the melodic intensity achieved in bars 9–12, Powell fashions mm. 13–16 to fall more or less predictably into two two-bar units. (The quarter note–half note figure on G in m. 15 seems to abruptly put brakes on the flow begun in m. 9, setting up the cadential figure of m. 16.)

Powell's rhetoric in the first sixteen bars of "Fool's Fancy" works profoundly on two levels: phrase structure and rhythm. In the phrase structure, Powell moves from a more or less unconventional, disjunctive melodic unit (2+2+2+2) to a longer unit (mm. 9–12) to an absolutely predictable 2+2 conclusion. In rhythmic activity, Powell moves from irregularity and unpredicatability (mm. 1–12) to the conventional. The basic phrase structure is regular, as noted above, but the rhythmic againstness continuously pushes the listener off balance. For example, m. 2 has no note on the downbeat and silence on beat 3. Likewise, m. 5 carries no note on its downbeat, and m. 7 has no note until the upbeat of beat 3. Powell crowns his departure from this disjunction on the downbeat of m. 13 with the G: the highest note of the piece so far. The note's placement has the effect of breaking through the barrier of rhythmic unpredictability and into more conventional motion toward the cadence in m. 16.

Powell's bridge section (mm. 17–24) also balances convention with againstness. The progression follows the rhythm changes, but with the tritone substitution technique employed in mm. 19 and 23: the G-flat 7 and E7 replace the C7 and B-flat 7, respectively. (During the solos, the band plays progression without the tritone substitution.) Powell's riff melody—consisting largely of pendular thirds—contrasts sharply with the rhythmic disjunction of A and B. The two four-measure phrases constitute a perfectly symmetrical antecedent-consequent relationship. Melodic tensions are used in a consistent way in each phrase: an accented cross-relation with the chord's third. Nevertheless, the pounding effect of Powell's percussive comping, Roach's polyrhythmic conception, and the cross-rhythms created by the riff's accents thicken the sonic environment without sacrificing either momentum or the feeling of contrast between the A and B sections. When B returns, the piece is off and running again like a locomotive. The melodic—and especially the rhythmic—excitement challenges each soloist to sustain or even surpass the level of interest created by the theme.

"Bud's Bubble"

"Bud's Bubble" is Powell's only composition on his January 10, 1947, Deluxe leader session; the piece is also known as "Crazeology" and is sometimes credited to Bennie Harris. Like "Fool's Fancy," "Bud's Bubble"'s progression is based on rhythm changes. Again, Powell puts his mark on the harmonic structure, this time by tinkering with the progression itself (example 14). After a fairly routine beginning, in bar 3 Powell approaches the C minor 7 in the next measure by a half step above (D-flat diminished 7). In mm. 5–6, Powell eliminates the subdominant arrival with substitution chords: ii7–V7–I of G-flat (m. 5) and ii7–V7–I of D-flat (m. 6). Powell closes the section with an important gesture—a full measure of melodic silence (m. 8)—wherein the tonic B-flat is played. In contrast to "Fool's Fancy," where the bridge

EXAMPLE 14. "Bud's Bubble."

and the main part of the head share little in common—in this piece, the abrupt breaking-off into silence at the end of the A section permeates the bridge in a regular and patterned way. Thus "Bud's Bubble" exhibits a higher degree of integration than "Fool's Fancy."

The phrase structure of "Bud's Bubble"'s A section begins with a pair of two-bar units. The first is made by a melodic sequence, the second member of which dovetails with a new figure, beginning on the upbeat of m. 3 and then repeated in sequence starting on the upbeat of m. 4. Powell continues with a second pair of two-bar units. The first is a continuation of the figure from mm. 3–4, but with a small rhythmic variation at the start to avoid monotony, and it fills mm. 5–6, in sequence with mm. 3–4. Once more, the idea of againstness helps to explain Powell's rhetoric here. First, instead of landing on C as before, Powell chooses B-natural, producing a harmonic tension before the cadence. Next the gesture ends abruptly, in contrast to its previous appearance, when it went on to form a new phrase. The bridge's melody is pure sequence: a transposed restatement of the mm. 17–20 melodic material composes mm. 21–24, with only slight variations in mm. 20 and 24.

"Bebop in Pastel"

"Bebop in Pastel" was first recorded on the same session as "Fool's Fancy." Powell also included the theme on a date in 1949 for Blue Note under the title "Bouncing with Bud."[57] "Bebop in Pastel" is a nonblues theme whose form is A-A´-B-A´ with an eight-bar interlude that is not played during the solos. Unlike "Fool's Fancy" and "Bud's Bubble," Powell's "Bebop in Pastel" contains an original progression, and his melodic inventions complement his harmonic explorations. The harmonic rhythm generally moves at the rate of two chords per measure, and the circle-of-fifths paradigm permeates the A section (example 15). However, when a harmonic gesture does not fit into the paradigm, Powell directs the listener's attention right to it. He accentuates the nondiatonic G-flat 7 (m. 2) with the first pause of the melody. The relatively long duration of the dissonant G-flat also helps to emphasize the A-flat 7 chord. In m. 4, Powell tonicizes a G minor 7 (m. 5) but follows in the next measure with a nondiatonic C-sharp diminished chord, apparently to begin shifting back to B-flat.

Again, Powell draws attention to the harmonic move with melody and rhythm. Both the G minor 7 and the C-sharp diminished chord receive four beats each, making a shift in the harmonic rhythm. The two-note motive that ends the second phrase (B-flat and G) in bar 5 is repeated in bar 6, again placed on the downbeat, a move that helps to emphasize the chord. The A section's phrase structure is irregular: a three-bar statement (mm. 1–3) followed by a one-bar unit (m. 4), which serves as a lead-in to a four-bar passage beginning in m. 5—itself consisting of two two-bar sections. (The melodic figure in m. 5 suggests Gillespie's bebop theme "Groovin' High.") The unequal length of the phrases brings an element of unpredictability to the melodic line as a whole.

Instead of restating the melody in the next eight bars, Powell paraphrases its first four measures (9–12), forming an A´ in the theme's schematic organization. The last four measures (13–16) simply restate bars 5–8. In the B section, Powell returns to the relative minor with the slowest harmonic rhythm of the piece: two bars on G minor 7 (mm. 17–18). The G minor tonal area is reinforced by a ii-V7 half-cadence

EXAMPLE 15. "Bebop in Pastel."

in bars 19–20, and then gradually weakened until mm. 23–25, where Powell shifts back into B-flat with a ii–V–I cadence. Although, in general, the bridge lacks a "real" melody, Powell writes sequences that emphasize harmonic tensions: m. 19 (an eleventh), m. 21 (a raised eleventh), m. 22 (a thirteenth), m. 23 (a ninth), and m. 24 (a lowered thirteenth and raised eleventh, both of which occur on beat 1).

After a restatement of the A section, Powell includes an eight-measure interlude, returning to G minor as a temporary tonal area (mm. 33–34). A B-diminished chord (vii°/ii) sets up a brief arrival in C minor (mm. 35–36), which in turn pivots into a prolonged cadential ii–V–I of the tonic B-flat. Three phrases make up the interlude's melodic line. The first two are composed of six beats each, and the third is an irregular nine-beat phrase whose prolonged G in mm. 37–38 emphasizes a melodic tension (a ninth) created with the root of the F7 chord. The final two measures of the section (mm. 39–40) provide a space for the solo break. The overall character of the interlude—especially its gospel-like harmonic progression[58]—seems to anticipate many such passages found in hard bop compositions of the 1950s and early 1960s.

"Webb City"

"Webb City" first appeared on a September 6, 1946, date with a group called Fats Navarro / Gil Fuller's Modernists. (Fuller is listed as the arranger of the session.) The combo included Kenny Dorham (trumpet), Sonny Stitt (alto saxophone), Morris Lane (tenor sax), Eddie DeVerteuil (baritone saxophone), Bud Powell (piano), Al Hall (bass), and Kenny Clarke (drums). The tune presents yet another exploration of rhythm changes. "Webb City"'s harmonic structure is based on two models: an A section built on rhythm changes and a B section that uses Gershwin's "Oh, Lady Be Good" as its basis (example 16). In the first three bars of the A section, Powell emphasizes the relationship of the melody to the root movement in the bass. After the pickup figure, the B-flat in the bass sounds with the melody's C-sharp, creating an accented lower neighbor tone that also makes a minor sonority; it clashes with the B-flat major tonality of the opening chord. The pitches function as "blue notes" that add a blues feel to passage. (The opening melodic gesture of the bridge in m. 17 achieves the same effect.) Powell continues that ascending gesture in parallel tenths until mm. 4–8, where he moves the two "parts" in contrary motion.

Again, Powell uses the B section for melodic and harmonic contrast,

EXAMPLE 16. "Webb City."

but not without hints of unity with previous sections. The most decisive change that takes place is a stable chord for two whole measures. At the beginning of each previous section, the harmony is changing at the half-note level. The original pickup lick becomes the opening motive of a rifflike sequence (mm. 17–19) that ends with a melodic fragment in m. 20. The entire four-bar phrase stresses melodic tensions over the E-flat 7, B-flat 7, and G7 (sharp-5) chords. Measures 21–24 form an antecedent/consequent unit; the consequent begins as a melodic sequence with the antecedent. Harmonic tensions usually arpeggiate, and each of these phrases concludes with the descending interval characteristic of many bebop pieces. In fact, Powell makes extensive use of descending-scale passages in his compositional style, as is evidenced in this piece (and in the others). In general, the melodic rhetoric of "Webb City" shows Powell fully engaged with the affirmation/againstness model present in earlier works. One salient example is found in the way the tune's A sections trade heavily on an alternation of measures with and without downbeat notes. For example, mm. 2, 4, 6, and 8 all lack a note on the downbeat, while odd-numbered measures contain notes on their downbeats.

Throughout "Webb City," Powell blends convention with his individuality. In fact, that holds true of all four of the compositions discussed here. Each one confirms Feather's notion that bebop themes and solos share important qualities. Moreover, Powell's compositions show an extremely orderly and disciplined musical mind at work— one capable of deftly balancing predictability and surprise. Powell developed ways to elaborate on standard harmonic progressions without making the harmonic structure unrecognizable to his audience. His pieces show that a mature bebop compositional style existed by 1946.

Over the course of several performances in Powell's oeuvre, we can hear him exploring the musical assemblage muse, achieving Ellison's eloquent expression of idea-emotions through technical mastery to great advantage. On a Blue Note session recorded in August 1953, we hear a representative span of this expression. The piece "Collard Greens and Black-Eyed Peas" (also known as "Blues in the Closet" and written by Oscar Pettiford), a medium-tempo twelve-bar blues, provides an example of how Powell handled this ubiquitous form. The theme is a sing-songy melody, repeated three times over each four-bar section of the form. Powell's penchant for compressing as much sonic information as possible into the soundscape is clearly present. After sounding each line, he dashes off fast scales or other ditty-full passages that crowd the theme's space, creating a bit of a claustrophobic atmosphere. As the melody entwines through the Latin rhythm, the overall result is a piece that invites dance even as it rescinds this invitation and demands that we just listen. After the head is played, the rhythmic organization switches effortlessly to straight swing during the solos, placing the piece under hard bop's stylistic umbrella. Two choruses of exquisite Powellian solo work follow: precise melodic statements set squarely in the idiom. The bassist then plays two choruses of solos against Powell's incessant arrangement of syncopated chords, rich with harmonic complexity. He is clearly not trying to stay completely "outta the way" here. The following chorus seems like a shout section as the drummer switches back to the Latin rhythm and Powell plays a strong, repetitive rhythmic figure that gains momentum until the return of the melody.

Powell's "Glass Enclosure," recorded in the same session as "Collard Greens," could not be more different. According to Alfred Lion, producer of the August 1953 session, the unpredictable Powell was at the time of this piece's creation "a little bit under house arrest."[59] During an extended gig at Birdland, Powell was supplied an apartment and other things he needed by Oscar Goodstein, who was at that time the manager of the spot. The arrangement assured the fulfillment of his performance contract by supplying some day-to-day needs. The doors locked, Powell was left to his own creative devices with a piano. Lion borrowed the key and visited him one day. After hearing the new piece, he asked Powell its title. "Glass Enclosure," Powell said after looking around his locked apartment.

The composition itself lasts under three minutes and is composed of four distinct sections, each only suggestive of larger possible developments or movements. The first is a fanfare alternating between single-line phrases and full chords in a robust march tempo. The harmonic language of section 1 combines diatonic with bitonal gestures, the latter of which are allowed to languish unresolved. The swinging section 2 moves between scalar gestures that emphasize I-to-IV harmonic patterns suggestive of a minor blues and chromatic sequences that tumble downward. In section 3, a duet with piano and arco double bass, Powell pounds away at a repetitive gesture reminiscent of the march but with different phrasing. It is also laden with chromatic chord passages forceful in their drive toward an implied tonal center of C, which, when it finally arrives, sounds as a C9-flat 13, a sonorous bebop signature. Section 4 restates the opening of the piece, framing this miniature flight with a unifying gesture.

One should also mention here "Dusk 'n' Sandy," another of Powell's compositions steeped in his love of western art music. Written for solo piano, its most striking quality is its rich use of bitonality, an approach reminiscent of "Glass Enclosure" but even more pronounced. A gentle and ethereal piece, it moves through time unevenly, as if in deep contemplation. "Dusk 'n' Sandy" is in A-A-B-A form, with an eight-bar bridge section that, as in many of Powell's other compositions, is organized around parallel sequences of circle-of-fifths gestures.

The scope of Powell's aesthetic reach is apparent in these last three examples. One is a blues piece so simple that two musicians could claim authorship in typical oral-culture, jam-session fashion. The two other pieces, one a compressed suite, the other a solo piano work, seem to express Powell's potential to write larger, grander compositions as Duke Ellington did, though in his own voice. Taken together, they point to the restless nature and many facets of Powell's muse.

When working in the typical bebop ensemble of the day—two horns and a rhythm section—his experimental muse does not fade. Two cases in point: "Dance of the Infidels" and "Bouncing with Bud," both recorded on Blue Note in August 1949 and featuring Powell, Roy Haynes (drums), Tommy Potter (bass), Fats Navarro (trumpet), and Sonny Rollins (tenor saxophone). "Dance of the Infidels" opens with Navarro and Rollins in an unaccompanied horn fanfare: two tidy two-bar phrases written mostly in parallel thirds and garnished with nonharmonic tones. A four-bar piano interlude with a repeating motif on top of a circle-of-fifths harmonic structure concludes the introduction. The unison theme emphasizes nonharmonic tones within the graceful yet uneven phrases that dance through a cycle of ii–V harmonies. Cast in an unusual fourteen bars, the theme (sounded twice) ends with three identical dyads that almost stall the forward motion of the theme because they constitute its only repetition. The remainder of the tune features quintessential bebop solos.

"Bouncing with Bud" is in A-A'-B-A-C, the second A section featuring a slight variation on the unison melody. The bridge has Powell soloing through a circle-of-fifths pattern emphasizing alterations of chords in the classic bebop style of his contemporaries. The eight-bar C section, which operates as an interlude into the solos, is composed of two ii–V–I passages with a cadential set-up featuring a Powell cadenza. Taken together, these pieces show how the pianist took the standard bebop formula of the moment and twisted it into individualized statements, tweaking here and there at the edges of convention.

Powell's most famous composition, "Un Poco Loco," shows yet another side of the pianist's aesthetic. Recorded on a Blue Note session from May 1951, it features Curley Russell (bass) and Max Roach (drums). The rhythm of the piece is a fast Latin beat, similar to that of Gillespie's "A Night in Tunisia" but quicker and more "in your face." Powell's opening chords, played in sync with Roach, are syncopated and rich with harmonic extensions that no doubt made the song sound thoroughly modern to contemporary listeners. The fact that he plunges head-first into this gesture makes the entrance startling and uncompromising. Together with an unstable harmonic environment created by the lack of a clear cadence to the Cmaj7b9(#11), the presumed tonic is itself so decorated with harmonic tensions that it never quite sounds like "home." The bridge features a string of ii–V–I harmonies (beginning on Fm7) that promise tonal stability with a Dm11 to G+(#11) gesture in the last measure. Our expectation for a C tonic is ultimately frustrated by the abrupt and insistent-sounding of a Ebmaj7(#11). The grounding of the stable Latin beat and the unsettling harmonic language of the piece make for a delicious tension. It is not until Powell's solo, a repetitive *montuno* section, that the groove and harmonic environment sync up. Indeed, before the solo, the Powellian againstness approach is in robust full effect.

In his compositions, Powell relished augmenting the standard A-A-B-A popular song form with a C section, an interlude that leads us into the solos. In "Un Poco Loco," the interlude provides a directed landing in the *montuno* with its strong, syncopated chords that harmonically insist that tonic C is the destination. His composition "Celia," named for his daughter, also has a C section that concludes with a two-bar cadenza, a marvel of compression. It is a stunning flourish primarily because the run is packed with sixteenth notes, a double-time passage in the context of a relaxed, elegant theme that moves steadily along, predominantly in easy eighth-note and triplet figures. Even in the lightning-fast "Tempus Fugue-It," Powell crams in a four-bar interlude before launching into what surely should be considered one of his greatest recorded solos: sure-footed, rhetorically rich, and setting an incredibly high standard for subsequent bebop pianists.

Bud Powell's musical avant-garde was a mosaic of sonic and ideological shards taken from blues culture, jam session aesthetics, and inventive juxtapositions of Afrological and Eurological sensibilities—all embedded in the formal conventions (and mercenary priorities) of American popular music. For several reasons, the notion of "assemblage" (an idea borrowed from the world of visual arts) works well as an analogue to encapsulate my understanding of his music. *Assemblage* has been defined in the broadest sense by one of its chief theorists as "the fitting together of parts and pieces," a "juxtaposition of at least two different materials" that have been "discarded or purloined."[60] At first blush, this definition—and my use of it here—is reminiscent of other well-known theories of African American expressive culture such as creolization, hybridity, bricolage, and even Olly Wilson's famous formulation "the heterogeneous ideal." All these have been used in various ways to theorize African American cultural practices from its narratives of origin and processes of acculturation to various theories of interpretation grounded in African legacies or through the lens of postmodernism's irreverence toward established social categories.

I am making, however, a more specific alliance between Powell's bebop and another art praxis, albeit a visual one. Powell's "fitting together of parts and pieces" and combination of heterogeneous sonic materials and sensibilities made a compelling artistic statement, not by obliterating the sources of the things used (an action that distinguishes the assembler in art, for example, from the sculptor), but by allowing them to be recognized by the competent listener. The "communal-folk" continuities of the blues are juxtaposed to the highly individualized promotion of "self" from the virtuosic battles of jam-session cutting contests; popular song forms—analogous to found objects in visual assemblage—are repurposed and adorned with the technical extravagances of western art music; and traces of African-derived practices and attitudes become fodder not for ritual in its strictest sense, but as a fresh commodity for the marketplace. To this last point, bebop did not obscure the fact that it was connected to mass culture in its dependence on popular song form for some of its aesthetic logic.[61] But it insisted at the same time that "the everyday" should not be limited to narrow, predictable patterns of creation and consumption.

And yet "Experiment-bebop" was indelibly linked to numerous social, literary, and creative realignments, including the awakening of African Americans' sociopolitical standing; evolving critical discourses surrounding jazz; shifts in the gendered and racial dimensions of artistic practice; and the codification and dispersal of a new modern jazz language. Indeed, Langston Hughes's fictional Jesse B. Semple's glib assertion that bebop had been "beaten right out of some Negro's head" must certainly be considered a satirical understatement. Bebop's sonic and social logic was assembled from the entire fabric of its time. And Powell's personalized expression of it radiated all the traces of this historic, social, artistic, personal, and ideological complex. It was, quite simply, a poetic and potent force.

Cultural Validation and Requiem for a Heavyweight

When Bud Powell made his first performing tour to Europe, in 1956, he had been a well-established modernist figure for a decade. As rock 'n' roll and rhythm and blues, two new related styles of pop dance music, threatened to overtake jazz's economic clout, Powell continued to eke out a living in what was supposed to have been the prime of his life. He was fighting many personal and professional battles. In June, he had lost his brother Richie Powell in a tragic car accident that also claimed the life of trumpeter supreme Clifford Brown. A couple of months earlier, he had been named in a paternity suit by Buttercup Edwards, his common-law wife. And a year earlier—in March 1955—Powell had managed to become part of the unfortunate side of bebop lore when he and Charlie Parker, both reportedly drunk, clashed onstage during an engagement. Powell abruptly left, and a little over a week later, Parker died. And, to make matters worse, the checkered quality of Powell's performances, his emotional state, demeanor, and physical decline drew all the wrong kinds of press attention for someone who needed to be considered stable enough to be hired.[1]

But he was still known as one of modern jazz's founders, and therefore he could be counted on to draw audiences overseas. As such, he was included in the European 1956 Birdland tour (he would return to Paris in November 1957 for another engagement). Reports confirm that Powell both thrilled and alarmed audiences abroad, becoming something of a spectacle as his work and comportment were, at best, unpredictable. Writers could not help but respond with dramatic prose that telescoped interpretations of his music with knowledge of his health struggles and personal, offstage idiosyncrasies.

All was fair game in public discussions of the pianist: his medical condition, treatments, weight, dress, walk, stare, and drinking habits. Every private matter became a pivot for discussions of his music, and therefore his personal life was used as a lens for trying to understand his work. Powell himself continued his movement among familiar institutions: nightclubs, recording sessions, and mental hospitals. It's no wonder that he and Buttercup, with whom he had apparently settled legal differences, decided to move to Paris, no doubt with hopes of escaping the difficult business of jazz in late 1950s New York.

Paris, of course, was by the time of Powell's tours and eventual expatriation synonymous with a particular view of jazz as a serious art. If New York was the music's creative hothouse, a symbol of its gritty urbanity, modernity, and commercial industry, then Paris (and Europe as a whole) represented Jazz-Art's connection to an Old World pedigree of artistic authenticity. For musicians in Paris, the story goes, New York's commercial and racial grinds receded, unnecessary distractions from the exalted cultural work of jazz. Although Powell ultimately could not escape the ravages of his alcoholism and mental heath challenges, he would gain from his four-year sojourn in the City of Lights. He became close friends with his champion and devoted caretaker, the graphic artist Francis Paudras. And his reputation as the consummate "artist" (both during his life and posthumously) would be greatly enhanced by his Parisian address, limited French vocabulary, and fondness for French pastries, as well as a list of European musical exploits filling out his résumé.

BLUE PARIS

A number of factors prepared the way for Powell's Parisian adventures. When Dizzy Gillespie had taken live modern jazz to France in February 1948, one writer declared that the music had triumphed in Paris. It soon became the music favored by the postwar existentialists who populated the cafés of Saint-Germain-des-Prés, the post–World War II center of the Parisian left and home to many jazz clubs. Although swing and Dixieland jazz could still be heard in the city, bebop became associated with a bohemian arts scene that included scores of African American writers and visual artists during the 1940s and 1950s. Gone were the days of France's primitivist engagements with African and African American cultures. Many of the African American visual artists who had gone to Paris were abstractionists. They found it easy to study there but difficult to get galleries to show their work because it appeared devoid of the political content expected of black artists. It just seemed like "American" modernism. On the other hand, and quite interestingly, bebop abstractions, according to Tyler Stovall, were perfectly suited to the mood of postwar existentialists.[2]

How far bebop had come: from the days when the press had described it as a subterranean "cult" of drugs and subversive extravagance to its arrival as an art formation that played a role in international conversations about modernism. Both the hipster image cultivated from within and without bebop's inner circle and the U.S. government's fraught Jazz Ambassadors initiative (designed to make American culture a global export) worked hard to shape overseas impressions about American culture. With a community of expatriate jazz musicians living and working successfully there (including bebop drummer Kenny Clarke) and France's history of serious critical jazz writing, Paris seemed designed for Powell to make a successful go of it. In other words, the stage was set for him to complete another component of his "cultural validation": He was becoming an international artist.

Between December 1959 and the summer of 1964, Powell recorded in various settings, and this body of work affirms his herculean push for artistic viability. He recorded with a mix of American and European musicians in varied settings: the studio, club dates, jam sessions, music festivals, and Paudras's home. He performed in Paris, Stockholm, Edenville, Copenhagen, and Belgium—an impressive itinerary given his serious health struggles, which would have sidelined a weaker soul. But Powell's will to play his music was legendary. The relative quality of some of the records (mostly bebop chestnuts), as I've already pointed out, was grist for the mill for reviewers and other observers. Powell seemed to embody the spiritual essence of bebop experimentation, a language and artistic stance that true fans wanted to remain a vital part of a jazz scene that was being changed by new stylistic idioms subsumed under the label "jazz" (not to mention rock 'n' roll). Everyone— fans, writers, and musicians—would have been thrilled to see a glimpse of Powell's earlier killer virtuosity, and they cringed when he couldn't deliver it.

The years he spent in Paris are the basis for Francis Paudras's testimony-as-book, *Dance of the Infidels*. It, and the feature film *'Round Midnight*, based loosely on the book, riffs off both the details of Powell's life and the larger symbolism of a gifted black jazz musician abroad. As film historian and jazz scholar Krin Gabbard has argued, *'Round Midnight* turns on reliable stereotypes of the self-destructive jazz musician, the idea that European audiences had better insight into jazz's aesthetic values than Americans did, and, of course, the ubiquitous, empathetic white gaze.[3]

A film from Powell's Paris period ratchets Gabbard's concept up a notch or two. The intriguing *Stopforbud* (1962) is a twelve-minute, independently produced, and highly experimental short by Jørgen Leth. The black-and-white film—Leth's first—features Powell as a curious, silent figure, mostly lumbering through Copenhagen and playing the piano in a trio setting in a shadow-filled room. More poetic meditation on its subject than developed narrative, the film's cinematography seems to invite both Powell's objectification and his celebration.[4]

The film opens with the camera trained on Powell's stylish shoes and slowly pans up his suited body, stopping with a view upward from shoulder height. A male narrator, Dexter Gordon, interjects: "This is Bud Powell—the Amazing Bud Powell. Pianist. Composer. Innovator." Powell, placed against a white screen for contrast, avoids the camera's gaze and peers upward. Together with the narration, the visual set-up—the white background, the avoidance of the camera, the didactic narration—makes Powell seem to be some kind of specimen, albeit an exceptional one. In the next scenes, he's dressed in a dark suit, an overcoat, and a black beret, with a cigarette for accent. Powell makes quite a study as he moves almost rhythmically through various locations. His taciturn facial expression and blank stare keep his inner thoughts a mystery, although the deliberate ballad underscoring most of the film tips the scale toward a despairing mood.

In the performance sequence of the film, camera angles accentuate the beautiful, liquid movement of Powell's hands over the keyboard. Dexter Gordon adds disjointed thoughts at one point, speaking of Powell's large left hand, George Shearing's comparative earnings, and his own memories of meeting Bud in 1940s New York. The final scene shows Powell walking slowly behind what looks like a metallic wall; this is immediately followed by a shot of a white male appearing from behind the wall, walking in the opposite direction while shaking condensation out of a tenor saxophone. One cannot help but conflate this treatment with Leth's best-known film, *The Perfect Human* (1967), another black-and-white short with narration and music, this time using a man and woman as its subjects, both under the same art-school aesthetic of "examination."

In spite of his hopes for a Parisian salvation, Powell struggled in Europe. His problems are well documented: the serious hospitalizations, his valiant bout with tuberculosis (which required long-term care), and his relentless battle with alcoholism. Mounting debt inspired two benefit concerts (one in New York and one in Paris) to defray the costs of his health care and rehabilitations. As his relationship with Buttercup apparently deteriorated, Powell moved in with Paudras and his young family. Together they plotted yet another comeback, and Oscar Goodstein extended his fateful invitation for a residency at Birdland. Powell could, in theory at least, return musically victorious, put his U.S. career back on track, and earn enough money to pay off some debts.

Bud Powell never gave up hope that his amazing art would make a way for him.

And his audience, in turn, was always thrilled to be amazed by him.

Notes

INTRODUCTION

1. Quotations from "Dizzy and Local 802 to Bury Bud Powell," *New York Amsterdam News*, August 6, 1966: 3. The narrative of Bud Powell's return to New York and the events leading up to his death and burial has been constructed from the following sources: "Bud Powell to Return to Birdland," *New York Amsterdam News*, August 1, 1964: 46; "Bud Powell: Condition Improved," *New York Amsterdam News*, July 24, 1965: 27; "Bud Powell: Still Listed as Critical," *New York Amsterdam News*, July 17, 1965: 27; "Bud's in Bloom," *New York Amsterdam News*, August 14, 1965: 25; George Todd, "Bud Welcomed Home by Daughter, Friends," *New York Amsterdam News*, August 21, 1965: 1A; Simon Anekwe, "Bud Powell Plays Final Performance," *New York Amsterdam News*, August 13, 1966: 1; "Young Praises Community for Bud's Funeral," *New York Amsterdam News*, August 20, 1966: 6; and Francis Paudras, *Dance of the Infidels: A Portrait of Bud Powell* (New York: Da Capo Press, 1986).

2. "Bud's O.K.," *Time* (September 4, 1964): 84.

3. Paudras, *Dance of the Infidels*, 235.

4. Ibid., 23.

5. Todd, "Bud Welcomed Home," *New York Amsterdam News*, 1A.

6. Paudras, *Dance of the Infidels*, 347.

7. "Requiescat in Pace: Bud Powell—1924–66," *Down Beat* (September 8, 1966): 13.

8. David Brackett, "(In Search of) Musical Meaning: Genres, Categories, and Crossover," in *Popular Music Studies: International Perspectives*, David Hesmondhalgh and Keith Negus, eds. (London: Arnold, 2002), 67.

9. My discussion of genre in this introduction is based on the work of Jeffery Kallberg, *Chopin at the Boundaries: Sex, History, and Musical Genre*

(Cambridge, MA: Harvard University Press, 1996), 3–29; David Brackett, "Questions of Genre in Black Popular Music," *Black Music Research Journal* 25 (2005): 73–92; Allan F. Moore, "Categorical Conventions in Music Discourse: Style and Genre," *Music and Letters* 82 (2001): 432–42; and Franco Fabbri, "A Theory of Musical Genres: Two Applications," in *Popular Music Perspectives*, David Horn and Philip Tagg, eds. (Göteborg and Exeter: International Association for the Study of Popular Music, 1981), 52–81.

10. Eric Porter, *What Is This Thing Called Jazz?: African American Musicians as Artists, Critics, and Activists* (Berkeley: University of California Press, 2002), 57.

11. See Moore, "Categorical Conventions in Music Discourse"; and Fabbri, "A Theory of Musical Genres."

12. Samuel A. Floyd, Jr., *The Power of Black Music: Interpreting Its History from Africa to the United States* (New York: Oxford University Press, 1995).

13. Gunther Schuller, *Early Jazz: Its Roots and Musical Development* (New York: Oxford University Press, [1968] 1986), 3.

14. LeRoi Jones (Amiri Baraka), "Jazz and the White Critic" (1963), in *Black Music* (New York: William Morrow, 1968), 13, 14.

15. Ibid., 20.

16. Bruce Tucker, "Editor's Introduction: Black Music after Theory," *Black Music Research Journal* 11 (1991): v. Richard Crawford sees Baraka's work (and also that of W. E. B. Dubois, Ralph Ellison, Harold Cruse, and Albert Murray) as belonging to a "literary tradition" of writings about black music. These writers treat black music, Crawford writes, "as a reflection of [the] Afro-American experience." Richard Crawford, "On Two Traditions of Black Music Research," *Black Music Research Journal* (1986): 1–9. What unifies their work is that their approach to black music lies "outside the realm of formal music scholarship" (5).

17. Ralph Ellison, *"Blues People,"* in *Shadow and Act* (New York: Vintage, 1964), 257.

1. "CULLUD BOYS WITH BEARDS"

1. Celia Powell, "Bud Powell, My Father: I Miss You," *The Complete Bud Powell on Verve*, 314–521–669–2, 1994, liner notes, 92.

2. Eric Lott, "Double V, Double-Time: Bebop's Politics of Style," *Callaloo*, no. 36 (July 1, 1988): 599.

3. See Joseph Kerman, "How We Got into Analysis, and How to Get Out," *Critical Inquiry* 7 (1980): 313; and Janet Wolff, "The Ideology of Autonomous Art," foreword to *Music and Society: The Politics of Composition, Performance and Reception*, Richard Leppert and Susan McClary, eds. (Cambridge: Cambridge University Press, 1987), 1–2.

4. Frank Tirro, *Jazz: A History*, 2nd ed. (New York: W. W. Norton, 1993), 287; Cornel West, *Prophetic Fragments: Illuminations of the Crisis in American Religion and Culture* (Grand Rapids, MI: Eerdmans, 1988), 178; Nelson George, *The Death of Rhythm and Blues* (New York: Pantheon, 1988),

25; William W. Austin, *Music in the 20th Century: From Debussy through Stravinsky* (New York: W. W. Norton, 1966), 291; and Wilfred Mellers, *Music in a New Found Land: Two Hundred Years of American Music* (New York: Oxford University Press, 1987), 339.

5. Martin Williams, *The Jazz Tradition,* new rev. ed. (New York: Mentor, [1970] 1983), 140.

6. Ibid., 152; see also Scott DeVeaux, "The Emergence of the Jazz Concert, 1935–1945," *American Music* 7 (1989): 24–25.

7. Williams, *The Jazz Tradition,* 7.

8. Raymond Williams, *Keywords: A Vocabulary of Culture and Society,* rev. ed. (New York: Oxford University Press, [1976] 1983), 112–13.

9. Gilbert McKean, "The Diz and the Bebop," *Esquire* (October 1947): 121. Nat Shapiro and Nat Hentoff, *Hear Me Talkin' to Ya* (New York: Dover, [1955] 1966), note that while Dizzy Gillespie was closely identified with the bebop look, Mary Lou Williams stated that Thelonious Monk actually started the trend (350).

10. Bruce M. Tyler, "Black Jive and White Repression," *Journal of Ethnic Studies* 16 (1989): 32.

11. Ibid., 31.

12. Robin D. G. Kelley, "Malcolm X," in *Malcolm X: In Our Own Image,* Joe Wood, ed. (New York: St. Martin's Press, 1992), 156.

13. Miles Davis with Quincy Troupe, *Miles: The Autobiography* (New York: Touchstone, 1989), 111.

14. Kelley, "Malcolm X," 160.

15. Quoted in George Lipsitz, *Class and Culture in Cold War America* (New York: Praeger, 1981), 189.

16. Judith Becker, "Is Western Art Music Superior?," *Musical Quarterly* 72, no. 3 (January 1, 1986): 342.

17. Susan McClary, "Terminal Prestige: The Case of Avant-Garde Music Composition," *Cultural Critique* 12 (April 1, 1989): 60.

18. Richard Crawford, *The American Musical Landscape* (Berkeley: University of California Press, 1993), 41.

19. Dizzy Gillespie and Al Fraser, *To Be or Not to Bop: Memoirs of Dizzy Gillespie* (New York: Da Capo Press, 1985), 297.

20. Albert Murray, *Stomping the Blues,* rev. ed. (New York: Da Capo Press, 1989), 164–65.

21. Samuel A. Floyd, Jr., "Ring Shout! Literary Studies, Historical Studies, and Black Music Inquiry," *Black Music Research Journal* 11, no. 2 (Fall 1991): 278.

22. Quoted in Suzanne McElfresh, "Max Attack," *Down Beat* (November 1993): 18.

23. See, for example, Rose Rosengard Subotnik, "Romantic Music as Post-Kantian Critique: Classicism, Romanticism, and the Concept of the Semiotic Universe," in *Developing Variations: Style and Ideology in Western Music* (Minneapolis: University of Minnesota Press, 1990), 118.

24. William Weber, "Mass Culture and the Reshaping of European Musical Taste, 1770–1870," *International Review of the Aesthetics and Sociology*

of Music 8, no. 1 (June 1, 1977): 6. I thank Robert Walser for bringing this article to my attention.

25. See Roger Lax and Frederick Smith, *The Great Song Thesaurus* (New York: Oxford University Press, 1984), xi–xiii, for an explanation of how the authors determined the "popularity" of a song.

26. Katherine McKittrick, *Demonic Grounds: Black Women and the Cartographies of Struggle* (Minneapolis: University of Minnesota Press, 2006), xi. I thank Kellie Jones for pointing out the usefulness of this work to the present project.

27. Ibid., xiii.

28. Quoted in Shapiro and Hentoff, *Hear Me Talkin' to Ya,* 340–41.

29. Nat Hentoff, *The Jazz Life* (New York: Da Capo Press, [1961] 1975), 195. Hentoff describes the story of "the young insurgents like Monk, Parker and Gillespie . . . carefully planning raids on the established harmonic and rhythmic order" as a "fanciful condensation" (195). He equates it to the same oversimplification that states jazz came up the Mississippi River from New Orleans. LeRoi Jones (Amiri Baraka) echoes this sentiment in *Blues People* (New York: William Morrow, 1963). He calls the story a stereotypical legend that "sounds almost like the beginnings of modern American writing among the emigres of Paris" (197–98). Monk asserted in 1961 that he "was just playing a gig, trying to play music. While I was at Minton's anybody sat in if he could play. . . . I had no particular feeling that anything new was being built" (Hentoff, *The Jazz Life,* 195).

30. DeVeaux, "The Emergence of the Jazz Concert," 11.

31. Ibid. Also see Danny Barker, *A Life in Jazz,* Alyn Shipton, ed. (New York: Oxford University Press, 1986), 113–16.

32. Ralph Ellison, *Shadow and Act* (New York: Vintage, [1953] 1972), 207.

33. Ralph Ellison, *Living with Music: Ralph Ellison's Jazz Writings,* ed. Robert O'Meally (New York: Modern Library, 2001), 61.

34. Samuel Barclay Charters and Leonard Kunstadt, *Jazz: A History of the New York Scene* (New York: Da Capo Press, 1984), 314.

35. Quoted in Shapiro and Hentoff, *Hear Me Talkin' to Ya,* 339.

36. Quoted in ibid., 338.

37. Davis with Troupe, *Miles,* 53.

38. Charters and Kunstadt, *Jazz,* 314.

39. Lott, "Double V, Double-Time," 599.

40. Malcolm X and Alex Haley, *The Autobiography of Malcolm X* (New York: Grove Press, 1964), 74.

41. Quoted in Arnold Shaw, *52nd Street: The Street of Jazz* (New York: Da Capo Press, 1977), 279–80.

42. Quoted in ibid., 263.

43. Davis with Troupe, *Miles,* 53–55.

44. Patrick Burke, *Come in and Hear the Truth: Jazz and Race on 52nd Street* (Chicago: University of Chicago Press, 2008), 3.

45. Ibid., 173–79; Ingrid Monson, "The Problem with White Hipness: Race, Gender, and Cultural Conceptions in Jazz Historical Discourse," *Journal of the American Musicological Society* 48, no. 3 (October 1, 1995):

396–422; and Robin D. G. Kelley, "The Riddle of the Zoot: Malcolm Little and Black Cultural Politics during World War II," in *American Studies: An Anthology,* Janice A. Radway, Kevin Gaines, Barry Shank, and Penny von Eschen, eds. (Hoboken, NJ: John Wiley & Sons, 2009), 281–89. See also Norman Mailer, *The White Negro* (New York: City Lights Books, [1957] 1970).

46. Davis with Troupe, *Miles,* 67.

47. Bernard Gendron, *Between Montmartre and the Mudd Club: Popular Music and the Avant-Garde* (Chicago: University of Chicago Press, 2002), 139.

48. See Amiri Baraka, "Jazz and the White Critic" (1963), in *The LeRoi Jones / Amiri Baraka Reader* (New York: Basic Books, 1999), 179–86; and John Gennari, *Blowin' Hot and Cool: Jazz and Its Critics* (Chicago: University of Chicago Press, 2006).

49. Gendron, *Between Montmartre and the Mudd Club,* 126.

50. Ibid., 125.

51. See Scott DeVeaux, "Constructing the Jazz Tradition: Jazz Historiography," *Black American Literature Forum* 25, no. 3 (October 1, 1991): 525–60.

52. Gendron, *Between Montmartre and the Mudd Club,* 125.

53. Charles Miller, "Bebop and Old Masters," *New Republic* (June 30, 1947): 37.

54. Ibid., 37.

55. Wilder Hobson, "Hits and Misses," *Saturday Review* (March 26, 1949): 32. Hobson was reviewing four sides by a combo he calls the "high priests of bebop." The group, which included Charlie Parker, recorded under the name Metronome All Stars. The tunes included "Victory Ball," "Overtime," "Lover Come Back to Me," and the "Cuban-style" piece "Gurachi Guaro."

56. "Bopera on Broadway," *Time* (December 20, 1948): 64.

57. Quoted in "B. G. and Bebop," *Newsweek* (December 27, 1948): 67.

58. Quoted in Stuart Allen, "What Is Bop? It's the Way I Think and Feel about Jazz," *Melody Maker* (February, 12, 1949): 3.

59. Michael Levin and John S. Wilson, "No Bop Roots in Jazz: Parker," *Down Beat* (September 9, 1949): 1.

60. "Bird Wrong; Bop Must Get a Beat: Diz," *Down Beat* (October 7, 1949): 1. Other significant articles of this period include an insightful essay on Gillespie and the bop movement by Richard O. Boyer, "Profiles (Bop)," *New Yorker* (July 3, 1948): 28–37; and a review of Leonard Feather's *Inside Bebop*: Irving Kolodin, "A Feather in the Cap of Bop," *Saturday Review* (July 30, 1949): 45. Both devote at least part of their articles to a definition of bebop, complete with commentary about the style.

61. Gendron, *Between Montmartre and the Mudd Club,* 155–56.

62. Benjamin Cawthra, *Blue Notes in Black and White: Photography and Jazz* (Chicago: University of Chicago Press, 2011), 10.

63. Ibid., 13.

64. Theodor W. Adorno with the assistance of George Simpson, "On Popular Music" (1941), in *On Record: Rock, Pop, and the Written Word,* Simon Frith and Andrew Goodwin, eds. (New York: Pantheon, 1990), 305.

65. Ibid.

66. Mark C. Gridley, *Jazz Styles: History and Analysis,* 5th ed. (Englewood Cliffs, NJ: Prentice Hall, 1994), 9. Gridley does, however, admit that *some* jazz should be considered popular music "because people use it as party music, film music, and dance music" (10).

67. Ibid., 11.

68. See Scott DeVeaux, *Jazz in America: Who's Listening?* (Washington, DC: Research Division Report / National Endowment for the Arts, 1992).

69. See McClary, "Terminal Prestige," 57–81.

70. Martin Williams, "The Bystander," *Down Beat* (April 9, 1964): 6. Williams designed these remarks as a bold (if problematic) reaction to three works: Sidney Walter Finkelstein, *Jazz: A People's Music* (New York: International Publications, 1951); Francis Newton, *The Jazz Scene* (New York: Penguin Books, 1961); and LeRoi Jones, *Blues People,* books with strong Marxist underpinnings that all possess merits as well as shortcomings.

71. Quoted in Gillespie and Fraser, *To Be or Not to Bop,* 192.

72. Quoted in Shapiro and Hentoff, *Hear Me Talkin' to Ya,* 351.

73. Lawrence Levine, *Highbrow/Lowbrow: The Emergence of Cultural Hierarchy in America* (Cambridge, MA: Harvard University Press, 1988), 86.

74. Martin Williams, "Jazz Composition: What Is It?," *Down Beat* (February 15, 1962): 20.

75. DeVeaux, "Constructing the Jazz Tradition," 498. It is important to note here that both Louis Armstrong's improvisational abilities and Duke Ellington's compositions had earlier inspired the idea that jazz was an art music.

76. See Robert Walser, ed., *Keeping Time: Readings in Jazz History* (New York: Oxford University Press, 1999); and Gennari, *Blowin' Hot and Cool.*

77. See Robert O'Meally, Brent Hayes Edwards, and Farah Jasmine Griffin, eds., *Uptown Conversation: The New Jazz Studies* (New York: Columbia University Press, 2004).

78. Scott DeVeaux, *The Birth of Bebop: A Social and Musical History* (Berkeley: University of California Press, 1997); Ingrid Monson, *Saying Something: Jazz Improvisation and Interaction* (Chicago: University of Chicago Press, 1996); Eric Porter, *What Is This Thing Called Jazz? African American Musicians as Artists, Critics, and Activists* (Berkeley: University of California Press, 2002); Gendron, *Between Montmartre and the Mudd Club;* Eddie Meadows, *Bebop to Cool: Context, Ideology, and Musical Identity* (Westport, CT: Greenwood Press, 2003); and Guthrie P. Ramsey, Jr., *Race Music: Black Cultures from Bebop to Hip-Hop,* new ed. (Berkeley: University of California Press, 2003).

79. Kellie Jones, "Lost in Translation: Jean-Michel in the (Re)Mix," in *Basquiat,* Marc Mayer, ed. (London: Brooklyn Museum and Merrell, 2005), 163–79.

80. For a discussion of Marsalis's emergence in jazz discourse, see Porter, *What Is This Thing Called Jazz?,* 287–334. On philanthropy and western art music in America, see Crawford, *The American Musical Landscape.*

81. Gennari, *Blowin' Hot and Cool,* 13.

2. SOMETHING ELSE

1. Arthur T. Davidson, "A History of Harlem Hospital," *Journal of the National Medical Association* 56, no. 5 (September 1964): 373–80.

2. Chad Heap, *Slumming: Sexual and Racial Encounters in American Nightlife, 1885–1940* (Chicago: University of Chicago, 2009), 1. See also Clare Corbould, *Becoming African Americans: Black Public Life in Harlem, 1919–1939* (Cambridge, MA: Harvard University Press, 2009).

3. Eugene Holley, Jr., "The Education of Bud Powell," *Village Voice* (June 28, 1994): SS7. See also Gary Giddins, *The Genius of Bud Powell*, Verve VE-2-2506, 1976, liner notes; and telephone interview with the author, November 9, 1993.

4. Holley, "The Education of Bud Powell."

5. Francis Paudras, *Earl Bud Powell: Early Years of a Genius*, 44–48, Mythic Sound MS 6001–2, 1989, liner notes. Of all who have written about Powell, Paudras was the first to mention Rawlins by name. The first chapter of Peter Pullman's excellent 2012 e-book biography of Powell contains information about Rawlins's pedagogical techniques: Peter Pullman, *Wail: The Life of Bud Powell* (Peter Pullman, LLC, 2012).

6. Jackie McLean, interview with the author, January 27, 1994.

7. See Doris Evans McGinty, ed., *A Documentary History of the National Association of Negro Musicians* (Chicago: Columbia College / Center for Black Music Research, 2004).

8. Sharon A. Pease, "Bud Powell's Unique Style Has Widespread Influence," *Down Beat* (June 15, 1951): 16.

9. Ira Gitler, *Jazz Masters of the Forties* (New York: Da Capo Press, 1982), 112.

10. Giddins, *The Genius of Bud Powell*.

11. Paudras, *Earl Bud Powell*.

12. "Harlem Mourns: Bud Powell Funeral Jazz Requiem," *Newark Evening News* (August 6, 1966): 11; and Requiem Mass Program for Bud Powell, St. Charles Roman Catholic Church, August 8, 1966, Institute of Jazz Studies (IJS), Rutgers University, Vertical File.

13. "Harlem Mourns," 11.

14. Bob Doerschuk, "Bud Powell," *Keyboard* 10 (June 1984): 28.

15. John Chilton, *Who's Who of Jazz: Storyville to Swing Street* (New York: Time-Life Records, 1978).

16. Quoted in Holley, "The Education of Bud Powell," SS7.

17. Pease, "Bud Powell's Unique Style," 16.

18. Ole J. Astrup, "The Forgotten Ones: Billy Kyle," *Jazz Journal International* 37, no. 8 (1984): 10.

19. Holley, "The Education of Bud Powell."

20. Robin D. G. Kelley, *Thelonious Monk: The Life and Times of an American Original* (New York: Free Press, 2009), 79–82.

21. Ibid., xv.

22. Ibid., 14, 22.

23. Ibid., 39.

24. Ibid., xvii.

25. Gitler, *Jazz Masters of the Forties*, 112–13.

26. Ibid., 113.

27. Kelley, *Thelonious Monk*, 81.

28. Quoted in Gitler, *Jazz Masters of the Forties*, 113.

29. Quoted in Ira Gitler, *Swing to Bop: An Oral History of the Transition in Jazz in the 1940s* (New York: Oxford University Press, 1987), 102–03.

30. Chilton, *Who's Who of Jazz*, 309; see also Pullman, *Wail*, chap. 2, for a detailed description of Powell's early professional alliances.

31. Doerschuk, "Bud Powell," 28.

32. Lewis Porter, Michael Ullman, and Edward Hazell, *Jazz: From Its Origins to the Present* (New York: Prentice Hall, 1992), 199–200.

33. Gunther Schuller, *Early Jazz: Its Roots and Musical Development*, new ed. (New York: Oxford University Press, [1968] 1986), 355; and James Lincoln Collier, *The Making of Jazz: A Comprehensive History* (Boston: Houghton Mifflin, 1978), 244. According to Ellington, Williams was "kidded a lot" by his peers for switching to the plunger and growl style: "But he didn't pay them any mind. He caught onto a lot from Tricky Sam [Nanton], and before you knew it everyone was saying nobody could work with a plunger like Cootie" (Nat Shapiro and Nat Hentoff, *Hear Me Talkin' to Ya: The Story of Jazz as Told by the Men Who Made It* [Mineola, NY: Dover Publications, 1966], 215).

34. Schuller, *Early Jazz*, 118, n. 39. For writing that seeks to understand the aesthetic value and cultural work of jazz beyond its similarities to western art music, see, for example, Samuel A. Floyd, Jr., *The Power of Black Music: Interpreting Its History from Africa to the United States* (New York: Oxford University Press, 1996); Ingrid Monson, *Saying Something: Jazz Improvisation and Interaction* (Chicago: University of Chicago Press, 1996); David Ake, *Jazz Cultures* (Berkeley: University of California Press, 2002); and Robert Walser, "Deep Jazz: Notes on Interiority, Race, and Criticism," in *Inventing the Psychological: Toward a Cultural History of Emotional Life in America*, Joel Pfister and Nancy Schnog, eds. (New Haven, CT: Yale University Press, 1997), 271–96.

35. Shapiro and Hentoff, *Hear Me Talkin' to Ya*, 321–22.

36. Cootie Williams, IJS, Rutgers University, Oral History Project interview.

37. Quoted in Stanley Dance, *The World of Swing: An Oral History of Big Band Jazz* (New York: Scribner, 1974), 255–56.

38. Quoted in Vern Montgomery, "Jaws Unlocks," *Jazz Journal International* 36 (July 1983): 14.

39. Williams, IJS Oral History interview.

40. See Montgomery, "Jaws Unlocks," 14; and Bob Rusch, "Eddie Lockjaw Davis," *Cadence* (January 1988): 13.

41. David Stowe, *Swing Changes: Big-Band Jazz in New Deal America* (Cambridge, MA: Harvard University Press, 1994), 17–49.

42. Langston Hughes, *Montage of a Dream Deferred* (New York: Holt, 1951).

43. Guthrie P. Ramsey, Jr., *Race Music: Black Cultures From Bebop to Hip-Hop* (Berkeley: University of California Press, 2003), 96–130.

44. Quoted in Eileen Southern, *The Music of Black Americans: A History,* 2nd ed. (New York: W. W. Norton, 1983), 477.

45. Eric Lott, "Double V, Double-Time: Bebop's Politics of Style," *Callaloo* 36 (1988): 598.

46. Leonard Feather, *Inside Jazz* (originally published as *Inside Bebop*) (New York: Da Capo Press, [1949] 1977), 8.

47. See Elaine Hayes, "To Bebop or to Be Pop: Sarah Vaughan and the Politics of Crossover," PhD diss., University of Pennsylvania, 2004.

48. Ralph Ellison, *Invisible Man,* 2nd ed. (New York: Vintage, [1952] 1981).

49. Arnold Shaw, *52nd Street: The Street of Jazz* (New York: Da Capo Press, 1977), 257.

50. Hentoff and Shapiro, *Hear Me Talkin' to Ya,* 367; and Gitler, *Swing to Bop,* 123.

51. Shaw, *52nd Street,* 270.

52. Quoted in ibid., 173.

53. See Shaw, *52nd Street,* 259–60, for Gillespie's description of a racial confrontation from that time. For Miles Davis's account of police brutality, see Miles Davis and Quincy Troupe, *Miles: The Autobiography* (New York: Simon & Schuster, 1989), 238–40.

54. Roach quoted in Scott DeVeaux, "Bebop and the Recording Industry: The 1942 AFM Recording Ban Reconsidered," *Journal of the American Musicological Society* 41, no. 1 (April 1, 1988): 156; see also Feather, *Inside Jazz,* 29.

55. *Charlie Parker: The Complete Savoy Studio Sessions,* Savoy S5J-5500, 1988.

56. DeVeaux, "Bebop and the Recording Industry," 157–58.

57. Ibid., 159, n. 83.

58. Williams, IJS Oral History Project interview.

59. Ibid.; and Allan Morrison, "Can a Musician Return from the Brink of Insanity?," *Ebony* (August 1953): 71.

60. Morrison, "Can a Musician Return?," 71.

61. Quoted in Shaw, *52nd Street,* 271–72.

62. Dizzy Gillespie and Al Fraser, *To Be or Not to Bop: Memoirs of Dizzy Gillespie* (New York: Da Capo Press, 1985), 222. See also Samuel Charters and Leonard Kunstadt, *Jazz: A History of the New York Scene* (Garden City, NY: Doubleday, 1962), 324.

63. Quoted in Gillespie and Fraser, *To Be or Not to Bop,* 224–25.

64. Ibid., 231.

65. Quoted in ibid., 236.

66. Quoted in ibid., 237.

67. Shaw, *52nd Street,* 271.

68. Gillespie and Fraser, *To Be or Not to Bop,* 237–38.

69. Quoted in James Patrick, *Charlie Parker: The Complete Savoy Studio Sessions,* S5J-5500, liner notes, 1988. Patrick's accounts are drawn from the Savoy archives, Teddy Reig's recollections, and the musical evidence on the recordings.

70. Quoted in ibid. Also see Teddy Reig and Edward Berger, *Reminiscing in Tempo: The Life and Times of a Jazz Hustler* (Metuchen, NJ: Scarecrow Press and Institute of Jazz Studies, 1990).

71. Patrick, *Charlie Parker.*

72. Ross Russell, *Bird Lives!: The High Life and Hard Times of Charlie (Yardbird) Parker* (New York: Da Capo Press, 1996), 195–97.

73. Ibid., 195. Russell states that Monk was the intended pianist. Miles Davis could not recall whether it was Monk or Powell who "couldn't or wouldn't make it." Davis with Troupe, *Miles,* 75.

74. Ross Russell, *The Chase,* Dexter Gordon and Wardell Gray, Arista Records SJL 2222, liner notes, 1977.

75. Scott DeVeaux, "Jazz in Transition: Coleman Hawkins and Howard McGhee, 1935–1945," Ph.D. diss., University of California at Berkeley, 1985, 292–349. See also Scott DeVeaux and Howard McGhee, "Conversation with Howard McGhee: Jazz in the Forties," *Black Perspective in Music* 15 (Spring 1987): 69–71; and Gioia, *West Coast Jazz,* 10–15.

76. Gitler, *Swing to Bop,* 160.

77. Gillespie and Fraser, *To Be or Not to Bop,* 250.

78. Ibid., 243.

79. Quoted in ibid.

80. Ibid., 250.

81. "Dizzy's Combo Comes Back to New York," *Down Beat* (January 28, 1946): 1.

82. Gillespie and Fraser, *To Be or Not to Bop,* 251.

83. Advertisement, *Down Beat* (February 11, 1946): 4.

84. Gillespie and Fraser, *To Be or Not to Bop,* 251.

85. Shaw, *52nd Street.* RCA Victor's requirement "brought drummer J.C. Heard and tenor saxophonist Don Byas into a session that produced four bebop recordings: 'Anthropology,' 'Night in Tunisia,' 'Ol' Man Bebop,' and '52d Street Theme'" (273).

86. Quoted in ibid., 276.

87. Shaw, *52nd Street,* 273–76.

88. Gunther Schuller's endpoint in the subtitle of his monumental study *The Swing Era: The Development of Jazz, 1930–1945* (New York: Oxford University Press, 1989), suggests the same periodization of jazz history.

89. See Claude Schlouch, *Once upon a Time: Bud Powell: A Discography* (Marseille: Claude Schlouch, 1983).

90. Howard Rye, "De Luxe," in *The New Grove Dictionary of Jazz,* 2nd ed., Barry Kernfeld, ed., Grove Music Online, Oxford Music Online http://proxy.library.upenn.edu:4680/subscriber/article/grove/music/J118400 (accessed September 3, 2009).

91. Charters and Kunstadt, *Jazz,* 326; and Gillespie and Fraser, *To Be or Not to Bop,* 314.

92. Gilbert S. McKean, "The Diz and the Bebop" (1947), in *Jam Session: An Anthology of Jazz,* Ralph Gleason, ed. (New York: G.P. Putnam's Sons, 1958), 125.

93. Richard Boyer, "Bop," *New Yorker* (July 3, 1948): 28.

94. Myron Swartzman, *Romare Bearden: His Life and Art* (New York: H.N. Abrams, 1990), 78–82.

95. Romare Bearden, *Riffs and Takes: Music in the Art of Romare Bearden* (Raleigh: North Carolina Museum of Art, 1988), 1–2.

96. Richard J. Powell, *Homecoming: The Art and Life of William H. Johnson* (Washington, DC: National Museum of American Art, Smithsonian Institution, 1991), 16.

97. Kellie Jones, "Norman Lewis: The Black Paintings," *Norman Lewis, 1909–1979* (Newark: State University of New Jersey, Rutgers, 1985), 2. Exhibit held January 31 to March 7, 1985.

98. Ann Gibson, "Recasting the Canon: Norman Lewis and Jackson Pollock," *Artforum* 22 (1984): 64–70. See also Jones, "Norman Lewis."

99. Henry McBride quoted in Gibson, "Recasting the Canon," 67.

100. Lowery Stokes Sims, *Challenge of the Modern: African-American Artists, 1925–1945* (New York: Studio Museum in Harlem, 2003), 109.

101. Quoted in ibid., 110.

102. See Arnold Rampersad, *The Life of Langston Hughes*, vol. 2, *1941–1967* (New York: Oxford University Press, 1988), 151.

103. Arna Bontemps quoted in ibid., 113.

104. Langston Hughes, *The Best of Simple* (New York: Hill and Wang, 1961), 118.

105. Rampersad, *The Life of Langston Hughes*, vol. 2, 152.

106. Hughes, *Montage of a Dream Deferred*, 3.

107. Rampersad, *The Life of Langston Hughes*, vol. 2, 152, 151.

108. Gwendolyn Brooks, *The Essential Gwendolyn Brooks*, Elizabeth Alexander, ed. (New York: Library of America, 2005), xv.

109. Ibid., xvii.

110. Jonathan M. Metzl, *The Protest Psychosis: How Schizophrenia Became a Black Disease* (Boston: Beacon Press, 2009), 82. See also Morrison, "Can a Musician Return?," 71.

111. Morrison, "Can a Musician Return?," 71.

112. Feather, *Inside Jazz*, 95.

113. Alan Groves and Alyn Shipton, *The Glass Enclosure: The Life of Bud Powell* (Oxford, MS: Bayou Press, 1993), 16.

114. Quoted in ibid., 23.

115. Morrison, "Can a Musician Return?"

116. Ibid., 73.

117. Groves and Shipton, *The Glass Enclosure*, 53.

118. Ibid., 75.

119. For more on the women of jazz musicians, see Robin D.G. Kelley, "The Jazz Wife: Muse and Manager," *New York Times* (July 21, 2002): 21, 24. The article questions the stereotype of jazz musicians as roving womanizers and sheds light on the crucial role that wives played in the financial and personal stability of their family lives. Kelley quotes Maxine Gordon, widow of saxophonist Dexter Gordon, who recalled that during the years that she managed her husband's career, she was considered "pushy, domineering or worse, but dismissed such criticism as part of the job."

120. For an excellent critique, see Ingrid Monson, *Freedom Sounds: Civil Rights Call Out to Jazz and Africa* (New York: Oxford University Press, 2007). Scott DeVeaux, *The Birth of Bebop: A Social and Musical History* (Berkeley: University of California Press, 1999), provides a thorough description of the business of bebop.

121. Celia Powell, telephone interview with the author, April 16, 1994.

122. Carl Smith, *Bouncing with Bud: All the Recordings of Bud Powell* (Brunswick, ME: Biddle, 1997); Schlouch, *Once upon a Time;* and Alyn Shipton, "Recording Chronology," in Groves and Shipton, *The Glass Enclosure,* 117–38. Like most discographies focused on a single subject, Smith's *Bouncing with Bud* provides commentary on specific recordings but focuses mostly on Powell's contributions. Smith's inclusion of the cover art and vinyl labels of Powell recordings highlight how important material culture is to the history of jazz: fans cherished album cover art as an important component of jazz's reception.

123. Schuller, *The Swing Era,* 267.

124. Frank Tirro, *Jazz: A History,* 2nd ed. (New York: W. W. Norton, 1993), 292.

3. NOTES AND TONES

1. Ruth A. Solie, ed., *Musicology and Difference: Gender and Sexuality in Music Scholarship* (Berkeley: University of California Press, 1995), 2.

2. See Ingrid Monson, *Freedom Sounds: Civil Rights Call Out to Jazz and Africa* (New York: Oxford University Press, 2010), 71. See also Guthrie P. Ramsey, Jr., *Race Music: Black Cultures from Bebop to Hip-Hop* (Berkeley: University of California Press, 2004), 96–130.

3. As Sonny Rollins attests, Powell's peers (and those who succeeded him) routinely referred to him as a genius. Interestingly, Thelonious Monk's Blue Note recording of 1947 was titled *Genius of Modern Music,* BLP 5002.

4. See Janet Wolff, "The Ideology of Autonomous Art," foreword in *Music and Society: The Politics of Composition, Performance and Reception,* Richard Leppert and Susan McClary, eds. (Cambridge: Cambridge University Press, 1987), 1–12.

5. See, for example, Peter Kivy IV, *The Possessor and the Possessed: Handel, Mozart, Beethoven, and the Idea of Musical Genius* (New Haven, CT: Yale University Press, 2001).

6. It is interesting to note in this context the jazz musicians who have been granted the MacArthur "genius" Award. Among them are Regina Carter, John Zorn, George Lewis, Max Roach, George Russell, Cecil Taylor, Gunther Schuller, Steve Lacy, Ken Vandermark, Miguel Zenon, and Ornette Coleman. I thank John Meyers for this observation.

7. Paula Higgins, "The Apotheosis of Josquin des Prez and Other Mythologies of Musical Genius," *Journal of the American Musicological Society* 57, no. 3 (December 1, 2004): 443–510; and Roland Barthes and Richard Howard, *Mythologies: The Complete Edition, in a New Translation,* trans. Annette Lavers (New York: Hill and Wang, 1972).

8. One might mention here the Experience Music Project and the Rock and Roll Hall of Fame and Museum, among other institutions.

9. Nicholas Kenyon, "The Careful Construction of a Child Prodigy," *New York Times,* Arts and Leisure section (July 24, 2005): 24.

10. Ibid.

11. Robert Walser, *Running with the Devil: Power, Gender, and Madness in Heavy Metal Music* (Middletown, CT: Wesleyan University Press, 1993), 75.

12. Walser, *Running with the Devil,* 76. See also Leon Plantinga, "The Virtuosos," in his *Romantic Music: A History of Musical Style in Nineteenth-Century Europe* (New York: W. W. Norton, 1984), 173–203.

13. Walser, *Running with the Devil,* ibid. See also Gunther Schuller's discussion of various reactions to Art Tatum's technical abilities in *The Swing Era: The Development of Jazz, 1930–1945* (New York: Oxford University Press, 1991), 477–502.

14. Quincy Jones, *Q: The Autobiography of Quincy Jones* (New York: Doubleday, 2001), 284.

15. Robin D. G. Kelley, "Miles Davis: The Chameleon of Cool: A Jazz Genius in the Guise of a Hustler," *New York Times,* Arts & Leisure section (May 13, 2001): 1. See, for example Pearl Cleage, *Mad at Miles: A Black Woman's Guide to Truth* (Atlanta: Cleage Group, 1990).

16. Sharon A. Pease, "Bud Powell's Unique Style Has Widespread Influence," *Down Beat* (June 15, 1951): 16.

17. Alan Groves and Alyn Shipton, *The Glass Enclosure: The Life of Bud Powell* (Oxford, MS: Bayou Press, 1993), 43–44.

18. David Ake, *Jazz Cultures* (Berkeley: University of California Press, 2002), 83.

19. Groves and Shipton, *The Glass Enclosure,* 44.

20. Ibid., 45.

21. Ibid., 47.

22. Francis Paudras, *Dance of the Infidels: A Portrait of Bud Powell* (New York: Da Capo Press, 1986), 19.

23. Groves and Shipton, *The Glass Enclosure,* 41.

24. Robin D. G. Kelley, *Thelonious Monk: The Life and Times of an American Original* (New York: Free Press, 2009), 155–57.

25. Groves and Shipton, *The Glass Enclosure,* 49.

26. Paudras, *Dance of the Infidels,* 14.

27. Ibid., 11.

28. Ibid., x.

29. See Monson, *Freedom Sounds,* 107–51; and George E. Lewis, "Improvised Music after 1950: Afrological and Eurological Perspectives," *Black Music Research Journal* 16, no. 1 (Spring 1996): 93.

30. Lewis, "Improvised Music after 1950," 217.

31. Charles Hamm, *Music in the New World* (New York: W. W. Norton, 1983), 655.

32. Samuel A. Floyd, Jr., *The Power of Black Music: Interpreting Its History from Africa to the United States* (New York: Oxford University Press,

1995); and Ronald M. Radano, *Lying Up a Nation: Race and Black Music* (Chicago: University of Chicago Press, 2003).

33. Floyd, *The Power of Black Music*, 5.

34. See, for example, Melville Herskovits, *The Myth of the Negro Past* (New York: Beacon Press, 1941). See also Olly Wilson, "The Significance of the Relationship between Afro-American Music and West African Music," *Black Perspective in Music* 2, no. 1 (Spring 1974): 3–22; and Portia Maultsby, "Africanisms in African American Music," in *Africanisms in American Culture,* Joseph E. Holloway, ed. (Bloomington: Indiana University Press, 1990), 185–210.

35. Radano, *Lying Up a Nation,* 10.

36. Ibid., 39, 49.

37. Ibid., 37.

38. James Sidbury, *Becoming African in America: Race and Nation in the Early Black Atlantic* (New York: Oxford University Press, 2007), 6.

39. Ibid., 18, 22–23.

40. Ibid., 7.

41. Gerardo Mosquera, "Eleggúa at the (Post?)Modern Crossroads: The Presence of Africa in the Visual Art of Cuba," in *Santería Aesthetics in Contemporary Latin American Art,* Arturo Lindsay, ed. (Washington, DC, and London: Smithsonian Institution Press, 1996), 226. I thank Kellie Jones for alerting me to this reference.

42. Stuart Hall, "Cultural Identity and Diaspora," in *Diaspora and Visual Culture: Representing Africans and Jews,* Nicholas Mirzoeff, ed. (New York: Routledge, 2000), 23.

43. Ibid., 22.

44. St. Clair Drake, *Black Folk Here and There: An Essay in History and Anthropology,* vol. 1 (Berkeley: University of California Press, 1987), 1.

45. Ibid.

46. James Lincoln Collier, *The Reception of Jazz in America: A New View* (New York: ISAM, 1988), provides an overview of this body of literature.

47. The term *essentialist* is used here to denote the belief that some things (races, in this case) have essences that serve to define them.

48. Henry O. Osgood, *So This Is Jazz* (Boston: Little, Brown, 1926), 11, 10.

49. See Ted Gioia, *The Imperfect Art: Reflections on Jazz and Modern Culture* (New York: Oxford University Press, 1990), 19–49; and John Gennari, "Jazz Criticism: Its Development and Ideologies," *Black American Literature Forum* 25, no. 3 (Autumn 1991): 465–67.

50. Winthrop Sargeant, *Jazz, Hot and Hybrid,* 3rd ed. (New York: Da Capo Press, [1938] 1975), 7.

51. Ibid., 22, 23.

52. Ibid., 211.

53. Frederick Ramsey, Jr., and Charles Edward Smith, *Jazzmen: The Story of Jazz Told in the Lives of the Men Who Created It* (New York: Limelight Editions, [1939] 1985), 9, and its useful literature review by Roger Pryor Dodge, "Consider the Critics."

54. See Herskovits, *The Myth of the Negro Past;* and Gunnar Myrdal, *An American Dilemma: The Negro Problem and Modern Democracy* (New York: Harper & Row, [1942] 1962).

55. Rudi Blesh, *Shining Trumpets: A History of Jazz,* 2nd ed. (New York: Da Capo Press, [1946] 1958).

56. Ibid., ix–x.

57. Ibid., 25, 3.

58. Ibid., 4.

59. Ibid., 5.

60. Ibid., 25.

61. Ibid., 48; emphasis original.

62. Sidney Finkelstein, *Jazz: A People's Music* (New York: Citadel Press, 1948), 13.

63. Barry Ulanov, *A History of Jazz in America* (New York: Viking Press, 1952), ix.

64. Ibid., 9.

65. Ibid., 12–13.

66. Ibid., 7.

67. Gennari, "Jazz Criticism," 478–80. See also Jeremy Yudkin, *The Lenox School of Jazz: A Vital Chapter in the History of American Music and Race Relations* (South Egremont, MA: Farshaw, 2006).

68. Alan Morrison, "Can a Musician Return from the Brink of Insanity?," *Ebony* (August 1953): 72.

69. Quoted in Paudras, *Dance of the Infidels,* 4.

70. Quoted in ibid., 3.

71. Ellen Dwyer, "Psychiatry and Race during World War II," *Journal of the History of Medicine and Allied Sciences* 61, no. 2 (2006): 122.

72. Jonathan M. Metzl, *The Protest Psychosis: How Schizophrenia Became a Black Disease* (Boston: Beacon Press, 2009), ix.

73. Ibid., xiii.

74. Morrison, "Can a Musician Return?," 72.

75. Paudras, *Dance of the Infidels,* 15.

76. Eric C. Schneider, *Smack: Heroin and the American City* (Philadelphia: University of Pennsylvania Press, 2008), 17.

77. Ibid., 31.

78. Ibid., 27. David Ake, *Jazz Cultures* (Berkeley: University of California, 2002); Ingrid Monson, *Freedom Sounds: Civil Rights Call Out to Jazz and Africa* (New York: Oxford University Press, 2007); Farah Jasmine Griffin and Salim Washington, *Clawing at the Limits of Cool: Miles Davis, John Coltrane, and the Greatest Jazz Collaboration Ever* (New York: St. Martin's Press, 2008); and Robin D. G. Kelley, *Thelonious Monk: The Life and Times of an American Original* (New York: Free Press, 2009).

79. Ibid., 28.

80. Ibid., 29, 32.

81. Quoted in Morrison, "Can a Musician Return?," 68, 72.

82. Eugene Holley, Jr., "The Education of Bud Powell," *Village Voice* (June 28, 1994): SS7.

83. Maely Daniele Dufty, "The Sound of Truth," undated, Bud Powell file, Institute of Jazz Studies archives; Kelley, *Thelonious Monk,* 156.

84. Paudras, *Dance of the Infidels,* 15.

85. Quoted in Michael Cuscuna and Michel Ruppli, *The Blue Note Label:*

A Discography, Revised and Expanded (Westport, CT: Greenwood Press, 2001), xii.

86. Quoted in ibid., xiii.

87. Quoted in Mark Gardner, *The Complete Bud Powell Blue Note Recordings (1949–1958),* Mosaic 116, 1986, liner notes.

88. Quoted in ibid.

89. Ibid.

90. For a full account of this storied concert, see Mark Miller, *Cool Blues: Charlie Parker in Canada, 1953* (London, ON: Nightwood Editions, 1989).

91. Quoted in ibid., 79.

92. Marshall W. Stearns, *The Story of Jazz* (New York: Oxford University Press, 1956), 16.

93. André Hodeir, *Jazz: Its Evolution and Essence,* updated ed. (New York: Grove Press, 1956), 42 (originally published as *Hommes et problèmes du jazz* [Paris: Flammarion, 1954]).

94. Gennari, "Jazz Criticism," 477.

95. Donald J. Childs, "New Criticism," in *Encyclopedia of Contemporary Literary Theory: Approaches, Scholars, Terms,* Irena R. Makaryk, ed. (Toronto: University of Toronto Press, 1993), 122.

96. Terry Eagleton, *Literary Theory: An Introduction,* 3rd ed. (Minneapolis: University of Minnesota Press, 1983), 49.

97. See Richard Crawford, "Martin Williams: An Appreciation," *Sonneck Society Bulletin* 18 (1992): 50.

98. Martin T. Williams, ed., *The Art of Jazz: Essays on the Nature and Development of Jazz* (New York: Oxford University Press, 1959).

99. Eagleton, *Literary Theory,* 48.

100. Gunther Schuller, "The Future of Form in Jazz," in *Musings: The Musical Worlds of Gunther Schuller* (New York: Oxford University Press, 1986), 18.

101. Gunther Schuller, "Sonny Rollins and the Challenge of Thematic Improvisation," in ibid., 86, 88.

102. Ibid., 94.

103. Mark Tucker, "Musicology and the New Jazz Studies," *Journal of the American Musicological Society* 51 (1998): 131–48.

104. Stan Britt, "The First Lady of Jazz: Mary Lou Williams," *Jazz Journal International* 34, no. 9 (September 1981): 12.

105. Art Taylor, *Notes and Tones: Musician-to-Musician Interviews* (New York: Da Capo Press, [1977] 1993).

106. Edward Berger, *Basically Speaking: An Oral History of George Duvivier* (Metuchen, NJ: Scarecrow Press, 1993), 90–91.

107. Paudras, *Dance of the Infidels,* 18.

108. Ibid., 20.

4. MAKING THE CHANGES

1. See Eric Lott, "Double V, Double-Time: Bebop's Politics of Style," *Callaloo,* no. 36 (July 1, 1988).

2. Peter Pullman, *Wail: The Life of Bud Powell* (Peter Pullman, LLC, 2012), Kindle edition.

3. Scott DeVeaux, "'Nice Work If You Can Get It': Thelonious Monk and Popular Song," *Black Music Research Journal* 19, no. 2 (October 1, 1999): 169.

4. Richard Wang, "Jazz circa 1945: A Confluence of Styles," *Musical Quarterly* 59, no. 4 (October 1, 1973): 545.

5. Ingrid Monson, *Saying Something: Jazz Improvisation and Interaction* (Chicago: University of Chicago Press, 1996), 2.

6. Patrick Burke, "Oasis of Swing: The Onyx Club, Jazz, and White Masculinity in the Early 1930s," *American Music* 24, no. 3 (Autumn 2006): 321.

7. See John Gennari, *Blowin' Hot and Cool: Jazz and Its Critics* (Chicago: University of Chicago Press, 2006). Also see E. Taylor Atkins, ed., *Jazz Planet* (Jackson: University Press of Mississippi, 2003).

8. See also Richard Mook, "White Masculinity in Barbershop Quartet Singing," *Journal of the Society of American Music* 1 (2007): 453–83.

9. Quoted in Allan Morrison, "Can a Musician Return from the Brink of Insanity?," *Ebony* (August 1953): 68.

10. Katrina Hazzard-Gordon, *Jookin': The Rise of Social Dance Formations in African-American Culture* (Philadelphia: Temple University Press, 1990), 63–119.

11. Richard Crawford, *An Introduction to America's Music* (New York: W. W. Norton, 2001), 191–92.

12. Gavin James Campbell, "Classical Music and the Politics of Gender in America, 1900–1925," *American Music* 21, no. 4 (December 1, 2003): 466.

13. Ibid.

14. Crawford, *An Introduction to America's Music,* 291.

15. Alan Lomax, *Mister Jelly Roll: The Fortunes of Jelly Roll Morton, New Orleans Creole and the "Inventor" of Jazz* (New York: Pantheon, [1950] 1993), quoted in Robert Walser, ed., *Keeping Time: Readings in Jazz History* (New York: Oxford University Press, 1999), 16–17.

16. Jeffrey Magee, *The Uncrowned King of Swing: Fletcher Henderson and Big Band Jazz* (New York: Oxford University Press, 2005), 16–17.

17. Ibid., 13.

18. Hazel Carby, "'It Jus' Be's Dat Way Sometime': The Sexual Politics of Women's Blues," in Ellen Carol DuBois and Vicki L. Ruiz, eds., *Unequal Sisters: A Multicultural Reader in U.S. Women's History* (New York: Routledge, 1990), quoted in Walser, *Keeping Time,* 353.

19. I thank Jeffrey Magee for the reference and conversations about these ideas.

20. Ross Russell, "Bebop," in Martin Williams, ed., *The Art of Jazz: Essays on the Nature and Development of Jazz* (New York: Oxford University Press, 1959), 188–89; Leonard Feather, *Inside Jazz* (originally published as *Inside Bebop*) (New York: Da Capo Press, [1949] 1977), 57–58.

21. The same effect, however, was also achieved at slower tempos.

22. Russell, "Bebop," 189.

23. Maureen Mahon, *Right to Rock: The Black Rock Coalition and the Cultural Politics of Race* (Durham, NC: Duke University Press, 2004), 8.

24. See Eileen Southern, ed., *Readings in Black American Music,* 2nd

ed. (New York: W. W. Norton, 1983), 318–32. See also David N. Baker, Lida Belt, and Herman Hudson, eds., *The Black Composer Speaks* (Metuchen, NJ: Scarecrow Press, 1977). For a contemporary assessment, see William C. Banfield, *Musical Landscapes in Color: Conversations with Black American Composers* (Lanham, MD: Scarecrow Press, 2003).

25. Like many of their white counterparts, black concert composers in the 1940s had been working as primarily university professors. In many ways, the historically black colleges—the primary employers of these composers—filled a role for black concert composers similar to the one that Minton's and other black theaters and clubs filled for black jazz musicians. It was a cultural space in which they could work out their creative ideas on their own terms.

26. Quoted in Judith Tick, "Charles Ives and Gender Ideology," in *Musicology and Difference: Gender and Sexuality in Music Scholarship,* Ruth A. Solie, ed. (Berkeley: University of California Press, 1993), 92.

27. Eileen Southern, *The Music of Black Americans: A History,* 3rd ed. (New York: W. W. Norton, 1983), 543–44.

28. Ronald Byrnside, "The Performer as Creator: Jazz Improvisation," in Charles Hamm, Bruno Nettl, and Ronald Byrnside, eds., *Contemporary Music and Music Cultures* (Englewood Cliffs, NJ: Prentice-Hall, 1975), 224. See also Bruno Nettl and Melinda Russell, eds., *In the Course of Performance: Studies in the World of Musical Improvisation* (Chicago: University of Chicago Press, 1998).

29. Feather, *Inside Jazz,* 49–56.

30. James Patrick describes bebop musicians' use of borrowed chord progressions:

> The general procedure of the borrowed-harmony technique is well-known: an original piece is selected; the original harmony is retained and the original melody is discarded; a new melody is then fitted to the borrowed chord structure, yielding a new composition. Thus, George Gershwin's "I Got Rhythm" (1930) may be transformed into Sidney Bechet's "Shag" (1932) or into Charlie Parker's "Dexterity" (1947). Similarly, new blues compositions may be created by fitting a newly-composed melodic line to a basic I-IV-I-V-I harmonic scheme. By analogy to text substitution in medieval music, I call this general technique the "melodic contrafact" (contrafactum).

James Patrick, "Charlie Parker and Harmonic Sources of Bebop Composition: Thoughts on the Repertory of New Jazz in the 1940s," *Journal of Jazz Studies* 2 (June 1975): 3.

31. Patrick, 4–5. See also Eileen Southern, "An Origin for the Negro Spiritual," *Black Scholar* 3 (1972): 8–13, for a concise discussion of antebellum African American religious music. In the case of black religious music, singers drew on numerous sources to create new music, though there is no evidence that harmonic progressions formed the basis of these borrowings. In 1819, John Fanning Watson, a Methodist minister, criticized the black-inspired singing in camp meetings in a New Jersey–published tract, complaining: "We have too, a growing evil, in the practice of singing in our places of public and society worship, merry airs, adapted from old songs, to hymns of our composing . . . and most frequently composed and first sung by the illiterate blacks of the society" (quoted in ibid., 11).

32. Feather, *Inside Jazz,* 50.

33. Quoted in Dizzy Gillespie and Al Fraser, *To Be or Not to Bop: Memoirs of Dizzy Gillespie* (New York: Da Capo Press, 1985), 209.

34. James Patrick, *Charlie Parker: The Complete Savoy Studio Sessions,* Savoy Jazz S5J-5500, 1988, liner notes, offers a meticulous description of this compositional process and its relationship to both Parker's Savoy recordings and to existing copyright laws.

35. Quoted in Robert George Reisner, ed., *Bird: The Legend of Charlie Parker* (New York: Da Capo Press, [1962] 1977), 183.

36. Gillespie and Fraser, *To Be or Not to Bop,* 208.

37. Quoted in ibid., 208.

38. See Richard Crawford, *America's Musical Life: A History* (New York: W.W. Norton & Company, 2001).

39. Gillespie and Fraser, *To Be or Not to Bop,* 301.

40. See Patrick, "Charlie Parker and Harmonic Sources of Bebop Composition," for a discussion of Savoy's payment procedures with melodic contrafacts.

41. Tick, "Charles Ives and Gender Ideology," 105.

42. Frank Tirro, "The Silent Theme Tradition," *Musical Quarterly* 53 (July 1967): 313.

43. Ibid., 290.

44. Richard Crawford, *The American Musical Landscape: The Business of Musicianship from Billings to Gershwin, Updated With a New Preface* (Berkeley: University of California Press, 1993), 231–32.

45. DeVeaux, "'Nice Work If You Can Get It'," 172–73.

46. Ibid., 174.

47. Theodor W. Adorno, with the assistance of George Simpson, "On Popular Music," in Simon Frith and Andrew Goodwin, eds., *On Record: Rock, Pop, and the Written Word* (New York: Pantheon, 1990), 308. See also Richard Middleton, *Studying Popular Music* (Milton Keynes, UK, and Philadelphia: Open University Press, 1990), 34–63.

48. Henry Louis Gates, Jr., *The Signifying Monkey: A Theory of African-American Literary Criticism* (New York: Oxford University Press, 1989), 52.

49. Anne Danielsen, *Presence and Pleasure: The Funk Grooves of James Brown and Parliament* (Middletown, CT: Wesleyan University Press, 2006), 59. On the term *musicking,* see Christopher Small, *Musicking: The Meanings of Performing and Listening* (Hanover, NH: University of New England Press for Wesleyan University Press, 1998).

50. Danielsen, *Presence and Pleasure,* 60.

51. See Jeffrey Magee, "Kinds of Blue: Miles Davis, Afro-Modernism, and the Blues," *Jazz Perspectives* 1, no. 2 (2007): 5–27.

52. Gillespie and Fraser, *To Be or Not to Bop,* 206–07.

53. J. Bradford Robinson calls this aspect of Powell's style "almost anti-pianistic." See "Bud Powell," in *The New Grove Dictionary of Jazz,* 3 vols., Barry Kernfeld, ed., 2nd ed. (London: Macmillan, 2002), 319.

54. I thank Richard Crawford for leading me to this concept during our many discussions about Powell's musicianship.

55. Jeffrey J. Taylor, "Earl Hines's Piano Style in the 1920s: A Historical and Analytical Perspective," *Black Music Research Journal* 12, no. 1 (April 1, 1992): 59.

56. See, for example, Christine Brattersby, *Gender and Genius: Towards a Feminist Aesthetic* (London: Women's Press, 1989).

57. Farah Jasmine Griffin, *If You Can't Be Free, Be a Mystery: In Search of Billie Holiday* (New York: One World / Ballantine, 2002), 14.

58. Nichole T. Rustin, "Mary Lou Williams Plays Like a Man!: Gender, Genius, and Difference in Black Music Discourse," *South Atlantic Quarterly* 104, no. 3 (Summer 2005): 443–62.

59. Among them are Sherrie Tucker, *Swing Shift: "All-Girl" Bands of the 1940s* (Durham, NC: Duke University Press, 2000); and idem, "Big Ears: Listening for Gender in Jazz Studies," *Current Musicology,* nos. 71–73 (Spring 2001–02): 375–408. An excellent addition to the gender and jazz literature is Nichole T. Rustin and Sherrie Tucker, eds., *Big Ears: Listening for Gender in Jazz Studies* (Durham, NC: Duke University Press, 2008).

60. Tucker, "Big Ears," 387.

61. Ibid., 379.

62. Sherrie Ortner, ed., *The Fate of "Culture": Geertz and Beyond* (Berkeley: University of California Press, 1999), 6.

63. Ibid., 7.

64. Susan McClary, *Feminine Endings: Music, Gender, and Sexuality* (Minneapolis: University of Minnesota Press, 1991). This work investigates five sweeping points of intervention:

1. Musical constructions of gender and sexuality

2. Gendered aspects of traditional theory

3. Gender and sexuality in musical narrative

4. Music as a gendered discourse

5. Discursive strategies of women musicians

65. Ibid., 27.

66. David Ake, *Jazz Cultures* (Berkeley: University of California Press, 2002), 67.

5. EXPLODING NARRATIVES AND STRUCTURES IN THE ART OF BUD POWELL

1. Salim Washington, "'All the Things You Could Be by Now': Charlie Mingus Presents and the Limits of Avant-Garde Jazz," in *Uptown Conversation: The New Jazz Studies,* Robert G. O'Meally, Brent Hayes Edwards, and Farah Jasmine Griffin, eds. (New York: Columbia University Press, 2004), 28.

2. Vijay Iyer, "Exploding the Narrative in Jazz Improvisation," in *Uptown Conversation: The New Jazz Studies,* Robert G. O'Meally, Brent Hayes Edwards, and Farah Jasmine Griffin, eds. (New York: Columbia University Press, 2004), 393–403.

3. Ibid., 395.

4. Ibid.

5. Ibid., 401.

6. Ibid., 401–02.

7. Susan McClary, *Conventional Wisdom: The Content of Musical Form* (Berkeley: University of California Press, 2000), 6.

8. See Roger Lax and Frederick Smith, *The Great Song Thesaurus,* 2nd ed. (New York: Oxford University Press, 1989), 299.

9. See Brian A. Rust, *Jazz and Ragtime Records, 1897–1942,* 5th ed. (Littleton, CO: Mainspring Press, 2002).

10. See Gunther Schuller, *The Swing Era: The Development of Jazz, 1930–1945* (New York: Oxford University Press, 1991), 84–86, for a discussion of the original recording.

11. See Richard Crawford and Jeffrey Magee, *Jazz Standards on Record, 1900–1942: A Core Repertory* (Chicago: Columbia College / Center for Black Music Research, 1992), 29–30, for a list of the tune's recordings before Williams's version.

12. The personnel includes Cootie Williams, Ermit Perry, George Treadwell, and Harold "Money" Johnson, trumpets; Ed Burke, Bob Horton, and George Stevenson, trombones; Eddie "Cleanhead" Vinson, alto sax, vocals; Charlie Holmes, alto sax; Lee Pope and Eddie "Lockjaw" Davis, tenor sax; Eddie DeVerteuil, baritone sax; Bud Powell, piano; Norman Keenan, bass; Vess Payne, drums; and Pearl Bailey, vocals.

13. Leonard Feather, *Inside Jazz* (originally published as *Inside Bebop*) (New York: Da Capo Press, [1949] 1977), 36.

14. For more on center collectivities, see Fabian Holt, *Genre in Popular Music* (Chicago: University of Chicago Press, 2007), 20–21.

15. According to jazz historian and critic Michael Ullman, Gordon once stated that the pieces on this session (and many others) were arbitrarily named by the management at Savoy. Interview with the author, October 3, 1993.

16. Monk's "Epistrophy," for example, represents an A-B-C-B formal scheme. See James Kent Williams, "Themes Composed by Jazz Musicians of the Bebop Era: A Study of Harmony, Rhythm, and Melody," PhD diss., Indiana University, 1982, for examples of the variants.

17. For a discussion on quotation in jazz solos, see Krin Gabbard, "The Quoter and His Culture," in *Jazz in Mind: Essays on the History and Meanings of Jazz,* Reginald T. Buckner and Steven Weiland, eds. (Detroit: Wayne State University Press, 1991), 92–111.

18. Anthony Brown, "Modern Jazz Drumset Artistry," *Black Perspective in Music* 18 (1990): 40; emphasis original.

19. Ibid., 54.

20. Ibid., 46.

21. Ibid., 43.

22. Ibid., 44.

23. Ibid., 56.

24. Ibid. Brown also stresses that Roach combined the earlier styles of drummers Sid Catlett, Chick Webb, and Jo Jones and "distilled these elements through the conceptual parameters of Clarke's polyrhythmical innovations" (ibid., 56).

25. Ross Russell, "Bebop," in Martin Williams, ed., *The Art of Jazz:*

Essays on the Nature and Development of Jazz (New York: Oxford University Press, 1959), 190.

26. Ibid., 193.

27. Williams, "Themes Composed by Jazz Musicians of the Bebop Era," 44.

28. Ibid., 45.

29. Ibid., 68.

30. See ibid., 72–80, for a discussion of these examples and their variants.

31. Lax and Smith, *The Great Song Thesaurus,* 236.

32. See Rust, *Jazz and Ragtime Records.*

33. Dizzy Gillespie and Al Fraser, *To Be or Not to Bop: Memoirs of Dizzy Gillespie* (New York: Da Capo Press, 1985), 251.

34. Ibid., 252–53.

35. Quoted in Ira Gitler, *Jazz Masters of the Forties* (New York: Da Capo Press, 1982), 120–21.

36. John McDonough, "Sarah Vaughan, 1924–90," *Down Beat* (June 1990): 11.

37. Leslie Gourse, *Sassy: The Life of Sarah Vaughan* (New York: Scribner, 1993), 48.

38. Claude Schlouch, *Once upon a Time: Bud Powell: A Discography* (Marseille: Claude Schlouch, 1983), 3. Besides Powell, the quintet included Freddie Webster, trumpet; Leroy Harris, alto saxophone; Cecil Payne, baritone saxophone; Ted Sturgis, bass; and Kenny Clarke, drums.

39. Other songs included "I Can Make You Love Me," "You're Not the Kind," and "My Kinda' Love." See *Tenderly,* Musicraft MVSCD-57, 1946.

40. George E. Lewis, "Improvised Music after 1950: Afrological and Eurological Perspectives," *Black Music Research Journal* 22(2002): 218.

41. Lax and Smith, *The Great Song Thesaurus,* 302.

42. Rust, *Jazz and Ragtime Records.*

43. Henry Martin, "Jazz Harmony: A Syntactic Background," *Annual Review of Jazz Studies* 4 (1988): 12.

44. Quoted in Gitler, *Jazz Masters of the Forties,* 138–39.

45. George Hoefer, "Early J.J.," *Down Beat* (January 28, 1965): 33.

46. Ira Gitler, "The Remarkable J.J. Johnson," *Down Beat* (May 11, 1961): 17.

47. Hoefer, "Early J.J.," 33.

48. Quoted in Gillespie and Fraser, *To Be or Not to Bop,* 254.

49. Thomas Owens, s.v. "Bebop," *The New Grove Dictionary of Jazz,* vol. 2, 494; see also Feather, *Inside Jazz,* 98.

50. Quoted in George Hoefer, "The Significance of Fats Navarro," *Down Beat* (January 27, 1966): 16.

51. Quoted in Dan Morgenstern, *Fats Navarro, Fat Girl: The Savoy Sessions,* Savoy Jazz SJL 2216, 1947, liner notes.

52. Henry Louis Gates, Jr. *The Signifying Monkey: A Theory of African-American Literary Criticism* (New York: Oxford University Press, 1989), 53.

53. Ibid., 63.

54. John P. Murphy, "Jazz Improvisation: The Joy of Influence," *Black Perspective in Music* 18, nos. 1–2 (1990): 7–19.

55. Gitler, *Jazz Masters of the Forties,* 130–34, notes that Al Haig, Dodo Marmarosa, and Clyde Hart all adopted the bebop style around the same time that Powell did. But by the late 1940s, Gitler writes, "a raft of Negro pianists, strongly influenced by Powell, became active." In 1957, pianist John Lewis called Powell "the most influential pianist of the last ten years" (quoted in Gitler, *Jazz Masters of the Forties,* 135).

56. Quoted in A.B. Spellman, *Four Lives in the Bebop Business* (New York: Limelight Editions, [1966] 1990), 56.

57. The August 8, 1949, recordings can be heard on *The Amazing Bud Powell,* vol. 1, Blue Note CDP 7–81503–2, 1995. On the Stitt session, "Bebop in Pastel" is listed in some places as Stitt's composition, but all subsequent versions of the tune list Powell as composer.

58. The bridge's melody is also harmonized by Stitt and Dorham.

59. Quoted in *The Amazing Bud Powell,* Mosaic Records, 1986 (reissue), liner notes.

60. William Seitz quoted in Anna Dezeuze, "Assemblage, Bricolage, and the Practice of Everyday Life," *Art Journal* (Spring 2008): 31. See also William Chapin Seitz, *The Art of Assemblage* (New York: Museum of Modern Art, 1961). My thinking about the topic of assemblage and music is indebted to Kellie Jones.

61. Like bebop, assemblage also (1) spurred critical debates about "recognizability and transformation"; (2) encouraged a critique of the object versus the performance/process basis in debates about what is considered "high art"; and (3) inspired a rethinking of the relationship between the idea of art and the everyday. See Dezeuze, "Assemblage, Bricolage, and the Practice of Everyday Life," 31–37; and Arnold Rubin, "Accumulation: Power and Display in African Sculpture," *Art Forum* 13, no. 9 (May 1975): 35–47.

CODA

1. The interpretation of the events of Powell's life in this chapter is taken from Alan Groves and Alyn Shipton, *The Glass Enclosure: The Life of Bud Powell* (Oxford, MS: Bayou Press, 1993); Francis Paudras, *Dance of the Infidels: A Portrait of Bud Powell* (New York: Da Capo Press, 1986); and Claude Schlouch, *Once upon a Time: Bud Powell: A Discography* (Marseille: Claude Schlouch, 1983).

2. See Tyler Stovall, *Paris Noir: African Americans in the City of Light* (Boston: Houghton Mifflin, 1996), 130–81.

3. See Krin Gabbard, *Jammin' at the Margins: Jazz and the American Cinema* (Chicago: University of Chicago Press, 1996), 64–100, for a discussion of jazz biopics.

4. www.youtube.com/watch?v=DtBAHTXTy9E (accessed April 9, 2012).

Selected Bibliography

Adorno, Theodor W., with the assistance of George Simpson. "On Popular Music." In *On Record: Rock, Pop, and the Written Word*. Edited by Simon Frith and Andrew Goodwin. New York: Pantheon, 1990, 301–14.

Ake, David. *Jazz Cultures*. Berkeley: University of California Press, 2002.

Allen, Stuart. "What Is Bop? It's the Way I Think and Feel about Jazz." *Melody Maker*, February 12, 1949, 3.

Astrup, Ole J. "The Forgotten Ones: Billy Kyle." *Jazz Journal International* 37, no. 8 (1984): 10.

Austin, William W. *Music in the 20th Century: From Debussy through Stravinsky*. New York: W.W. Norton, 1966.

Baker, David N., Lida Belt, and Herman Hudson, eds. *The Black Composer Speaks*. Metuchen, NJ: Scarecrow Press, 1977.

Banfield, William C. *Musical Landscapes in Color: Conversations with Black American Composers*. Lanham, MD: Scarecrow Press, 2003.

Barker, Danny. *A Life in Jazz*. Edited by Alyn Shipton. New York: Oxford University Press, 1986.

Barthes, Roland, and Richard Howard. *Mythologies: The Complete Edition, in a New Translation*. Translated by Annette Lavers. New York: Hill and Wang, 1972.

Battersby, Christine. *Gender and Genius: Towards a Feminist Aesthetics*. London: Womens Press Ltd, 1999.

Bearden, Romare. *Riffs and Takes: Music in the Art of Romare Bearden*. Raleigh: North Carolina Museum of Art, 1988.

Becker, Judith. "Is Western Art Music Superior?" *Musical Quarterly* 72, no. 3 (January 1, 1986): 341–59.

Berger, Edward. *Basically Speaking: An Oral History of George Duvivier*. Metuchen, NJ: Scarecrow Press, 1993.

"B. G. and Bebop." *Newsweek*, December 27, 1948, 66–67.

Blesh, Rudi. *Shining Trumpets: A History of Jazz*. New York: Da Capo Press, [1946] 1958.

"Bopera on Broadway." *Time*, December 20, 1948, 63–64.

Boyer, Richard O. "Bop." *New Yorker*, July 3, 1948, 28.

Brattersby, Christine. *Gender and Genius: Towards a Feminist Aesthetic*. London: Women's Press, 1989.

Britt, Stan. "The First Lady of Jazz: Mary Lou Williams." *Jazz Journal International* 34, no. 9 (September 1981): 10–12.

Brooks, Gwendolyn. *The Essential Gwendolyn Brooks*. Edited by Elizabeth Alexander. New York: Library of America, 2005.

Brown, Anthony. "Modern Jazz Drumset Artistry." *Black Perspective in Music* 18 (1990): 39–58.

Burke, Patrick. "Oasis of Swing: The Onyx Club, Jazz, and White Masculinity in the Early 1930s." *American Music* 24, no. 3 (Autumn 2006): 320–46.

———. *Come in and Hear the Truth: Jazz and Race on 52nd Street*. Chicago: University of Chicago Press, 2008.

Byrnside, Ronald. "The Performer as Creator: Jazz Improvisation." In *Contemporary Music and Music Cultures*. Edited by Charles Hamm, Bruno Nettl, and Ronald Byrnside. Englewood Cliffs, NJ: Prentice-Hall, 1975, 223–51.

Campbell, Gavin James. "Classical Music and the Politics of Gender in America, 1900–1925." *American Music* 21, no. 4 (December 1, 2003): 446–73.

Carby, Hazel. "'It Jus' Be's Dat Way Sometime': The Sexual Politics of Women's Blues." In *Keeping Time: Readings in Jazz History*. Edited by Robert Walser. New York: Oxford University Press, 1999, 351–65.

Charters, Samuel, and Leonard Kunstadt. *Jazz: A History of the New York Scene*. Garden City, NY: Doubleday, 1962.

Childs, Donald J. "New Criticism." In *Encyclopedia of Contemporary Literary Theory: Approaches, Scholars, Terms*. Edited by Irena Makaryk. Toronto: University of Toronto Press, 1993, 118–32.

Chilton, John. *Who's Who of Jazz: Storyville to Swing Street*. New York: Time-Life Records, 1978.

Cleage, Pearl. *Mad at Miles: A Black Woman's Guide to Truth*. Atlanta: Cleage Group, 1990.

Collier, James Lincoln. *The Making of Jazz: A Comprehensive History*. Boston: Houghton Mifflin, 1978.

———. *The Reception of Jazz in America: A New View*. New York: ISAM, 1988.

Corbould, Clare. *Becoming African Americans: Black Public Life in Harlem, 1919–1939*. Cambridge, MA: Harvard University Press, 2009.

Crawford, Richard. "Martin Williams: An Appreciation." *Sonneck Society Bulletin* 18 (1992): 50.

———. *The American Musical Landscape: The Business of Musicianship from Billings to Gershwin, Updated With a New Preface*. Berkeley: University of California Press, 1993.

———. *An Introduction to America's Music*. New York: W. W. Norton, 2001.

Crawford, Richard, and Jeffrey Magee. *Jazz Standards on Record, 1900–1942: A Core Repertory.* Chicago: Columbia College / Center for Black Music Research, 1992.

Cuscuna, Michael, and Michel Ruppli. *The Blue Note Label: A Discography, Revised and Expanded.* Westport, CT: Greenwood Press, 2001.

Dance, Stanley. *The World of Swing: An Oral History of Big Band Jazz.* New York: Scribner, 1974.

Danielsen, Anne. *Presence and Pleasure: The Funk Grooves of James Brown and Parliament.* Middletown, CT: Wesleyan University Press, 2006.

Davidson, Arthur T. "A History of Harlem Hospital." *Journal of the National Medical Association* 56, no. 5 (September 1964): 373–80.

Davis, Miles, and Quincy Troupe. *Miles: The Autobiography.* Simon & Schuster, 1989.

DeVeaux, Scott. "Bebop and the Recording Industry: The 1942 AFM Recording Ban Reconsidered." *Journal of the American Musicological Society* 41, no. 1 (April 1, 1988): 126–65.

———. "The Emergence of the Jazz Concert, 1935–1945." *American Music* 7, no. 1 (April 1, 1989): 6–29.

———. "Constructing the Jazz Tradition: Jazz Historiography." *Black American Literature Forum* 25, no. 3 (October 1, 1991): 525–60.

———. *Jazz in America: Who's Listening?* Washington, DC: Research Division Report / National Endowment for the Arts, 1992.

———. *The Birth of Bebop: A Social and Musical History.* Berkeley: University of California Press, 1997.

———. "'Nice Work If You Can Get It': Thelonious Monk and Popular Song." *Black Music Research Journal* 19, no. 2 (October 1, 1999): 169–86.

DeVeaux, Scott, and Howard McGhee. "Conversation with Howard McGhee: Jazz in the Forties." *Black Perspective in Music* 15 (Spring 1987): 65–78.

Dezeuze, Anna. "Assemblage, Bricolage, and the Practice of Everyday Life." *Art Journal* (Spring 2008): 31–37.

"Dizzy's Combo Comes Back to New York." *Down Beat,* January 28, 1946.

Doerschuk, Bob. "Bud Powell." *Keyboard* 10 (June 1984): 26–32.

Drake, St. Clair. *Black Folk Here and There: An Essay in History and Anthropology.* Vol. 1. Berkeley: University of California Press, 1987.

DuBois, Ellen Carol, and Vicki L. Ruiz, eds. *Unequal Sisters: A Multicultural Reader in U.S. Women's History.* New York: Routledge, 1990.

Dwyer, Ellen. "Psychiatry and Race during World War II." *Journal of the History of Medicine and Allied Sciences* 61, no. 2 (2006): 117–43.

Eagleton, Terry. *Literary Theory: An Introduction.* 3rd ed. Minneapolis: University of Minnesota Press, 1983.

Ellison, Ralph. *Invisible Man.* 2nd ed. New York: Vintage, [1952] 1981.

———. *"Blues People."* In Ralph Ellison, *Shadow and Act.* New York: Vintage, 1964.

———. *Shadow and Act.* New York: Vintage, 1964.

———. *Living with Music: Ralph Ellison's Jazz Writings.* Edited by Robert O'Meally. New York: Modern Library, 2001.

Feather, Leonard. *Inside Jazz*. Originally published as *Inside Bebop*. New York: Da Capo Press, [1949] 1977.

Finkelstein, Sidney. *Jazz: A People's Music*. New York: Citadel Press, 1948.

Floyd, Samuel A., Jr. "Ring Shout! Literary Studies, Historical Studies, and Black Music Inquiry." *Black Music Research Journal* 11, no. 2 (Fall 1991): 265–87.

———. *The Power of Black Music: Interpreting Its History from Africa to the United States*. New York: Oxford University Press, 1995.

Gabbard, Krin. "The Quoter and His Culture." In *Jazz in Mind: Essays on the History and Meanings of Jazz*. Edited by Reginald T. Buckner and Steven Weiland. Detroit: Wayne State University Press, 1991, 92–111.

Gates, Henry Louis Jr. *The Signifying Monkey: A Theory of African-American Literary Criticism*. New York: Oxford University Press, 1989.

Gendron, Bernard. *Between Montmartre and the Mudd Club: Popular Music and the Avant-Garde*. Chicago: University of Chicago Press, 2002.

Gennari, John. "Jazz Criticism: Its Development and Ideologies." *Black American Literature Forum* 25, no. 3 (Autumn 1991): 449–523.

———. *Blowin' Hot and Cool: Jazz and Its Critics*. Chicago: University of Chicago Press, 2006.

George, Nelson. *The Death of Rhythm and Blues*. New York: Pantheon, 1988.

Gibson, Ann. "Recasting the Canon: Norman Lewis and Jackson Pollock." *Artforum* 22 (1984): 64–70.

Giddins, Gary. Liner notes to *The Genius of Bud Powell*. Bud Powell. Verve VE-2-2506. CD. 1988.

Gillespie, Dizzy, and Al Fraser. *To Be or Not to Bop: Memoirs of Dizzy Gillespie*. New York: Da Capo Press, 1985.

Gioia, Ted. *The Imperfect Art: Reflections on Jazz and Modern Culture*. New York: Oxford University Press, 1990.

———. *West Coast Jazz: Modern Jazz in California, 1945–1960*. New York: Oxford University Press, 1992.

Gitler, Ira. "The Remarkable J. J. Johnson." *Down Beat*, May 11, 1961, 17.

———. *Jazz Masters of the Forties*. New York: Da Capo Press, 1982.

———. *Swing to Bop: An Oral History of the Transition in Jazz in the 1940s*. New York: Oxford University Press, 1987.

Gourse, Leslie. *Sassy: The Life of Sarah Vaughan*. New York: Scribner, 1993.

Gridley, Mark C. *Jazz Styles: History and Analysis*. 5th ed. Englewood Cliffs, NJ: Prentice Hall, 1994.

Griffin, Farah Jasmine. *If You Can't Be Free, Be a Mystery: In Search of Billie Holiday*. New York: One World / Ballantine, 2002.

Groves, Alan, and Alyn Shipton. *The Glass Enclosure: The Life of Bud Powell*. Oxford, MS: Bayou Press, 1993.

Hall, Stuart. "Cultural Identity and Diaspora." In *Diaspora and Visual Culture: Representing Africans and Jews*. Edited by Nicholas Mirzoeff. New York: Routledge, 2000, 21–34.

Hamm, Charles. *Music in the New World*. New York: W. W. Norton, 1983.

Hamm, Charles, Bruno Nettl, and Ronald Byrnside, eds. *Contemporary Music and Music Cultures*. Englewood Cliffs, NJ: Prentice-Hall, 1975.

Bibliography page

"Harlem Mourns: Bud Powell Funeral Jazz Requiem." *Newark Evening News,* August 6, 1966, 11.

Hayes, Elaine. "To Bebop or to Be Pop: Sarah Vaughan and the Politics of Crossover." PhD diss., University of Pennsylvania, 2004.

Hazzard-Gordon, Katrina. *Jookin': The Rise of Social Dance Formations in African-American Culture.* Philadelphia: Temple University Press, 1990.

Heap, Chad. *Slumming: Sexual and Racial Encounters in American Nightlife, 1885–1940.* Chicago: University of Chicago Press, 2009.

Hentoff, Nat. *The Jazz Life.* New York: Da Capo Press, [1961] 1975.

Herskovits, Melville. *The Myth of The Negro Past.* New York: Beacon Press, 1941.

Higgins, Paula. "The Apotheosis of Josquin des Prez and Other Mythologies of Musical Genius." *Journal of the American Musicological Society* 57, no. 3 (December 1, 2004): 443–510.

Hobson, Wilder. "Hits and Misses." *Saturday Review,* March 26, 1949, 32.

Hodeir, André. *Jazz: Its Evolution and Essence.* Updated ed. Originally published as *Hommes et problèmes du jazz* (Paris: Flammarion, 1954). New York: Grove Press, 1956.

Hoefer, George. "Early J.J." *Down Beat,* January 28, 1965, 33.

———. "The Significance of Fats Navarro." *Down Beat,* January 27, 1966.

Holley, Eugene Jr. "The Education of Bud Powell." *Village Voice,* June 28, 1994, SS7.

Holt, Fabian. *Genre in Popular Music.* Chicago: University of Chicago Press, 2007.

Hughes, Langston. *Montage of a Dream Deferred.* New York: Holt, 1951.

———. *The Best of Simple.* New York: Hill and Wang, 1961.

Iyer, Vijay. "Exploding the Narrative in Jazz Improvisation." In *Uptown Conversation: The New Jazz Studies.* Edited by Robert O'Meally, Brent Hayes Edwards, and Farah Jasmine Griffin. New York: Columbia University Press, 2004, 393–403.

Jones, Kellie. "Norman Lewis: The Black Paintings." In *Norman Lewis, 1909–1979.* Newark: State University of New Jersey, Rutgers, 1985, 1–8. Exhibition held January 31–March 7, 1985.

———. "Lost in Translation: Jean-Michel in the (Re)Mix." In *Basquiat.* Edited by Marc Mayer. London: Brooklyn Museum and Merrell, 2005, 163–79.

Jones, LeRoi (Amiri Baraka). *Blues People: Negro Music in White America.* New York: William Morrow, 1963.

———. "Jazz and the White Critic" (1963). In LeRoi Jones, *Black Music.* New York: William Morrow, 1968, 11–20.

Kelley, Robin D. G. "Malcolm X." In *Malcolm X: In Our Own Image.* Edited by Joe Wood. New York: St. Martin's Press, 1992, 155–82.

———. "Miles Davis: The Chameleon of Cool: A Jazz Genius in the Guise of a Hustler." *New York Times,* Arts & Leisure section, May 13, 2001, 1.

———. "The Jazz Wife: Muse and Manager." *New York Times,* July 21, 2002, 21, 24.

———. "The Riddle of the Zoot: Malcolm Little and Black Cultural Politics during World War II." In *American Studies: An Anthology.* Edited by Janice A. Radway, Kevin Gaines, Barry Shank, and Penny von Eschen. Hoboken, NJ: John Wiley & Sons, 2009, 281–89.

——. *Thelonious Monk: The Life and Times of an American Original.* New York: Free Press, 2009.

Kenyon, Nicholas. "The Careful Construction of a Child Prodigy." Arts & Leisure section, July 24, 2005, 24.

Kernfeld, Barry, ed. *The New Grove Dictionary of Jazz.* 2nd ed. 3 vols. London: Macmillan, 2002.

Kivy, Peter IV. *The Possessor and the Possessed: Handel, Mozart, Beethoven, and the Idea of Musical Genius.* New Haven, CT: Yale University Press, 2001.

Kolodin, Irving. "A Feather in the Cap of Bop." *Saturday Review,* July 30, 1949, 45.

Lax, Roger, and Frederick Smith. *The Great Song Thesaurus.* 2nd ed. New York: Oxford University Press, 1989.

Levin, Michael, and John S. Wilson. "No Bop Roots in Jazz: Parker." *Down Beat,* September 9, 1949, 1.

Levine, Lawrence. *Highbrow/Lowbrow: The Emergence of Cultural Hierarchy in America.* Cambridge, MA: Harvard University Press, 1988.

Lewis, George E. "Improvised Music after 1950: Afrological and Eurological Perspectives." *Black Music Research Journal* 16, no. 1 (Spring 1996): 91–122; reprinted in *Black Music Research Journal* 22, suppl. (2002).

Lipsitz, George. *Class and Culture in Cold War America: A Rainbow at Midnight.* New York: Praeger, 1981.

Lomax, Alan. *Mister Jelly Roll: The Fortunes of Jelly Roll Morton, New Orleans Creole and the "Inventor" of Jazz.* New York: Pantheon, [1950] 1993.

Lott, Eric. "Double V, Double-Time: Bebop's Politics of Style." *Callaloo,* no. 36 (July 1, 1988): 597–605.

Magee, Jeffrey. *The Uncrowned King of Swing: Fletcher Henderson and Big Band Jazz.* New York: Oxford University Press, 2005.

——. "Kinds of Blue: Miles Davis, Afro-Modernism, and the Blues." *Jazz Perspectives* 1, no. 2 (2007): 5–27.

Mahon, Maureen. *Right to Rock: The Black Rock Coalition and the Cultural Politics of Race.* Durham, NC: Duke University Press, 2004.

Mailer, Norman. *The White Negro.* New York: City Lights Books, [1957] 1970.

Martin, Henry. "Jazz Harmony: A Syntactic Background." *Annual Review of Jazz Studies* 4 (1988): 9–30.

McClary, Susan. "Terminal Prestige: The Case of Avant-Garde Music Composition." *Cultural Critique* 12 (April 1, 1989): 57–81.

——. *Feminine Endings: Music, Gender, and Sexuality.* Minneapolis: University of Minnesota Press, 1991.

——. *Conventional Wisdom: The Content of Musical Form.* Berkeley: University of California Press, 2000.

McDonough, John. "Sarah Vaughan, 1924–90." *Down Beat,* June 1990, 11.

McElfresh, Suzanne. "Max Attack." *Down Beat,* November 1993, 18.

McGinty, Doris Evans, ed. *A Documentary History of the National Association of Negro Musicians*. Chicago: Columbia College / Center for Black Music Research, 2004.

McKean, Gilbert. "The Diz and the Bebop." In *Jam Session: An Anthology of Jazz*. Edited by Ralph Gleason. New York: G.P. Putnam's Sons, 1958, 120–26.

McKittrick, Katherine. *Demonic Grounds: Black Women and the Cartographies of Struggle*. Minneapolis: University of Minnesota Press, 2006.

Meadows, Eddie. *Bebop to Cool: Context, Ideology, and Musical Identity*. Westport, CT: Greenwood Press, 2003.

Mellers, Wilfred. *Music in a New Found Land: Two Hundred Years of American Music*. New York: Oxford University Press, 1987.

Metzl, Jonathan M. *The Protest Psychosis: How Schizophrenia Became a Black Disease*. Boston: Beacon Press, 2009.

Middleton, Richard. *Studying Popular Music*. Milton Keynes, UK, and Philadelphia: Open University Press, 1990.

Miller, Charles. "Bebop and Old Masters." *New Republic*, June 30, 1947, 37.

Miller, Mark. *Cool Blues: Charlie Parker in Canada, 1953*. London, ON: Nightwood Editions, 1989.

Monson, Ingrid. "The Problem with White Hipness: Race, Gender, and Cultural Conceptions in Jazz Historical Discourse." *Journal of the American Musicological Society* 48, no. 3 (October 1, 1995): 396–422.

———. *Saying Something: Jazz Improvisation and Interaction*. Chicago: University of Chicago Press, 1996.

———. *Freedom Sounds: Civil Rights Call Out to Jazz and Africa*. New York: Oxford University Press, 2007.

Montgomery, Vern. "Jaws Unlocks." *Jazz Journal International* 36 (July 1983): 14.

Mook, Richard. "White Masculinity in Barbershop Quartet Singing." *Journal of the Society of American Music* 1 (2007): 453–83.

Morgenstern, Dan. Liner notes to *Fats Navarro, Fat Girl: The Savoy Sessions*. Fats Navarro. Savoy Jazz SJL 2216. CD. 1947.

Morrison, Allan. "Can a Musician Return from the Brink of Insanity?" *Ebony*, August 1953, 67–74.

Mosquera, Gerardo. "Elegguá at the (Post?)Modern Crossroads: The Presence of Africa in the Visual Art of Cuba." In *Santería Aesthetics in Contemporary Latin American Art*. Edited by Arturo Lindsay. Washington, DC, and London: Smithsonian Institution Press, 1996, 225–58.

Murphy, John P. "Jazz Improvisation: The Joy of Influence." *Black Perspective in Music* 18, nos. 1–2 (1990): 7–19.

Murray, Albert. *Stomping The Blues*. Rev. ed. New York: Da Capo Press, 1989.

Myrdal, Gunnar. *An American Dilemma: The Negro Problem and Modern Democracy*. New York: Harper & Row, [1942] 1962.

Nettl, Bruno, and Melinda Russell, eds. *In the Course of Performance: Studies in the World of Musical Improvisation*. Chicago: University of Chicago Press, 1998.

Newton, Francis. *The Jazz Scene.* New York: Penguin Books, 1961.

O'Meally, Robert, Brent Hayes Edwards, and Farah Jasmine Griffin, eds. *Uptown Conversation: The New Jazz Studies.* New York: Columbia University Press, 2004.

Ortner, Sherrie, ed. *The Fate of "Culture": Geertz and Beyond.* Berkeley: University of California Press, 1999.

Osgood, Henry Osborne. *So This Is Jazz.* Boston: Little, Brown, 1926.

Patrick, James. "Charlie Parker and Harmonic Sources of Bebop Composition: Thoughts on the Repertory of New Jazz in the 1940s." *Journal of Jazz Studies* 2 (June 1975): 3–23.

———. Liner notes to *Charlie Parker: The Complete Savoy Studio Sessions.* Charlie Parker. Savoy Jazz S5J-5500. CD. 1988.

Paudras, Francis. *Dance of the Infidels: A Portrait of Bud Powell.* New York: Da Capo Press, 1986.

———. Liner notes to *Earl Bud Powell: Early Years of a Genius, 44–48.* Bud Powell. Mythic Sound MS 6001–2. CD. 1989.

Pease, Sharon A. "Bud Powell's Unique Style Has Widespread Influence." *Down Beat,* June 15, 1951, 16.

Plantinga, Leon. "The Virtuosos." In Leon Plantinga, *Romantic Music: A History of Musical Style in Nineteenth-Century Europe.* New York: W. W. Norton, 1984, 173–203.

Porter, Eric. *What Is This Thing Called Jazz?: African American Musicians as Artists, Critics, and Activists.* Berkeley: University of California Press, 2002.

Porter, Lewis, Michael Ullman, and Edward Hazell. *Jazz: From Its Origins to the Present.* New York: Prentice Hall, 1992.

Pullman, Peter. *Wail: The Life of Bud Powell.* Kindle ed. Peter Pullman, LLC, 2012.

Radano, Ronald M. *Lying Up a Nation: Race and Black Music.* Chicago: University of Chicago Press, 2003.

Rampersad, Arnold. *The Life of Langston Hughes.* Vol. 2: *1941–1967.* New York: Oxford University Press, 1988.

Ramsey, Frederick, Jr. and Charles Edward Smith. *Jazzmen: The Story of Jazz Told in the Lives of the Men Who Created It.* New York: Limelight Editions, [1939] 1985.

Ramsey, Guthrie P. Jr. *Race Music: Black Cultures from Bebop to Hip-Hop.* New ed. Berkeley: University of California Press, 2003.

Reig, Teddy, and Edward Berger. *Reminiscing in Tempo: The Life and Times of a Jazz Hustler.* Metuchen, NJ: Scarecrow Press and Institute of Jazz Studies, 1990.

Reisner, Robert George. *Bird: The Legend Of Charlie Parker.* New York: Da Capo Press, [1962] 1977.

Robinson, J. Bradford. "Bud Powell." In *The New Grove Dictionary of Jazz.* 2nd ed. Vol. 3. Edited by Barry Kernfeld. London: Macmillan, 2002, 319.

Rubin, Arnold. "Accumulation: Power and Display in African Sculpture." *Art Forum* 13 (May 1975): 35–47.

Rusch, Bob. "Eddie Lockjaw Davis." *Cadence* (January 1988): 13.

Russell, Ross. "Bebop." In *The Art of Jazz: Essays on the Nature and Development of Jazz*. Edited by Martin Williams. New York: Oxford University Press, 1959.

———. *Bird Lives!: The High Life and Hard Times of Charlie (Yardbird) Parker*. New York: Da Capo Press, 1996.

Rust, Brian A. *Jazz and Ragtime Records, 1897–1942*. 5th ed. Littleton, CO: Mainspring Press, 2002.

Rustin, Nichole T. "Mary Lou Williams Plays Like a Man!: Gender, Genius, and Difference in Black Music Discourse." *South Atlantic Quarterly* 104, no. 3 (Summer 2005): 443–62.

Rustin, Nichole T., and Sherrie Tucker, eds. *Big Ears: Listening for Gender in Jazz Studies*. Durham, NC: Duke University Press, 2008.

Sargeant, Winthrop. *Jazz, Hot and Hybrid*. 3rd ed. New York: Da Capo Press, [1938] 1975.

Schneider, Eric C. *Smack: Heroin and the American City*. Philadelphia: University of Pennsylvania Press, 2008.

Schuller, Gunther. *Early Jazz: Its Roots and Musical Development*. New ed. New York: Oxford University Press, [1968] 1986.

———. *Musings: The Musical Worlds of Gunther Schuller*. New York: Oxford University Press, 1986.

———. *The Swing Era: The Development of Jazz, 1930–1945*. New York: Oxford University Press, 1991.

Seitz, William Chapin. *The Art of Assemblage*. New York: Museum of Modern Art, 1961.

Shapiro, Nat, and Nat Hentoff. *Hear Me Talkin' to Ya: The Story of Jazz as Told by the Men Who Made It*. Mineola, NY: Dover Publications, 1966.

Shaw, Arnold. *52nd Street: The Street of Jazz*. New York: Da Capo Press, 1977.

Sidbury, James. *Becoming African in America: Race and Nation in the Early Black Atlantic*. New York: Oxford University Press, 2007.

Sims, Lowery Stokes. *Challenge of the Modern: African-American Artists, 1925–1945*. New York: Studio Museum in Harlem, 2003.

Small, Christopher. *Musicking: The Meanings of Performing and Listening*. Hanover, NH: University of New England Press for Wesleyan University Press, 1998.

Smith, Carl. *Bouncing with Bud: All the Recordings of Bud Powell*. Brunswick, ME: Biddle, 1997.

Solie, Ruth A., ed. *Musicology and Difference: Gender and Sexuality in Music Scholarship*. Berkeley: University of California Press, 1995.

Southern, Eileen. "An Origin for the Negro Spiritual." *Black Scholar* 3 (1972): 8–13.

———. *The Music of Black Americans: A History*. 3rd ed. New York: W. W. Norton, 1983.

———, ed. *Readings in Black American Music*. 2nd ed. New York: W. W. Norton, 1983.

Spellman, A. B. *Four Lives in the Bebop Business*. New York: Limelight Editions, [1966] 1990.

Stearns, Marshall W. *The Story of Jazz*. New York: Oxford University Press, 1956.

Stowe, David W. *Swing Changes: Big-Band Jazz in New Deal America*. Cambridge, MA: Harvard University Press, 1994.

Subotnik, Rose Rosengard. "Romantic Music as Post-Kantian Critique: Classicism, Romanticism, and the Concept of the Semiotic Universe." In Rose Rosengard Subotnik, *Developing Variations: Style and Ideology in Western Music*. Minneapolis: University of Minnesota Press, 1990, 112–40.

Swartzman, Myron. *Romare Bearden: His Life and Art*. New York: H.N. Abrams, 1990.

Taylor, Arthur. *Notes and Tones: Musician-to-Musician Interviews*. New York: Da Capo Press, [1977] 1993.

Taylor, Jeffrey J. "Earl Hines's Piano Style in the 1920s: A Historical and Analytical Perspective." *Black Music Research Journal* 12, no. 1 (April 1, 1992): 57–77.

Tick, Judith. "Charles Ives and Gender Ideology." In *Musicology and Difference: Gender and Sexuality in Music Scholarship*. Edited by Ruth A. Solie. Berkeley: University of California Press, 1993, 83–106.

Tirro, Frank. "The Silent Theme Composition." *Musical Quarterly* 53 (July 1967): 313–34.

———. *Jazz: A History*. 2nd ed. New York: W.W. Norton, 1993.

Tucker, Mark. "Musicology and the New Jazz Studies." *Journal of the American Musicological Society* 51 (1998): 131–48.

Tucker, Sherrie. *Swing Shift: "All-Girl" Bands of the 1940s*. Durham, NC: Duke University Press Books, 2000.

———. "Big Ears: Listening for Gender in Jazz Studies." *Current Musicology*, nos. 71–73 (Spring 2001–02): 375–408.

Tyler, Bruce M. "Black Jive and White Repression." *Journal of Ethnic Studies* 16 (1989): 31–66.

Ulanov, Barry. *A History of Jazz in America*. New York: Viking Press, 1952.

Walser, Robert. *Running with the Devil: Power, Gender, and Madness in Heavy Metal Music*. Middletown, CT: Wesleyan University Press, 1993.

———, ed. *Keeping Time: Readings in Jazz History*. New York: Oxford University Press, 1999.

Wang, Richard. "Jazz circa 1945: A Confluence of Styles." *Musical Quarterly* 59, no. 4 (October 1, 1973): 531–46.

Washington, Salim. "'All the Things You Could Be by Now': Charlie Mingus Presents and the Limits of Avant-Garde Jazz." In *Uptown Conversation: The New Jazz Studies*. Edited by Robert G. O'Meally, Brent Hayes Edwards, and Farah Jasmine Griffin. New York: Columbia University Press, 2004, 27–49.

Weber, William. "Mass Culture and the Reshaping of European Musical Taste, 1770–1870." *International Review of the Aesthetics and Sociology of Music* 8, no. 1 (June 1, 1977): 5–22.

West, Cornel. *Prophetic Fragments: Illuminations of the Crisis in American Religion and Culture*. Grand Rapids, MI: Eerdmans, 1988.

Williams, James Kent. "Themes Composed by Jazz Musicians of the Bebop

Era: A Study of Harmony, Rhythm, and Melody." PhD diss., Indiana University, 1982.

Williams, Martin T., ed. *The Art of Jazz: Essays on the Nature and Development of Jazz*. New York: Oxford University Press, 1959.

——. "Jazz Composition: What Is It?" *Down Beat*, February 15, 1962, 20.

——. "The Bystander." *Down Beat*, April 9, 1964, 6.

——. *The Jazz Tradition*. New rev. ed. New York: Mentor, [1970] 1983.

Williams, Raymond. *Keywords: A Vocabulary of Culture and Society*. Rev. ed. New York: Oxford University Press, [1976] 1983.

Wolff, Janet. "The Ideology of Autonomous Art." Foreword to *Music and Society: The Politics of Composition, Performance and Reception*. Edited by Richard Leppert and Susan McClary. New York: Cambridge University Press, 1987, 1–12.

X, Malcolm, and Alex Haley. *The Autobiography of Malcolm X*. New York: Grove Press, 1964.

Yudkin, Jeremy. *The Lenox School of Jazz: A Vital Chapter in the History of American Music and Race Relations*. South Egremont, MA: Farshaw, 2006.

Illustration Credits

Chapter 1. Bud Powell, New York City, 1949. © Mosaic Images. Photograph by Francis Wolff, used by permission.

Chapter 2. Page 44: Bud Powell, New York City, 1958. © Mosaic Images. Photograph by Francis Wolff, used by permission. Page 72: Norman Lewis, *Twilight Sounds*. Saint Louis Art Museum, funds given by Mr. and Mrs. John Peters MacCarthy, Mr. and Mrs. Havey Saligman, Billy E. Hodges, and the Art Enrichment Fund.

Chapter 3. Bud Powell, New York City, 1957. © Mosaic Images. Photograph by Francis Wolff, used by permission.

Chapter 4. Bud Powell, New York City, 1949. © Mosaic Images. Photograph by Francis Wolff, used by permission.

Chapter 5. Bud Powell, New York City, 1958. © Mosaic Images. Photograph by Francis Wolff, used by permission.

Chapter 6. Bud Powell, New York, ca. 1956. Photograph by Chuck Stewart, used by permission.

Index

acid jazz, 9
Adorno, Theodor, 34, 135
African Academy of Arts and Research, 95
African Diaspora, 97
African identification, 95–96
Africanisms, 101–3, 106, 114, 117
Afrological tradition, 96, 109, 119, 184
Afro-modernism, 38, 75, 86, 145
Ake, David, 91, 141–42
"All God's Chillun Got Rhythm" (Jurmann, Kahn, and Kaper), 82
Alston, Charles, 49
American Federation of Musicians, Local 802, 5, 27, 51
American Musicological Society, 40
Ammons, Gene, 61
Anderson, Marian, 130
Anderson, T. J., 129, 130
Andrews Sisters, 166
"Anitra's Dance" (Grieg), 48
Antheil, George, 101
"Anthropology" (Gillespie and Parker), 93, 202n85
Apollo Records, 61, 68
Apollo Theater (Harlem), 27, 49, 51
Armstrong, Louis, 24–25, 36, 87, 198n75
ASCAP, 132
assemblage, 12, 181, 184–85
Austin, William, 20

Bach, Carl Philipp Emanuel, 85

Bach, Johan Sebastian, 15, 17, 47, 114
Bailey, Pearl, 151
Baldwin, James, 49
Balliett, Whitney, 107
Baptist Church, 50, 164
Baraka, Amiri, 10, 11, 39, 107, 194n16, 196n29
Barnes, Celia, 4, 5, 17, 79, 81
Barnes, Frances, 4, 5, 79
Basie, Count, 60, 148, 171
Basquiat, Jean-Michel, 41–42
Bates, Alan, 5
Bearden, Romare, 70, 71
bebop, 6–7, 106, 185; academic approach to, 38–41; aesthetic of, 86–87, 121–22; archetypal musicians of. See Clarke, Kenny; Gillespie, Dizzy; Gordon, Dexter; Monk, Thelonius; Parker, Charlie; Powell, Bud; Roach, Max; artistic pedigree of, 20–21, 23–24, 39; audience for, 34–38; as avant-garde music of black youth culture, 24–30; in California, 66–67; collective formation in, 170–72; composition and performance practice in, 130–34, 159, 161–63, 165, 172; concerts of, 4, 37, 63, 114; critics' response to, 30–34; drug abuse and, 110; emergence of, 54–57; in Europe, 118, 188–89; and experiments in visual arts and literature, 70–75; in 52nd Street clubs, 57, 60–61, 63–65,

MUSIC OF THE AFRICAN DIASPORA

Guthrie P. Ramsey, Jr., Editor
Samuel A. Floyd, Jr., Editor Emeritus

TEXT:
10/13 Sabon

DISPLAY:
Sabon, Din

COMPOSITOR:
BookMatters, Berkeley

INDEXER:
Ruth Elwell

PRINTER AND BINDER:
Maple Press